To Barbie

2nd Warwick Sea Scouts.
A Group second to none.

With every best wish.
Roy Masini
Gilwell September 2011

SEA SCOUTING
A History
1909-2009

1st Tyne Sea Scouts sailing on the yacht Gladwyna, *1913. Northumberland.*

SEA SCOUTING
A History
1909-2009

Roy Masini

PHILLIMORE

2011
Published by
PHILLIMORE & CO. LTD
Andover, Hampshire, England
www.phillimore.co.uk

© Roy Masini, 2011

ISBN 978-1-86077-573-4

CONTENTS

LIST OF ILLUSTRATIONS

Frontispiece: 1st Tyne Sea Scouts sailing on the yacht *Gladwyna*, 1913, Northumberland.

ILLUSTRATION ACKNOWLEDGEMENTS

Michael Baden-Powell, 4; The Hon Michael Baden-Powell and The Scout Association, front cover, 11; Tony Bartlett, 117, 152, 154, 155, 156, 157; 64th Birkenhead Sea Scouts, 127; Frank Brittain, 53, 55, 56, 57; CC Publishers (1916), 44; John Player & Sons, 45; City of Chester, 41; Angela Cousins, 20, 22, 23; Dockland Scout Project, 91, 128, 129, 130; Dundee Heritage Trust, 96; Geoff Durand, 121, 122, 123; 3rd Frodsham Sea Scouts, 158; Maurice Gardener, 126; Lieutenant Commander David Griffiths, 160; Martin Habgood, 63, 70, 71, 149; Steven Harris, 16, 39, 61; Steven Harris, 74 (postcard source), 26 and 43 (*Headquarters Gazette* photographs); Bruce Horne, 75; Peter Hunt (artist's impressions), 37, 40; David Kellor (source: Friends of Nunhead Cemetery), 27; London Youth, 2004, 132; Roy Masini, 5 (postcard), 6, 12 (Ogdens cigarette cards), 21, 24 (postcard), 25, 29, 30, 31 (postcard), 35, 36 (postcard), 42, 46, 47, 50, 54, 68, 73 (press photograph), 92, 93, 94, 95, 97, 99, 133, 134, 136, 141, 143, 144, 148; 1st Mortlake Sea Scouts and Martin Habgood, 112; Mike Nadin, 72; Mike Parsons, 7; Geoff Preshner, 116, 118, 119, 120; *Reading Chronicle* Newspapers, 124 (sourced by Caroline Peach); Rickmansworth Sea Scouts, 142; The Scout Association, back cover, 1, 2, 3, 8, 9, 10, 13, 14, 15, 17, 18, 19, 32, 33, 34, 38, 51, 52, 58, 59, 60, 62, 64, 65, 66, 67, 69, 76, 77, 78, 79, 80, 81, 82, 83, 84, 85, 86, 87, 88, 89, 90, 98, 100, 101, 102, 103, 104, 105, 106, 107, 108, 109, 110, 111, 113, 114, 115, 125, 131, 135, 137, 138, 139, 140, 150, 151, 153; Scouts Offshore, Colchester, 159; Patricia Somerville, 48, 49, 145, 146, 147; Carole Tyrrell (source: Friends of Nunhead Cemetery), 28.

LIST OF SUBSCRIBERS

1st Blackfords Sea Scouts, RN 37
1st Heaton Vale Sea Scout Group
1st Southbourne Sea Scout Group
2nd Bexhill Scout Group
3rd Shoreham Sea Scouts
4th Knowle Sea Scout Group (RN Unit 75)
19th Exeter Sea Scouts
201st Islington Sea Scout Group
Rodney Adams
Clifford Adamson
Alan Afford
Derek Allday
Clare Ashen
Ian 'Daffy' de Ath
G.J. Baigent
Mohd Hilmi Bin Abu Bakar
Peter Barnes
Colin Beazley
Luke Van Beek CBE
Michael Billin
Brian Billington
John Bird
Malcolm Blowers
Mr M.J. Boyling
Mike Breakwell
Robert F. Brett
Frank Brittain
Geoff Brown
Ron Brown
Lee Budd

Mrs R.A. Bullough
Roger Butterick
Joy Carter
Pat Caws RVM
Steven Caws
Antoine Chataignon
Donald Cheyne – 7th South Shields
J.R. Clay
M.J. Cole
Ian Cooper
Tony Compton
Robin Corti
Ron Cox
Ken Crisp
George H. Crowl jnr
Allan Davey – 5th Gosport Sea Scouts
Michael James Davidson
Adrian Durrant – 5th Gosport Sea Scouts
Dick Eager
Brian Ewart
David Eyles
Carol Farnham
Craig Finch
Tony Ford
Douglas Francis
Donald Gibbons – 201st Islington
Doug Godlington
Claude Godwin – 1st Lilliput, 1938-45
T.D. Golder
Sonny Goudie

Tommy Goudie
John Griffin
David T. Griffiths
Clive Gritten
Denis Gudgeon
David H. Hallam
Vera Corner Halligan
Norman Hammond
Jamal Harim
Donald Harmes
Roger Harris
R.P. Hatton
John O. Hawthorn
Mick Heath
Mike Hogg
John A. Hollington
J. Alan Holmes
Marilyn Hudson
John Hunt
Peter Hunt
Simon Hunt
Brian G. Stan Jones
Brian Keller
J.G. Kershaw
Chris Klesel
Colin Knightley
Kuala Lumpur Charlie Rovers
Jean-Marie Lecointre
David G.Lewis
Paul & Marian Lonsdale
Michael Loomes
Nick Osborn
Tiny Matthews
John McAdams snr
Mary McAlister
John Mears
Brian Meyer
Douglas G. Meyers
Pasi Mikkonen
Richard J. Mitchell
Neil Munt S.L. – 11th Norwich Sea Scouts
Howard Paul Nelson
Stephen Newton
Sylvia Garnett Von Der Neyen
Denis A. Nicole
Bob Norfolk
Norfolk Scouts Archive
Anthony Norris
Colin Overington
Terence Pankhurst G.S.L.,
    Holy Trinity Sea Scout Group

M.N. Parker
C.J. Parr – 1st Barry Sea Scouts
M.R.C. Parr
R.F. Perkins
Neil Pitchford
Terry Porter
Lieut. Commander (SCC) Geoffrey Preshner MBE.
    RNR
James Preston
John Purser
Richard Redman
Frank Rice
David J. Rich –
    1st Cuddington (Warspite) Sea Scouts, SM RSL
George F. Rich
R.G.C. Robinson
Jeffrey V. Robson
Owen Rodgers
Michael Rose
Roger Rowe
Simon Rowland
Margaret Rutterford
Victoria St John-Easton
Khamaruzaman B. Samsudin
Philip Sandall
Kirsten Scott
Bob Stacey
Roger Starr
Ron Stead
Paul Stickland
John Stribblehill
David Sturdee
Mohd Ariff Bin Mohd Tajudin
Peter Tay
Ray Tennant
Dave Thompson – RN 48 Southbourne Sea Scouts
Jim Towndrow
John Towndrow
Peter Towndrow
Sue Towndrow
John Vallance
Mrs G. Walford
James Weeden
James A. Welsh
Barbara White
Rob Wiggins
Pete Wilson
David Wraight
J.M. & J.J. Wyatt – 1st Reading
Yalding Scout Group

ACKNOWLEDGEMENTS

Acknowledgements have proved extremely difficult – I have received many letters, documents and personal reminiscences. To those whose names do not appear I extend my sincere thanks, and my apologies that it has been impossible in the space available to mention every name. I am greatly indebted to many friends and acquaintances for their support, inspiration and information.

In particular, these are: Patricia Somerville, who has most generously given up so much of her time over the last seven years providing secretarial assistance, which included retyping draft chapters, checking details and clarifying information, together with a vast amount of proof reading and research – and providing transport to distant places.

Susan Fountaine, formerly of the Hampshire Library Service, who gave much of her own time and expertise over a lengthy period in researching Prime Ministerial papers and First World War biographies, the ensuing Peace Talks, together with other research.

Muriel Thomas who for three years provided secretarial help and, most importantly, visited, made arrangements and translated articles from local and national journals at the Médiathèque Municipale Calais about the loss of the 1st Mortlake Sea Scout whaler in 1950.

My daughter, Andrea Masini, whose friendship and company through the time-consuming writing of this book has been immeasurable.

The Scout Association have made this book possible by giving me full access to their Archives to assist my researches, and put at my disposal high-quality additional material not previously seen. Particularly I must thank the following from The Scout Association at Gilwell: the Archive and Heritage Manager, Daniel Scott-Davies, his colleague, now retired, Patricia Styles, and his predecessor, Paul Moynihan; and Chris James, the Brands Director and an editor of *Scouting* Magazine.

My sincere thanks also to the Hon. Michael Baden-Powell for writing the Foreword, Ron Bird, Frank Brittain, Lieutenant Commander David Griffiths RN, Steven Harris, Richard Ivens,

Michael Loomes, Michael Nadin, Geoffrey Preshner, Vic Rolfe and Colin Walker for their help and advice. To the following researchers: Len Barnett, Christine Thomas, Martin Stallion, Ruth Rothschild and Martin Earl.

Sadly, a number of people who contributed in various ways are no longer with us, and include the late Jane Brooks, Tony Bartlett, Martin Hapgood, Ivan Hazleton, Eric Musgrave, Ken Wright and June Dale.

RESEARCHING THE WRITTEN BOOK

I was most fortunate in being given a 'slot' on BBC Radio Two on 14 October 2001 to speak about my book and why I was writing it. This brought many replies from listeners worldwide. Minute books, Scout magazines, scrapbooks, albums, logbooks, photographs and press cuttings all began to arrive, followed by emails, telephone calls and invitations to events. To Liz Holden and Ed Stewart, BBC Radio 2, I am extremely grateful for the publicity this generated on the *Where are you Now?* part of Ed's programme.

In 2001, the late Mr John Fogg, Director of Communications at The Scout Association, circulated a mail-shot to all Scout County Secretaries in Great Britain, from whom I received a good response.

I viewed films, silent and sound; many photographs and slides were studied of local, national and international Sea Scouting events; and newspapers and magazines, particularly the *Navy News*, *Daily Express*, *South London Press*, *East London Advertiser, and Scouting* magazine, kindly published letters to trace participants and eye-witness accounts.

Research has taken me to many places in many countries – in the UK and Europe, the USA and Canada. More recently I went as a visitor to the World Jamboree in Essex in 2007, the European Sea Scout Seminar in Dublin in 2008, the rededication of the painting of Jack Cornwell VC at HMS *Raleigh*, Torpoint, Cornwall in 2009; I also visited the National Sea Scout Camp 2009 and the wreath-laying ceremony at the grave of Warington Baden-Powell at St Andrews in Scotland on 16 August 2009, all of which provided invaluable information.

My *Short History of Sea Scouting*, written in 2007, was placed on the internet, bringing welcome enquiries, providing further constructive material.

FINALLY:

To my publishers, Phillimore, who from the outset had belief in the publication of the book and who read through every page to bring it to its completion.

With the centenary of Sea Scouting in 2009, the Sea Scout Branch entered into a new phase of activity, and there is every expectation that Sea Scouts of the future should be at least as adventurous as those of the past.

I dedicate this book to the Scout Movement and to the many members, land, sea and air section, whose lives I have been privileged in part to share.

Sources and Credits

I am most grateful for the information contained in the following chapters. The Scout Association Archives and The National Archives, Kew supplied information used in most chapters

CHAPTER 1 – THE EARLY DAYS OF SEA SCOUTING, 1909-14
Stuart Garnett
The Rt Hon. Baroness Bottomley of Nettlestone, Julian Hunt, Peter Jay, the late Peggy Jay, Simon Hunt and Hans-Jürgen von der Neyen
Christopher Thornhill, Archivist, The Royal Cruising Club
Kate Bradley of the Barnett Research Centre, Toynbee Hall Library
Verity Andrews, Assistant Archivist, University of Reading Library, Bell Collection
Adam C. Green, Trinity College Library, Cambridge, *Alumni Cantabrigienses* (1947)
Simon May, Archivist, St Paul's School, Barnes, London
Dr Claire Rider, Archivist, The Honourable Society of the Inner Temple

The Loss of the Ketch Mirror, *1913*
Mrs Wyn Payne in relation to the family of Christopher Witt

The Rev. Everard Digby
Lambeth Palace Library
The Headquarters Gazette, 1912-1920

CHAPTER 2 – THE LEYSDOWN TRAGEDY, 1912 – 2ND WALWORTH TROOP, SUNDAY, 4 AUGUST 1912
2nd Walworth Scouts, Sidney Marsh
Rex Batten of the Friends of Nunhead Cemetery
Mrs Angela Cousins on the Filmer family
Father John Walker, St John's Parish Office, London SE17
Lois Pratt, Community Librarian, Swale District, Sittingbourne Library
Ruth Partis, Local Correspondent, *Sheerness Times*
Southwark Local History Library on Walworth
Naval Historical Branch, Ministry of Defence
The late Maggie Bird, Metropolitan Police Collection
The Dulwich College Archivists
East Sussex Record Office
Winchelsea Museum, East Sussex

CHAPTER 3 – COASTWATCHING DUTIES, 1914-20
Imperial War Museum

XVI   SEA SCOUTING: A HISTORY, 1909-2009

CHAPTER 4 – JACK CORNWELL VC, 1900-16
Mr Bob Strong, Royal British Legion, Manor Park, London
Mr Steven Snelling
Mrs Stephanie Nunn, London Borough of Newham
Colonel Michael J. Dudding OBE, TD, FCIS
HMS *Raleigh*, Torpoint, Cornwall

CHAPTER 5 – THE INTER-WAR YEARS, 1919-38 – CARRYING ON WITH VIGOUR
The National Archives, Kew

CHAPTER 6 – RRS *DISCOVERY*/HMS *DISCOVERY*, 1901-2009
Royal Botanic Gardens Library, Kew
Dusty Miller
Brian Ewart, 16th Ilford/1st Ilford North Sea Scouts
Mr Tim Parr
Discovery Point, RRS *Discovery*

CHAPTER 7 – THE SECOND WORLD WAR, 1939-45
Museum of London Docklands
Douglas Francis, 3rd Hillingdon Sea Scouts
Peter Davis, 3rd Chalkwell Bay Sea Scouts
Douglas Robertson, 22nd Walthamstow Sea Scouts
Ramsgate Maritime Museum
Cliff and Peter Adamson, Sea Scouting in Liverpool
Group History, 3rd Osterley Scouts
The late Ivan Hazleton, 21st Holy Trinity Sea Scouts
Bob Norfolk, Petersham & Ham Sea Scouts
Peter Wilcox, 2nd Wallasey Sea Scouts
Doug Godlington, 1st Dunkirk Sea Scouts
The History of the 3rd Shoreham Sea Scouts
Vic Rolfe, 71st Reading Sea Scouts
2nd Ryde Sea Scouts

CHAPTER 8 – SEA SCOUTING, 1946-2009
Mr Roy Tucker, information on the 1st Mortlake Sea Scouts
Miss C. Ashton, Sea Scout Jerseying
Thames River Police Museum
Girl Guiding Archives
Mrs Vera Corner Halligan, MBE, The Sea Ranger Association
Richard Hart, Julian Cartwright, Mike Nadin – Dockland Scout Project
Clive Fisher, Discovery Sailing Project
Southampton University Archives
The late Martin Hapgood on Sea Scouting in Mortlake
Mr James Weeden

CHAPTER 9 – SCOUTING INTERNATIONAL
Group History, 2nd Wallasey Sea Scouts
Michael Loomes, Be Prepared: The Story of Scouting Museum
Richard Chambers, 1st Blofield Sea Scouts, Nicholas Willment, 11th Norwich Sea Scouts
Ron Bird, Richard Hart, Steve Newton

CHAPTER 10 – THE ADMIRALTY AND SEA SCOUTS, 1910-2009
Hansard – Written Answer (Commons): Boys' Naval Brigades (13 March 1911)
2nd Wallasey Sea Scouts History
1st Mortlake Sea Scouts, Admiralty Inspection
Synopsis of Inspecting Officers' Reports (1951) (1955) (1965) (1975)
The Boy Scouts Association: Extracts from Inspecting Officers' Comments in Annual Reports (1956-60)
Paul Naish, 99th Bristol (Cabot) Sea Scouts
4th Streatham Sea Scouts
The Sea Scout Journal
2nd Beeston Sea Scouts
Lt Commander David Griffiths, RN: Admiralty Recognition/'Y' Scheme/RN Recognition

PREFACE

Sea Scouting: A History – 1909-2009 is officially endorsed by The Scout Association and the publication is written with its full co-operation and approval.

This book portrays Sea Scouting by selecting a record of events illustrating the development of the Sea Scouts during the last 100 years of its noteworthy existence. Ten years in the writing, my book is supported by over 30 years' research, its genesis inspired through a lifetime's involvement with Sea Scouting.

On 18 November 1979 I attended a memorial service arranged by London Sea Scouts and Sea Rangers for Lord Mountbatten, Commodore of Sea Scouts, who had lately been assassinated. The service was held at All Hallows by the Tower, London, a church closely connected with seafaring over the centuries. The congregation, united in grief, stood to mourn the passing of Lord Mountbatten.

I sat adjacent to a memorial dedicated to three London Sea Scouts and a Leader of the Daily Mirror Troop of Sea Scouts who perished on the ketch *Mirror* on 25 October 1913 at Gravesend. Little was known about the memorial, and my extended research into the history of Sea Scouting began – my book following a paper trail across Britain and elsewhere.

From the beginning, the rapidly-growing Scout Movement generated an imposing amount of fiction, its activities described in credible fashion but with varying degrees of accuracy. It was predicted that Sea Scouting would grow to 20,000 members within five years; numbers have remained generally static, current membership being around 10,000.

Many books have been written about the life of Robert Baden-Powell and the history of the Scout Movement. Scouting has always valued the written word; the Boy Scouts of America say, 'If the Romans had a word for it, the Boy Scouts would have written a book or pamphlet about it'. In the UK several books provided the impetus for the increasing popularity of Sea Scouting, mainly *Sea Scouting and Seamanship for Boys* (1912) by Warington Baden-Powell, elder brother of Robert B-P. This book provided a springboard for Sea Scouting, a distinct branch of the Scout Movement.

Seamanship for Scouts was written in 1914 by Lieutenant Commander Stuart Garnett, RNR, of the Royal Cruising Club and Ratcliff Sea Scouts. He should also be regarded as one of the co-founders of Sea Scouting, forming the 1st Ratcliff Sea Scouts in 1909/1910 at Toynbee Hall, East London. It is said that he wrote *Seamanship for Scouts* (1914) resulting from the loss of the ketch *Mirror*, which he was not skippering, on the fateful night, 25 October 1913. His book was reprinted in 1937, and completely revised in 1952 by Tom Browne MA, Headmaster of the Training Ship HMS *Conway*. Tom Browne also published his own work *Sea Scouting* (1951) in which he stated, 'Since its inception in 1910 [*sic*] Sea Scouting has enjoyed considerable popularity. The great traditions of a seafaring nation and the healthy bustle of life aboard alone account for this'.

Baden-Powell [B-P] continued testing the training of youth. An early aim was to develop a Sea Scout Branch in the Scout Movement. In July/August 1909 C.B. Fry placed his training ship, *Mercury*, for the use of B-P. One 'Troop' lived on the ship taking part in sea activities for one week, changing places with the other Troop camping near Buckler's Hard in Hampshire. Later many 'land' Scouts changed their Scout shirts to Sea Scout jerseys to become part of the wartime Coastwatching Service from 1914-20. Of the Scouts in wartime the Prime Minister, Lloyd George, said in 1917, 'The young boyhood of our country, represented by the Boy Scouts Association, shares the laurels for having been prepared with the old and trusted and tried British Army and Navy.'

Throughout the 1939-45 War Sea Scouts again carried out war service. During the post-war years Sea Scouting returned to peacetime activities and international events which continue into the 21st century.

There appears scant published history of Sea Scouting, other than that mainly found in some Scout Group, District and County histories published over the years. For more formal accounts of Sea Scouting events, copies of the *Headquarters Gazette*, *The Scouter* magazine and latterly *Scouting* magazine, logbooks and souvenir publications have proved invaluable.

This history has been written in chronological order, although in some of the chapters, by way of explanation, occasional references have been made to past or future events. I have not always stated specifically the sources of all quotations, due to editing or amalgamation, as the continuity of the narrative would be interrupted by a succession of footnotes.

Much information has been given to me, enough for further volumes, but unfortunately due to constraints on space it has been necessary to omit many excellent accounts, for which I apologise to those contributors.

Roy Masini

FOREWORD

by The Hon. Michael Baden-Powell

Having been a Sea Scouter in the UK for a short while and having served as an active Scouter over many years, I am delighted to have been invited to participate in this important project by writing the foreword for this book.

The production of this book is important because it records a hitherto little known account of how and why Sea Scouting commenced in the UK, an episode in Scouting history which regrettably over time has become one of Scouting's unsung events.

With 2009 being the Centenary of the Sea Scout section of the Movement, it is indeed timely to tell this remarkable story which is a major part of the Scouting story.

The Baden-Powell brothers grew up constantly reminded of their family's naval connections as their maternal grandfather was Admiral William Smyth. For my grandfather Robert Stephenson Smyth B-P, well known for his army exploits and latterly founding the Scout and Guide Movements, with this kind of family background it was only natural in starting the Sea Scouts that he turned to his older brother Warington for inspiration.

Warington was a remarkable and highly accomplished person, who might best be described as 'the quiet achiever'. Educated at St Paul's School, London, his early sea training commenced on board the naval training ship HMS *Conway*, a training establishment for boys intending to become officers in the British Merchant Service. It was whilst serving on HMS *Conway* that Warington qualified as a Master Mariner and was subsequently commissioned as a Lieutenant in the Royal Naval Reserve. With this background, it is hardly surprising that his fascination towards small boats and sailing canoes in particular developed. During 1871 at the age of 24, he paddled and sailed his canoe around the Baltic Sea which he describes in his book *Canoe Travelling*.

During 1876 Warington was called to the Bar, admitted as a barrister to the Inner Temple London, and was subsequently admitted to the Admiralty Bar and appointed a Queen's Council in December 1897, becoming King's Counsel on the accession of King Edward VII in 1901.

Amongst Warington's other achievements, he became a Fellow of the Royal Geological Society, a member of the Worshipful Company of Shipwrights and an Associate of the Institute of Naval Architects.

As a designer of yachts and as an amateur yachtsman, Warington won creditable acclamation from the then yachting fraternity notably the 'Royal Canoe Club' with his boats, *Diamond, Koh-I-Noor* and his sailing canoe *Nautilus*.

Warington was also largely responsible for establishing the Royal Naval Artillery Volunteers, a fighting unit which later was to play an important part in Britain's efforts during the Boer War.

Warington was an inspiration to his younger brother Robert, being an eminent lawyer, a sailor, an excellent yachtsman, a serving officer in the Royal Naval Reserve and the author of a number of manuals for young people notably his book *Sea Scouting and Seamanship for Boys*, designed to help the development of young people. As did the Founder, Warington appreciated that they lived – and we, as the current generation, would continue to live – in a rapidly changing world, thus it would become even more important over time to raise greater public awareness regarding the benefits and opportunities Scout and Guide training offers young people irrespective colour, class or creed. History has shown both brothers were correct.

I offer congratulations to Roy Masini for having the foresight and commitment to put the Sea Scouting story into print, thus recording once and for all the real story of Sea Scouting for the benefit of all current and future Scouts and Guides.

I hope you will enjoy reading this book as much as I did.

Michael Baden-Powell

ONE

THE EARLY DAYS OF SEA SCOUTING, 1909-14

INTRODUCTION

1909 is acknowledged as the year Sea Scouting started, a branch, and not a separate organisation, of the Scout Movement founded in 1908 by Robert Baden-Powell (B-P). It is difficult to disentangle the history of the formation of Sea Scouting from the early history of the Boy Scouts Association (later renamed The Scout Association) – the two are inextricably bound together through National Scout Headquarters which issues policy, organisation and rules.

LORD ROBERT BADEN-POWELL OM (1857-1941)

He was born on 22 February 1857 at 6 Stanhope Street, near Hyde Park. The surname Baden-Powell combined the surnames of two old-established families. Henrietta Powell, mother of B-P, had ten children of her own, only seven of whom survived infancy; additionally she cared for two stepchildren of the four from one of her husband's previous two marriages. Her own children were given the forename name Smyth, but not Baden; the surname of Baden was assumed on her initiative, by Royal Licence, in 1902 following the death of her husband.

In 1868, aged 11, B-P went to school at Rose Hill, Tunbridge Wells in Kent, which gave him the opportunity to explore the local woods and the surrounding fields. In 1869, aged 13, B-P was awarded a scholarship to Charterhouse School in London as a Gown Boy Foundationer.

1   *Lieutenant Sir Robert Baden-Powell, KCB, KCVO, CB, Chief Scout, 1912.*

HENRY WARINGTON SMYTH BADEN-POWELL KC (1847-1921)
The Founder of Sea Scouting

He was B-P's elder brother and the acknowledged founder of the Sea Scouts. This chapter redresses the fragmentary and sometimes incorrect information available.

B-P wrote, 'It was largely thanks to Warington Baden-Powell's interest in boys and seamanship that Sea Scouting became popular in the early days of the [Scout] Movement, "when the Great War came suddenly upon the nation, Sea Scouts proved able to take over the duties of the Coastguards when called away to man our fleet. Thus Sea Scouts watched our Coast from John O'Groats to Land's End during the whole period of the War". They so acquitted themselves that at the end of the war they received the public thanks of the Admiralty and of His Majesty the King himself.'

Warington Baden-Powell was born on 3 February 1847, 11 years before Robert. The eldest of the Baden-Powell sons, he was christened after his mother's eldest brother.

In 1855 the family purchased the yacht *Pearl*, built for the Marquess of Anglesey in 1820. Warington was not only winning races, but the yacht was a significant social asset, large enough to accommodate the family in winter when their house was rented out.

Following family tradition, from 1857 to 1861 Warington received free education at St Paul's School in London, his father having been a Liveryman of the Worshipful Company of Mercers, a City of London livery company.

Warington, grandson of an admiral and nephew of a serving captain in the Royal Navy, could easily have been nominated as a midshipman, but his mother, on financial grounds, put him into the Merchant Navy. In August 1861, aged 14, he joined the Naval Training Establishment, HMS *Conway*, moored on the River Mersey, as entry no 187. The ship opened in 1859 as the first pre-training establishment for boys intending to become officers in the British Merchant Service, and Warington achieved the highest marks ever awarded.

Almost 100 years later Tom Browne, Headmaster of HMS *Conway* and Group Scout Leader of the 1st Neston Sea Scouts, wrote that Warington's early reports said he had plenty of boyish spirit in his junior term, being described as 'rather troublesome'.

'But his sense of responsibility and leadership soon showed itself, and when he left the *Conway* in 1864 he carried with him not only a splendid all-round report but a Double Extra Certificate – they must truly have been giants in those days for there is nothing above an Extra Certificate today – and a prize for seamanship.'

In 1871 Warington, aged 24, sailed a canoe around the Baltic which involved stops in Germany, Denmark and Sweden, described in his book *Canoe Travelling* and another earlier book *Practical Hints on Building and Fitting Canoes*. His later book, *Sea Scouting and Seamanship for Boys*, has been used by thousands of Sea Scouts.

In 1872 the B-P brothers embarked on a cross-country expedition by collapsible canoe when they paddled up the River Thames to its source, paddled down the River Severn, then up the River Wye into Wales.

Warington began training at sea in the famous East Indiaman *Hotspur* of the Smith Line, sailing under Captain Toynbee to Calcutta in India. Later he joined the Peninsular & Oriental S.N. Co. line

2   *Warington Baden-Powell – Lieutenant, Royal Naval Artillery Volunteers (RNAV), c.1887.*

(P&O), serving as a 4th officer, but leaving at the age of 26. In many ways he had been the most adventurous son, in boyhood being the skipper of various small boats in which his brothers had acted as crew. His love of swimming, shooting and exploration had seemed to mark him out for an independent life but, as the eldest son whose father had died, it was seen as his duty to take his father's place in the family.

Warington was very keen on sailing, but the family did not have a great deal of spare money, so the brothers obtained old boats, put them in order and the four of them – Warington at the time aged 27, George 20, Francis 18 and Robert 16 – set off during the holidays in search of adventure cruising around the coast of Britain and to Norway.

In 1873, after 13 years at sea, Warington came home to live in London to help his mother bring up those of her young children remaining at home, and did not leave for another 40 years. The family slogan became 'Warington can do it!' He designed and supervised the building of a five-ton yacht, *The Diamond*, taking his brothers on extended summer cruises along the south coast.

In 1876 Warington, called to the Bar in the Inner Temple, practised in the Admiralty Court, specialising in Maritime Law. His technical knowledge of seamanship was an asset as few lawyers at that time had any practical knowledge of the sea. With his experience he became a popular figure, also practising in the Wreck Court and the Northern Circuit, advancing to become a Queen's Counsel.

As a designer of sailing yachts and an amateur yachtsman, he won a considerable reputation, notably with his boats *The Diamond*, *The Koh-i-Noor*, *The Pearl*, *The Vanessa*, and *The Nautilus* canoe. He took *The Nautilus* across by steamer to Sweden, and paddled it from Gothenburg to Stockholm. Tom Browne said about the book which Warington wrote about the journey:

> This makes fascinating reading for those who share his love of adventure afloat, and the opening paragraph of this surely breathes the very spirit of Sea Scouting: 'A stiff breeze, wild scenery, freedom of dress and action, how much more do I prefer this to being guided by a tourist handbook from a first class railway carriage to a comfortable monster hotel.' The book has been out of print … he sounded the call to find adventure and enjoyment in small boats exploring new waters.

3   *Warington Baden-Powell sailing his five-metre yacht,* Diamond, *c.1906.*

4   *Warington Baden-Powell's Royal Naval sword.*

The Nautilus became a new and popular type of sailing boat, used by the Royal Canoe Club situated on the River Thames opposite Kingston in Surrey. For many years Warington was on the council of the Yacht Racing Association, and largely responsible for the establishment of the Royal Naval Artillery Volunteers. He was known as an all-round fisherman, fishing for trout, salmon, pike or perch, and invented the prismatic fly for fishing.

Although a practising barrister, the sea stood at the centre of Warington's life and he became a member of several organisations focused on the sea. He was a Fellow of the Royal Geographical Society, a member of the Worshipful Company of Shipwrights, and an Associate of the Institute of Naval Architects. On 19 August 1884, Warington enlisted as a Lieutenant in the Royal Naval Reserve. By 1900 Warington was a successful barrister and Queen's Counsel.

Robert was promoted to Major General by order of Queen Victoria having had a distinguished military career, the peak of which was the Boer War (1899-1902). Home in England he was feted as the 'Hero of Mafeking' and 'Man of the Hour'; at 43 he was the youngest general in the British Army.

Robert became particularly concerned about the youth of Britain, and decided to use his name, which continued to be well known to the general public, to help boys grow into strong manhood. He adapted his boyhood adventures and military skills into a scheme he called 'Scouting', and in May 1906 he submitted a report to the Army about his proposal for the 'Boy Scouts'. In 1907 B-P wrote to various influential people including Admiral Lord Charles Beresford, GCB, MP, aboard HMS *Edward VII*, Channel Fleet, who acknowledged his proposals for the formation of a 'Boy Scout Corps' by saying he thought the ideas 'quite capital', 'good order and discipline would promote patriotism', 'Your ideas merit enthusiastic support'.

Scouting for Boys

In 1907 B-P was promoted to Lieutenant General, and also held an experimental camp for 22 boys at Brownsea Island, Dorset. B-P was familiar with Poole Harbour into which he had sailed with Warington and his brothers and knew Brownsea Island would be excellent – 560 acres of undulating land with two lakes.

On 15 January 1908 B-P wrote Part 1 of *Scouting for Boys*, published by Pearson in fortnightly parts, each costing 4d. The cover drawing by John Hassall was intended to be exciting to the lad of 1908, featuring a boy lying hidden behind a large rock above a sandy shore watching a landing party from a mysterious ship. Next to the boy lay his broad-brimmed hat and staff.

Scouting for Boys was warmly received by the national press. *The Times*, *The Spectator* and *The Daily Graphic* reviewed it as being 'most visionary'. The success of the publication was immediate; boys and girls formed themselves into patrols to put into practice what they had read in the book.

Letters for advice on Scouting poured in; an office was provided in London by the Managing Editor of Pearson to deal with the many enquiries. Amongst these was a letter sent by a group of boys living near the coast, enquiring whether they could do their Scouting in boats and canoes and fortunately the letter was passed directly to Robert Baden-Powell. B-P had developed a love for the sea, and saw how well nautical activities could complement basic Scouting.

An Appreciative Audience.

5   'An Appreciative Audience'. Three young Sea Scouts, with a Petty Officer RN, c.1909.

B-P was occupied trying to tie up the many ramifications of Scouting in the early days, and after a year he felt the need for Sea Scouts to be a section of the Movement in their own right. He turned for guidance to his brother Warington, late of the Royal Naval Reserve – the boys were there, water activities happening, and in 1909 a uniform was devised which is not vastly different from that worn today.

EARLY DEVELOPMENTS IN SEA SCOUTING

The term 'Sea Scout' was first used around December 1908. The Seaman Badge was amongst the first five efficiency badges (proficiency badges) introduced by the Boy Scout Association. B-P later said he adopted his Scout Badges of proficiency from those of the Royal Navy. The earliest badges resembled naval insignia branch badges and those for Lifesaving, Seamanship, Pioneering, and Marksmanship.

In 1908 there were also other Sea Scout-type formations – the 'British Boys' Naval Brigades', also known as the 'Sea Scouts of the Empire', was founded by Lieutenant Barratt, RN. Units were established in south London and their name was changed to the 'National Naval Cadets'. There is no trace of 'Sea Scouts of the Empire' beyond 1910 – they were most probably absorbed by Boys' Naval Brigades, the Boy Scouts Association and the 'British Boy Scouts' around 1910.

SEA SCOUTING, 1909

Robert Baden-Powell organised a camp between 7 and 21 August 1909 at Buckler's Hard near the mouth of the Beaulieu River, close to Southampton on the south coast of England and this is where Sea Scouting is said to have begun. The nautical aspect of the camp was carried out on the Training Ship *Mercury*, which had been put at the disposal of the Scout movement by C.B. Fry, the Captain and Superintendent of the ship. C.B. Fry was a polymath who had captained England at cricket, played soccer for England and Rugby football for Oxford. In 1900 he held the world long-jump record. He wrote several books, was one of the most successful and influential journalists of his day, had represented India at the League of Nations and was once offered the throne of Albania. Quite something.

The training ship was moored in the River Hamble, and the camp was on the site of the ancient slipways from which many of Admiral Lord Nelson's ships were constructed and launched. Two

6   TS Mercury *was replaced in 1914 by the former HMS* Gannet, *above, which is now preserved in Chatham Historic Dockyard. Russell George, a 'Mercury Boy' in the 1930s, vividly remembered the very harsh regime of the ship. The ship, by then a reformed establishment, closed in 1970.*

7   *TS* Mercury, *c.1910, formerly the barque* Illovo, *on the River Hamble, Hampshire.*

Troops were present at the camp, each spending one week at each site, then changing over. On board TS *Mercury* the boys slept in hammocks and were instructed in elementary boat work by the naval instructors from the ship. The *Mercury* camp was seen as 'a departure which proved acceptable to many adventurous lads who might not have been attracted to Scouting'. Rudyard Kipling's son Jack attended the camp.

From 1910 Sea Scouting developed further when B-P wrote to the Admiralty for permission to establish Sea Scouts 'Coastwatchers'. Approval was given and many Scout Troops on the coast changed over to become Sea Scouts, their adult instructors often coming from the ranks of the Coastguard.

In June 1911 B-P asked his brother Warington to head the first specialised branch of the Boy Scouts. The Sea Scout training scheme was formulated by Warington, Admiral Lord Charles Beresford and Lieutenant L.H. Hordern, RN, later to become Commissioner for Sea Scouts. Warington outlined his concept of Sea Scouting as follows:

8   *Sea Scouts at TS* Mercury *camp, 1909.*

Sea Scouting is not necessarily a scheme for turning out a boy as a ready-made sailor with a view to his going to sea, but rather to teach him, by means which attract him, to be a handy, quick and disciplined man, able to look after himself and to help others in danger … Boat handling, swimming and life saving in the water can be taught to inland Troops just as well as those belonging to the coast … When it is possible to get a floating club house, the sea spirit enters still more into the boy's mind.

In 1911 B-P wrote *Sea Scouting for Boys* with a distinguishing crossed Anchor Badge for Coastguard Scouts – a badge for Able Seaman and Sea Scout ranks of Coxwain (Patrol Leader), Bowman = Corporal, Leading Seaman = First Class Scout (AB), and Ordinary Seaman = Scout.

At that time the Kent Sea Scouts started coastwatching duties at Dymchurch, Kent. Scouts were encouraged to attend local drills with life-saving apparatus and to keep watch with coastguards. The Admiralty showed a friendly interest.

9 *Warington Baden-Powell (Henry Warington Smyth Baden-Powell), 1847-1921, in the uniform of the Royal Naval Reserve (RNR).*

10 *Sea Scouts of the 1st Ratcliff East London Troop carrying oars to be transported on board* Idler. *Note the 'Corporal' stripes on the Sea Scout (first right) and on the Sea Scout with rudder.*

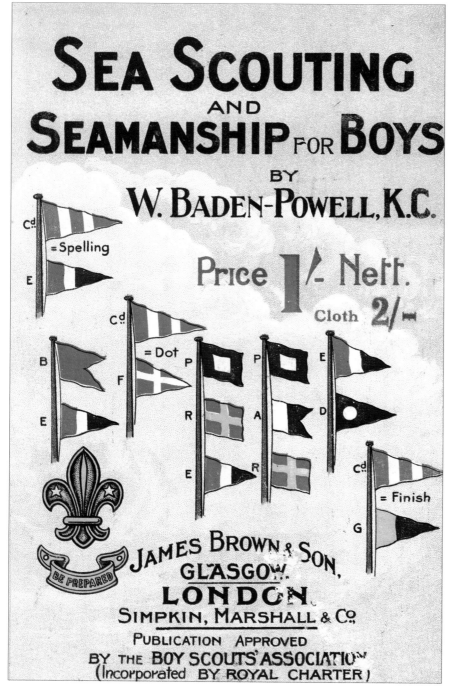

11   *The front cover of* Sea Scouting and Seamanship for Boys *by W. Baden-Powell, KC, 1912. The International Code Flags spell out 'Be Prepared', the Scout motto.*

In 1911 the Pool of London Sea Scouts Committee was formed under the Reverend Everard Digby, Commissioner for East London, to supervise the Scouts of the Thames. By March 1912, Sea Scout regulations had been issued to all Commissioners about the Sea Scout Badge Scheme.

In 1912, Sea Scouts from the 1st Ratcliff School Troop in Stepney, East London, and Sea Scouts from the Pool of London, appeared in the Lord Mayor of London's Show, and Sea Scouting by then had developed sufficiently to have a Sea Scout edition in the *Headquarters Gazette*, the official magazine published by The Scout Association.

ADMIRAL LORD CHARLES BERESFORD, GCB, GCVO, LLD, DCL, MP (1846-1919)

In 1912, Lord Charles Beresford, nicknamed 'Charlie B', was appointed first 'Headquarters Commissioner' for Sea Scouts, known as the Chief Sea Scout. B-P, The Chief Scout, wrote in his Outlook in the January 1912 edition of *Headquarters Gazette*:

> A practical scheme has been worked out for us by Mr Hordern, of which my brother, an old sailor, has compiled a book of instructions, and as Lord Charles Beresford has accepted office as Chief Sea Scout, we may look for big developments in this branch.

The choice of Lord Charles Beresford as Chief Sea Scout indicated Warington Baden-Powell did not wish to become too involved at that stage. B-P had known Lord Charles for several years, and had corresponded with him before the Brownsea Camp. Lord Charles's work as a MP precluded his active involvement in Sea Scouting, other than mainly ceremonial.

He was present at the first Sea Scout rally held at Earl's Court Lake on 20 July 1912, where a replica of Admiral Drake's flagship HMS *Revenge* had been built. Lord Charles and Lady Beresford were made welcome by a 100-strong Sea Scout guard of honour. There was a whale hunt, complete with mechanical whale, and a Red Indian attack by canoe, where all the participants, including adult leaders, ended up in the water.

12 *Lord Charles Beresford, GCB, GCVO, 1846-1919. First Chief Sea Scout, 1912-19. Ogdens issued a series of Guinea Golden cigarette cards between 1894 and 1907 covering events and personalities of the time.*

13   *Sea Scout buglers,*
Ratcliff Sea Scouts on
board yacht Idler, *c.1914.*

SEA SCOUTING AND SEAMANSHIP FOR BOYS

In 1912 *Sea Scouting and Seamanship for Boys*, written by Warington Baden-Powell, was published. In the preface to his book, he said, '"England expects that every man will do his duty." So signalled Admiral Lord Nelson on October 21st 1805, on going into action off Cape Trafalgar.'

'The book is to help boys to do their duty and is intended to be merely a chat with boys upon aquatic matters.'

Warington's book required a fairly high level of understanding to interpret its instructions. It only ran to one edition, but was re-published many times, for over 30 years being a main publication on Sea Scouting.

In the summer of 1913 Warington, aged 66, considered his duty to his family to have been accomplished, and in London he married Cecily Hilda Farmer from New Zealand, the woman to whom he had been secretly engaged for over two decades. His resolute mother, Henrietta, died aged 90 in London the following year.

Warington died in London on 24 April 1921 aged 74, his gravestone at St Andrews, Fife in Scotland recording that he was the founder of the Sea Scout Movement. After Warington's death his brother, Robert, wrote:

14 *Warington Baden-Powell and his wife, Cicely, 1914.*

He on whom I have always looked as the founder of Sea Scouting has just passed away. I realise that the Sea Scouting was an education in itself that has had much helpful influence on my career. It was from this personal experience of it that I have so persistently urged the development of Sea Scouting among our boys by men who knew something of sea life and who have the 'elder brother touch' in their nature.

It was under his [Warington B-P's] guidance that I, when a youngster, began my Sea Scouting as a Sea Scout. He was himself both a sailor and a boy at heart, and so his teaching told. It was largely thanks to his interest in boys and in seamanship that Sea Scouting became so popular … This book, by helping more boys in their turn to become handymen for their country, will stand as a fitting memorial to the life and character of its author.

Ill health of late years prevented him from taking as active a part in the training of Sea Scouts as he would like to have done, but his heart was always with them.

KETCH *MIRROR*, 1912-13

Robert Baden-Powell considered that, once trained, Sea Scouts would be excellent material to serve the British Empire. However the idea of Sea Scout training ships in every port did not materialise, due in part to the sinking of the ketch *Mirror* in 1913, and the outbreak of the First World War in 1914.

15 *The ketch* Mirror *was handed over to the Sea Scout Branch, received by Lieutenant Hordern, RN, for the Sea Scouts, in August 1912 at Greenwich, London. The* Daily Mirror *undertook to pay for the upkeep of the 52-ton ketch for the following 12 months.*

On 16 August 1912, following the Leysdown Tragedy, the *Daily Mirror* launched an appeal for the donation of training ships for Sea Scouts, and a 52-ton ketch, renamed *The Mirror*, was presented by the newspaper to Scout Headquarters.

In October 1913 *Mirror*, carrying 11 London Sea Scouts and two Assistant Leaders from the Daily Mirror Troop of Sea Scouts, recruited from boy messengers at the *Daily Mirror*, was run down by the steamer *Hogarth* in fog in the Thames estuary at Gravesend, Kent. Three Sea Scouts and one Assistant Scoutmaster drowned. The Coroner's Inquest recorded that *Mirror* had been navigated with proper and seamanlike care and the verdict recorded was Accidental Drowning. In correspondence between Prince Maurice of Battenberg, President of the Port of London Sea Scouts, and B-P, it was said that the boys 'had a good death'. Those drowned were Assistant Scoutmaster Roger S. Cornwall (24), Boatswain Christopher H. Witt (17), Sea Scouts Roland Purnell (17) Horace Rendell (14). Assistant Scoutmaster Fletcher Vowles, holder of a Second Master's Certificate, was awarded the Lloyds Silver Medal for Saving Life at Sea.

A memorial to the Sea Scouts drowned in this tragedy in 1913 is in the historic Church of All Hallows by the Tower.

The Oulton Broads Tragedy – Whit Monday, 1914

The *Norwich Mercury* reported a terrible fatality which occurred to Lowestoft Sea Scouts on Whit Monday, 1 June when their boat capsized on the River Waveney at Somerleyton. The crew of four Sea Scouts and three Leaders from the 1st Carleton left Oulton Broad on a sunny Saturday afternoon in a half-decked sailing boat, 16ft long and 4ft beam, and reached Somerleyton on the Sunday evening and pitched camp. They left on Whit Monday morning to spend the Bank holiday on the river with the intention of carrying out boating instruction.

The boat was heavily loaded with camping equipment, tent and their personal belongings. A strong wind was sweeping across the marshes. They rowed through the swing bridge and started to put up the sail. They got it up about three parts when a gust of wind caught it. The boat drove her stem into the water and went down bows first.

The only one to get clear was Stanley Woods who raised the alarm. The others, pinned down by the sail and drowned, were: Scoutmaster Mr Thornton Lory aged 32, a respected local solicitor, Mr James Lewington aged 38, Naval instructor ex-Royal Navy, Assistant Scoutmaster Sidney Searle aged 19, Arthur Beare aged 16, Sidney Thrower aged 16, and Reggie Middleton aged 14.

A Coroner's Inquest was to find the boat was overloaded for sailing and four of the Sea Scouts were poor swimmers.

It was recorded that thousands stood by the graveside at the funeral. A memorial cross of Cornish granite standing 15ft high was later erected in their memory.

Sidney Wood, the only one of the party to survive, was to die at the Battle of the Somme, aged nineteen.

16   *Memorial to Thornton Wrottesley Pendarves Lory (Scoutmaster and District Secretary), and five members of the 1st Carleton Patrol of Sea Scouts called to higher service through a boat accident on 1 June 1914.*

17 *Ratcliff Sea Scouts on the ketch* Idler *owned by Stuart Garnett, c.1914. The photograph was included in his book,* Seamanship for Scouts, *published in 1914.*

18 *Enrolment of 1st Portchester Sea Scouts on HMS* Victory, *Portsmouth. Admiral Sir James Startin, KCB, AM, with Scoutmaster W.L. Wyllie, a well-known seascape painter, c.1913.*

19   *1st Ratcliff Sea Scouts, c.1914.*

SEAMANSHIP FOR SCOUTS

In 1914 *Seamanship for Scouts* was published by Lieutenant Commander W.H. Stuart Garnett, RNR, of the Royal Cruising Club and the Ratcliff Sea Scouts.

Two

The Leysdown Tragedy
2nd Walworth Troop, Sunday, 4 August 1912

In 1912 Scouting stood for everything that was best in British youth, when it would soon be most needed.

Dulwich College Mission – 1905-9
The 2nd Walworth Troop evolved out of the Dulwich College Mission founded by Mr A.H. Gilkes and the Rev. G.C. Allen, which provided a home for orphan working boys in Walworth Road, south-east London. The Dulwich School Mission Troop was founded by Sidney John Marsh and others at 46, Brandon Street, Walworth.

The 2nd Walworth (Dulwich College Mission) Scout Troop
The Troop was formed at St John's Church, Larcom Street, Walworth. Church and street have changed little in the past 90 years, three lamps still hanging in the church as a memorial to preserve the memory of the nine boys who died. Local churchgoers and residents still speak as if this tragedy had only recently occurred, and many people living in the area know something of the event.

Sidney Marsh was a tall, well-set-up man of square build. He worked in the City of London for the Law Fire Society Ltd at 114 Chancery Lane, WC2, an impressive Victorian building now occupied by the Law Society. He was to remain there until 1946, having risen to superintendent within the company. He had been an officer in the Paymaster Branch of the Royal Naval Reserve since 15 November 1904.

Since 1908, Sidney Marsh had been devoted to helping the 'slum kids', as he called them, of the back streets of the neighbourhood. He became well known in the Walworth area for the way in which he would 'more-or-less drag some of the ragamuffins' from the street corners into his group. Unknown to him 'his' Scouts called him 'Old Marshee' – a term of some affection. He

20   *Photograph of the Filmer family taken shortly before the tragic accident, 1912.*

believed he was fulfilling a Christian mission in working with the less-privileged boys of Walworth. He regarded patriotism as part of his Christian duty, and his strong belief in a brand of muscular Christianity was sincerely held throughout his life.

He spent most of his free hours with the Scout Troop he had formed. The Scouts were expected to attend on most nights of the week, usual at that time, and for all fixed camps. He was referred to by his contemporaries as a man of uncommon sympathies, with great gifts of inspiration and organisation.

He lived at 46 Brandon Street, Walworth, a large, period house for the area which served also as the headquarters for the Troop. The rear garden had been covered over to provide a Scout hall for the Troop, and an area had also been converted into a carpenter's workshop and changing rooms.

21   *46 Brandon Street, south-east London, a fine Georgian house, home of Sidney Marsh and HQ of the 2nd Walworth Scouts; latterly Lord Somers' House, 1946-53.*

During August 1912, the worst summer month on record, an average of 183mm of rain had fallen, the temperature having been as low as 12.9°C (53°F) – London had only one day over 21°C (70°F).

Most of the Scouts in the crew of the 2nd Walworth were no strangers to sailing and had made the trip to Leysdown in 1911. Less than a month earlier they had given a display at the Sea Scout Rally at Earl's Court. Sidney Marsh had trained the boys to swim at the Manor Place Baths, Walworth, and to handle boats on the Thames.

The Leysdown Tragedy is an account of the disaster which befell the 2nd Walworth Scout Troop on Sunday, 4 August 1912. Eight Scouts, together with Frank Masters aged 14 from the Training Ship *Arethusa*, drowned in the choppy waters at Leysdown, Isle of Sheppey, off the north Kent coast.

A 32-foot cutter – taking 18 Scouts of the 2nd Walworth Troop, their Scoutmaster Sidney Marsh and four other adults to a week's camp at Leysdown – capsized. The 2nd Walworth boys who drowned were: William Beckham, Patrol Leader, 12, of 37 Eltham Street; Albert Dack, 11, of 17 Guinness Buildings, Brandon Street; Noel Filmer, 14 and Thompson (Tommy) Filmer, 12, both of 8 Brandon Road; Harry Gwynn, Patrol Leader, 13, of 46 Brandon Street; Percy Huxford, 12, of 133 Portland Street; James Skipsey, 12, of 43 Blackwood Street; Edward Smith, 11, of 100 Brandon Street. Most of the boys lived close to each other in these Walworth streets which mainly still exist. Frank Masters, 14, of the Training Ship *Arethusa*, Greenhithe, also drowned. Amongst the youngsters to survive were Scouts Baker, Phillips, Edward Beckham, Martin Schofield, and Patrick Taylor; the others are not recorded.

David Beckham, the renowned footballer, is closely related to the Beckhams of the '2nd Walworth' directly involved in the tragedy. If his great-grandfather, Edward, had not been saved from drowning, David Beckham would not have been born, and football history would have been written otherwise. Sadly, as shown above, William Beckham, aged 12, did not survive.

22   *The 2nd Walworth Troop, 1912 – shortly before the tragedy.*

SATURDAY, 3 AUGUST, 1912 –
THE CREW OF THE CUTTER

Sidney Marsh was at the helm in charge of the cutter, which in naval service had been rated to carry 40 armed men. The expedition crew of five adults and 18 boys was well within capacity. The cutter's oars made of ash were 14-15 feet long, and it would have been no mean feat for a 12- to 14-year-old to row with an oar of this length. It was therefore probable that there would have been two Scouts to each oar. Replacement oars were made in the workshop at 46, Brandon Street, Walworth. The cutter towed a small dinghy for ferrying the crew to land when they arrived at Leysdown.

The Scouts of the 2nd Walworth knew the River Thames around the London docks, particularly as they lived nearby and much employment in the area was connected with the docks.

23   *Sidney Marsh at the helm of the 2nd Walworth Scouts' cutter, July 1912.*

SATURDAY, 3 AUGUST 1912,
SUNSET AT 7.43 P.M.

The sky overcast, threatening rain. Shortly afterwards a fine drizzle fell and the Scouts used the sail to keep any further rain off, which had already soaked through their uniforms. By 9 p.m. it was dark and the crew reached Erith where they stopped for a rest and to stay for the night in the open boat covered by a sail and a shared blanket to keep off the chill night air.

DAY 2 – SUNDAY, 4 AUGUST 1912

By 4 a.m. it had stopped raining and would soon be first light. After a quick run ashore and a drink of water, they set sail down the river. It was still dark as sunrise was at 4.49 a.m., coinciding with high water, with the current starting to ebb (recede). The weather at the time was later described by Stuart Garnett, a leading Sea Scouter, as a stiff, easterly breeze blowing, and a steep sea.

SQUALL ONE

Abreast of (in line with) Warden Point a violent rain squall struck the cutter whilst the boat was on the starboard tack, causing her to 'lose way' (momentum). The first squall died down, but the rain continued. Sidney Marsh tacked and ran in close. As the cutter battled into each wave the crew were drenched with the spray. The heavy boat needed plenty of sail area to drive the craft through the flood tide, and would take time to respond to the commands given by the helmsman. The squall suddenly died down but it would return, and the rain continued. Despite all of this, the Scouts kept up their spirits by singing their Walworth Troop song, always a good way of raising spirits.

WARDEN POINT, ISLE OF SHEPPEY

Rounding Warden Point on the north-west coast of the Isle of Sheppey, the crew were close to their final destination. They could see land and the white cones of the pitched bell tents of the Scouts

08761.   WARDEN POINT, SHEPPEY.

24   *Postcard – scene of Warden Point, Leysdown, c.1912.*

from other Troops camping at Leysdown – near journey's end. On passing the 'Point', the wind had veered sufficiently to enable Sidney Marsh to carry on that tack (course) and at the same time fetch up (stop) close to the land.

Prior to the camp at Leysdown, Sidney Marsh had written to Chief Petty Officer Streeter of the Coastguard at Leysdown asking him to look out for the arrival of the Scouts' cutter. The watch reported the cutter, about two miles out, rounding Warden Point at approximately 1.30 p.m. It is not known why it had taken the cutter so long to travel from Waterloo to Warden Point, the crew having left Erith just after 4 a.m.

Sidney Marsh received the signal from the Coastguard onshore and gave the order to 'go about' (turn around). He put the mainsail over which became slack, and the foresail filled with wind. He kept on sufficiently to pass by the Coastguards' cottages, to enable the cutter to go about and run on the port tack to where a coastguard was signalling to where they were to come in. Sidney Marsh tacked again and ran in closer. The tide was on the flood, but he lost the tack on which he would have fetched up round Warden Point, when the crew would have downed sail and pulled in.

SQUALL TWO

Sidney Marsh tacked again, but on the starboard side the second squall hit them.

SQUALL THREE

2 p.m. Sidney Marsh lifted William Beckham over to the port side, to be ready to pull the main sheet when the helm was further over – the mainsail filled. At the moment when the boat had lost way, another squall struck the cutter. There was not enough way on the boat to force the cutter

forward, the wind coming in from Mussel Bank. John Filmer, an ex-navy man and father of Noel and Thompson Filmer, whom Sidney Marsh had asked to accompany them on the journey, was later to remark there was a 'nasty lop on the water' (a term used by sailors at the time meaning to break in short lump waves).

IN THE WATER

Attempting to remedy the situation, Sidney Marsh put the helm over and snatched the main sheet from William Beckham causing the cutter to come up a little. Before the vessel gathered way, it began to go over and filled with water. Mr Marsh was to say to the inquest that 'the extra puff shot right over the gunwales of the boat'.

2.10 – 2.12 – 2.13 P.M.

The water came in and the cutter filled up as though a wave had slid into it. Sidney Marsh fell out of the boat over the starboard side and into the sea. He later told the Margate inquest into the death of Percy Huxford on 14 August that he thought the accident had occurred between 2.10 and 2.13 p.m., as that was the time his watch stopped. The cutter righted itself but then capsized for a second time. Sidney Marsh was then rescued by the Coastguard gig 'as he was going down for the last time'.

25   Leysdown beach on a stormy August day.

At the inquest, Sidney Marsh said that Tom Filmer kept quite cool, considering everything, and was a good swimmer, but not accustomed to rough seas, and there was a lot of water which kept striking him in the face. Sidney Marsh turned him over and told him to keep hold of his shoulders, but the top of a wave came again, and 'I told him to swim and keep his head sideways. By that time he was pretty well done up.' Sidney Marsh held on to him but later said that he was rather done himself. At that time he estimated they were about half a mile from the shore. Those Scouts who had the strength to hang on to the dinghy were mainly saved; those Scouts who did not have the strength, tragically, did not survive.

Stuart Garnett, Leader of the 1st Ratcliff Troop of Sea Scouts, a barrister and experienced yachtsman who took part in the rescue, when writing in the *Royal Cruising Club Journal* in 1912 stated that the Scouts of the 2nd Walworth hung on to the rail, singing, shouting, and chafing as a Scout in a tight place should. The water was shallow, the bow weighed down by blankets (14 blankets and the boys' boots), anchor and gear, causing the cutter to grip the mud at that point. One of the Scouts jumped clear and the Scoutmaster (Sidney Marsh), who went to help him, was carried upstream by the tide. The stern swung slowly around, and the wind got under the peak of the sail. Suddenly the vessel righted and capsized to port. Three Scouts, caught beneath the sail, were drowned; one drifted away while Assistant Kidd went in pursuit of Albert Dack.

Sidney Marsh tried on several occasions to swim to rescue some of the Scouts but despite his efforts, later described as heroic, they were carried away by the offshore wind. The Scouts who were not strong enough to fight the tide drowned. Sidney Marsh nearly saved Tom Filmer, whose father John saw both his sons perish.

COURAGEOUS ACTIONS OF LEYSDOWN COASTGUARDS

More members of the 2nd Walworth Scouts would have died if Chief Petty Officer Streeter of the Leysdown Coastguard had not been asked by Sidney Marsh to keep a look-out for the arrival of the Walworth crew. From the Coastguard lookout tower he witnessed the tragedy unfold in the pouring rain.

The Coastguard 'lifeboat' was an 18-foot gig rated to carry 14 persons in all, and on this dramatic occasion its crew were able to rescue 21 souls from almost certain death – 16 Scouts and five adults had been in the water for half an hour and all were exhausted, some in a serious condition.

FIVE MINUTES TO TWO

During the rescue the Coastguard gig shipped 1½ tons of water which, with the crew and the survivors, could easily have caused it to turn over. Ironically, the squall vanished as quickly as it came.

The following is an extract from the *Daily Chronicle* of Monday, 5 August:

One of the greatest heroes of the camp of heroes is a woman. She is a Mrs Brummell, of Balham, and a member of a private party who are camping here. She was one of the first to see the boat capsize, and it was her actions that urged the rescuers to greater efforts. 'Why don't you swim out to the boys?' she asked some of the rescuers as the boat was being launched. It was pointed out to her that no swimmer could reach the capsized vessel, so strong was the force of the waves. 'But surely you can swim out with a line?' she cried, 'If you don't, I shall!' So saying, she started to wade out into the sea, but when the water was up to her neck she was compelled to stop. She stood her ground, and when the line was paid out by the Boy Scouts she held her length [of line] with the rest of them. Later when the victims were brought ashore, she worked valiantly at first aid and artificial respiration, and had the satisfaction of restoring several boys to life again.

No More Bodies

No more bodies were recovered up to 1.30 that morning. The rescued lads were carefully tended by the watch at the station, by the wives of the Coastguard at the cottages, and some at the Scout camp.

Government Tug Security

A torpedo destroyer and the Government Tug *Security* were dispatched from HMS *Actæon*, the Torpedo Training School and naval base at Sheerness to search for the other bodies and to attempt a recovery of the capsized cutter, which was in fact drifting towards Herne Bay. Later the cutter and its dinghy were found on the oyster grounds at Whitstable; the dinghy still contained various articles of clothing and a gold watch belonging to a member of the crew.

Inquest – Eight Victims – Leysdown, Kent

The *Guardian* and the *East Kent Advertiser*, Saturday, 10 August reported:

At 2 o'clock on Wednesday afternoon [7 August] Mr C.B. Harris, the Coroner for the North East Division of Kent, opened the Inquest on the eight victims whose bodies had been recovered on Monday.

The Coroner's Court was convened in the upper room of the last cottage. Mr Harris sat at a little table before which the school desks were ranged in a square. At these desks the jurymen sat. Mr Aylmer Digby, the barrister-at-law, attended the inquiry to represent the Boy Scouts Association. Behind the jury were the witnesses, several of whom were parents who had lost their sons in the catastrophe. Pressmen were accommodated at the desks built for infants. Crowding in at the door were picture men from the illustrated papers with cameras already set.

The jury promptly came to a decision, not waiting for the Coroner to sum up. The foreman, Mr Love, got up and said the jury were satisfied that the lads were accidentally drowned. They all agreed that Mr Marsh did his utmost under the conditions and that his conduct was very praiseworthy. Scoutmaster Woodburn, of No 9 (St Paul's Troop) Isle of Sheppey Boy Scouts, Sheerness, got up at the back of the Court and said he had come up to say they appreciated very highly the work of Scoutmaster Marsh and the valuable assistance given by No 1 Sheppey Troop in the catastrophe. The jury, through their foreman, expressed a vote of condolence with the bereaved parents, in which the Coroner joined.

Mr Digby, addressing the Court, said he was desired by Mr Marsh to say that no such thing as a half hitch was made whilst he was in charge of the boat, and he wished that to be understood. Mr Marsh stepped into the centre of the Court once more and said he and the lad Beckham had the mainsheet in hand and he put a boy next to him so that if there came an extra tug he could hold on too. He had never known a sailing ship to have half hitches round the block. On thinking the boat was going over he snatched the main sheet out of the boy's hand and would consider anything else as absolutely criminal. He would bring up other evidence to prove what he said if the Coroner thought it necessary.

Inquest – Percy Huxford – Margate, Kent

The *Thanet Times* of Friday, 16 August stated:

The last chapter of the sad story of the drowning of the Walworth Scouts off the Isle of Sheppey was completed on Tuesday [13 August], when the body of the ninth victim of the Leysdown disaster was washed ashore at Margate. It was that of Percy Baden-Powell Huxford [who was named after Baden-Powell, the Boer War hero]. The inquest was conducted at Margate Town Hall on Wednesday afternoon by Mr Coroner Boyes. Mr Edward Charles Austen was foreman of the jury.

The jury returned a verdict of 'Accidental death by drowning' and expressed their deep sympathy with the deceased's father. The Coroner associated himself with the jury's expression of sympathy. The Coroner called forward the witness Cox and told him he was entitled to the sum of five shillings for finding the body, but the coastguard said he would like the amount to be handed to the father for the purpose of helping to defray the expense.

HMS *Fervent*

As a tribute to the dead Scouts who drowned off the Isle of Sheppey, Mr Winston Churchill, MP, First Lord of the Admiralty, sent HMS *Fervent*, a torpedo-boat, to Leysdown to convey their coffins up the River Thames to Rotherhithe for burial at Nunhead. The bodies were taken out to the torpedo-boat by the Coastguard gig which rescued Scoutmaster Marsh and the other survivors. As the warship passed by, shipping on the River Thames lowered its flags in salute.

The *Sheerness Times* – Thursday, 8 August 1912; also the *Daily Express*, *Daily Chronicle* and the *Sphere*

Captain C.D. Johnson, Commanding Officer of HMS *Actæon*, had been directed by the Commander-in-Chief at the Nore to make arrangements and he selected the destroyer *Fervent* to act as a 'warship hearse', and attended himself at Leysdown to superintend the embarkation of the bodies. The nucleus crew of the *Fervent* was strengthened by seamen from the destroyer *Zephyr*.

The following is the exact entry in the Navigator's Log of HMS *Fervent* which is held in The National Archives at Kew:

Navigator's Log – Wednesday, 7 August 1912
She was at Stangate Creek, secured to a Number two buoy. Hands were called at 06.30. The forenoon was routine, although at 09.00 'lit fires in Nos 1 and 2 boilers'. At 13.15 she unshackled, slipping and proceeding half an hour later. By 14.45 she was making 15 knots. 'CO as Req for Leysdown' [Ship's company required for Leysdown.] At 15.50 she stopped and lowered her whaler. This was sent to CG [Coastguard] station". At 16.00 she anchored off Leysdown in 2 fathoms, putting ¾ shackle down. Her anchor bearings were Sheerness S28W and the CG station NW. This was short-lived however as she weighed [anchor] at 17.35. There was a moderate breeze from the SW force 4, the sky was blue with clouds, but the visibility was reduced due to haze or mist. Anyway, she re-anchored at 17.50. She 'Embarked bodies of Boy Scouts' at 18.00, weighing and proceeding at 18.15. At 20.00 she was again at 15 knots, 'CO as Req for Gravesend'. The wind was reduced to a

gentle breeze from the same direction by this time. The sky was overcast with clouds. At 21.00 she anchored off Gravesend in 15 fathoms. The fires were banked in number one boiler at 21.30 and in number two at 23.00.

Thursday, 8 August

At 03.15 fires were spread in number one boiler and 04.00 in number two. Hands were called at 05.15 with her weighing and proceeding an hour later. There was a gentle breeze, force 2, from the SW and it was overcast. Navigating up the Thames the speed was reduced to 12 knots. At 06.10 she secured to a buoy off Erith, but slipped and continued her way at 07.10. At 08.00 hands cleared into number one suits. One hour later she secured to Cherry Garden Pier (Rotherhithe) and 'disembarked remains of Boy Scouts'. Having done this 09.25 she slipped and proceeded down the Thames once more, with her 'hands employed repairing fenders'. At 12.50 she again secured to number two buoys in Stangate Creek.

THE SHEERNESS TIMES – THURSDAY, 8 AUGUST 1912.
ALSO THE DAILY EXPRESS, DAILY CHRONICLE AND THE SPHERE

On Cherry Garden Pier were gathered a handful of spectators headed by a white-surpliced clergyman. For a full hour they had strained their eyes through the gloom of the Pool of London for the first indication of the vessel. Four tiny Boy Scouts, wearing the official badge of mourning, presented themselves with a floral token, a *fleur-de-lis*, composed of red, violet, and white flowers, but they disappeared before the black hull of the destroyer was discerned rounding the bend of the river.

Ranged at the side of the vessel was a guard of honour of men from HMS *Zephyr* [a sister ship of HMS *Fervent*] and as a tiny coffin passed there rang out a sharp and crisp command 'Present arms!', the only words spoken during the proceedings.

Preceded by Mr Morris, the coffin was carried from the pier over the footbridge to the quayside and conveyed outside to Cherry Garden Street, where the seven hearses were standing [the brothers Filmer lay side by side]. The scene here was watched in respectful silence by a crowd of many thousands of sympathetic onlookers. Again and again, the melancholy procession was repeated. After the eight coffins came a bluejacket bearing a large white wreath – a tribute from the Leysdown Coastguards and their wives, who so carefully tended to the survivors of the disaster.

PROCESSION THROUGH CROWDED STREETS

Out in the street a dozen Boy Scouts belonging to the Port Authority Sea Scout Troop kept a way with their staves for the passage of the coffins. Then, when the last body came ashore, they fell in behind the hearse and formed part of the mournful procession. Along Cherry Garden Street and Jamaica Road the procession passed through dense crowds. Carmen drew to one side and uncapped. The trams stood still and the passengers rose to their feet. It was so all the way through Bermondsey to Walworth, where another huge crowd had gathered around St John's Church, which serves as a resting place for the coffins until Saturday.

A public notice was issued to the Southwark Battalion of the National Reserve:

NATIONAL RESERVE.

———

Southwark Battalion.

———

COL. G. RUMSEY, V.D., Commanding.
E.G.L ALLBERRY, Organising Officer.

———————

FUNERAL PARADE.

———————

BOY SCOUTS.

The Battalion will Parade as strong as possible in Larcom Street (Brandon Street End), at 2.30 p.m.,
On Saturday the 10th inst. Medals and Badges to be worn.
Members are requested to be punctual to time.

A. E. WATTS

A Fund of One Hundred Thousand Pennies

On Wednesday, 7 August the *Daily Express* announced the organisation of a fund of 100,000 pennies in order to erect a fitting memorial to the dead Scouts; this appeal was endorsed by Lieutenant General Edmond Ellis, Chief Commissioner of the Boy Scouts Association, who was acting for Lieutenant General Baden-Powell, the Association's founder and Chief Scout, who was at the time out of the country visiting South Africa.

'The Funeral Day, The Saddest Day'

Despite continuous rain on the day of the funeral on Saturday, 10 August, the route was lined many deep – the *Daily Express* estimated that 'over a million mourners' were present; at St John's Church, Walworth, and 100,000 people filed past the coffins paying their respects.

The funeral started from St John's Church, Walworth. Crowds lined each side of the route, starting from the church. Flags were at half-mast, and many shops were closed and shuttered in token of mourning. Crowds of people were looking from their windows. The procession was a very long one. The missing boy [Percy Huxford] still had not been found. He was to be interred with the others later. Each family had its own horse and carriage, and an open carriage for flowers.

FUNERAL SERVICE

The *Daily Mail* of Monday, 12 August stated:

The weather was pitiless. Heavy thunder showers broke over the district and while the service was in progress rain drenched the waiting thousands; but none of the onlookers seemed troubled by the weather. Half a dozen people sat through it all on a roof ridge. The little Scouts standing as a guard of honour in the churchyard were soaked and water dripping from their bare arms, but they bore the discomforts cheerfully. In the church Scoutmaster Marsh and the little band of survivors of the sailing trip were a conspicuous group. They were stationed near the coffins and they knelt in prayer immediately after entering the church.

The *Daily Telegraph* of 14 August reported the following:

The Reverend J.C. Morris, Vicar of St John's, read the funeral service, to which there were several choral additions. The coffins were lifted onto the shoulders of Scouts [Scout Officers] and borne to waiting hearses, while *The Dead March from Saul* was played on the organ. The white coffins, draped with the Union Jack [Union Flag] and almost hidden by flowers, were a touching sight as they passed through the crowded streets, now bright with sunshine.

The choral funeral service, in which the Bishop of Woolwich took part, was solemn and beautiful, but it could not assuage the emotion of anguished mothers, who sobbed aloud.

As the coffins, each enfolded in a Union Jack, were borne from the church, one or two [of the smaller] Scouts who had themselves been snatched from a watery grave at the side of their dead comrades cried bitterly, and several of the mothers were so distressed they had to be assisted to the carriage.

It was a procession of seven hearses – the bodies of the brothers Filmer were side by side in one hearse – that set out on the long route to the cemetery.

The Chief Scout, General Sir Robert Baden-Powell [who was abroad], had sent the most beautiful wreath of blue and white flowers in the shape of a lifebuoy to rest amid other floral tributes on the coffin of every Scout.

26   *The 2nd Walworth Scouts' funeral, Nunhead Cemetery, south-east London, August 1912. Crowds stood eight deep for five miles.*

27   *Postcard, The Leysdown Memorial – The Resting Scout, 1914.*

The appearance of the street on the long route to the cemetery was an eloquent tribute of public sympathy. Troops of Boy Scouts, Sea Scouts and Boys' Naval Brigade from all parts of London had come to line the roadway, and behind them the people were gathered, in places four or five deep. Outside the cemetery there were thousands of people.

The bodies are buried on a hilltop beneath the shade of a large elm tree. They were interred two-by-two; the graveside service, at which four clergymen officiated, occupied the greater part of an hour.

PATHÉ-ANIMATED GAZETTE – 16 AUGUST 1912

Because of the interest, *Pathé-Animated Gazette* made a newsreel film of the event, a copy of which still exists in the British Film Library. The newsreel was shown as being a weekly record of the world's events in motion pictures and was seen by more than 20 million people. Having viewed the film, the author was able to verify many details about the funeral day.

The *Thanet Times* of Friday, 16 August reported:

Yesterday [Thursday, 15 August] the body of Percy Huxford was removed from Margate for interment at Walworth. The local Scouts, whose forces were augmented by those encamped in the District, assembled at 11 a.m. at the Buffs [East Kent Regiment] Drill Hall, and proceeded to the premises of Messrs Gore where a brief, pathetic service was conducted by the Rev. J.D. Stewart, the Secretary of The Scouts Association. Some 125 Boy Scouts participated in a melancholy ceremony.

MEMORIAL TO THE 2ND WALWORTH SCOUT TROOP – 1914

The sacrifice made by the boys buried in 1912 under the moss-green banks of the burial plot would not be forgotten. There would be a fitting memorial to the Scouts whom the nation had mourned. It was decided that Frank Masters of the *Arethusa* be treated as a Scout.

The memorial was commissioned by the *Daily Express*, but it was not until the summer of 1914, two years after the boys were buried, that the magnificent 'cenotaph' was erected on a plot, also at Nunhead cemetery, in a prime position on an avenue visible to all. It was designed by Sir Giles Gilbert Scott RA – whose drawings are preserved in the Royal Institute of British Architects' library in London – and sculpted by Miss Lillie Reed, who had worked on the new Anglican Cathedral in Liverpool with Scott. The original monument in 1914 cost £500 (around £21,500 today) and

28 *The new Scout memorial to the 2nd Walworth, erected 1992 to replace the original memorial designed by Sir Giles Gilbert Scott and stolen in 1969.*

comprised a life-sized bronze figure of a resting Scout standing with head lowered in mourning holding his stave in salute directly before him. The figure measured approximately five feet high, and overall the marble monument was about eight feet high.

MEMORIAL TO THE 2ND WALWORTH – 1969

In July 1969 the statue of the 'Resting Scout' in Nunhead Cemetery was sawn through at the ankles and stolen, leaving only the boots remaining. The scrap value of the bronze statue was estimated by the police to be at about £40 (about £400 today). The London *Evening Standard* described the theft as 'easy cash for someone without qualms about breaking into the cemetery' and 'we know East Dulwich police feel it has almost certainly been melted down. Extensive enquiries revealed nothing.' However, not all hope has been lost that the statue, or the mould from which it was cast, may one day be recovered.

Other enquiries revealed there had been serious vandalism in the cemetery during the previous 30 years with some associated talk of 'black magic' ceremonies. These stories are strongly refuted by people connected with the cemetery.

In late 1970 after Nunhead Cemetery had been reopened, the marble plinth and the cenotaph were destroyed in the process of clearing up the cemetery. The marble chips lie along an adjacent path and can be seen without too much difficulty. When the Friends of Nunhead Cemetery (FONC) was formed in 1981 only a few bricks still marked the grave of the 2nd Walworth Scouts. As a boy of five Kim Mayo, later a Scout Commissioner, saw the Scouts' funeral in 1912, and he instigated the research into the Leysdown tragedy. Kim Mayo died in 1999, but he lived to see the original bronze plaque brought to the Nunhead Cemetery Open Day in 1998.

REPLACEMENT MEMORIAL TO THE 2ND WALWORTH – 1992

In 1992 very fine white Carrara marble carved in the shape of an open book was donated.

> TO COMMEMORATE
> THE SCOUTS OF
> THE 2ND WALWORTH TROOP
> DROWNED OFF LEYSDOWN,
> ISLE OF SHEPPEY
> ON 4TH AUGUST 1912

On the opposite pages there is a carved Scout badge in the style used in 1912, and underneath is written:

THIS STONE ERECTED
IN 1992 REPLACES THE
MEMORIAL DESIGNED
BY
SIR GILES GILBERT SCOTT

DONATED BY
KELLAWAYS FUNERAL SERVICES
& FRANCIS CHAPPELL
MONUMENTAL MASONS LTD
WITH THE HELP OF
THE FRIENDS OF
NUNHEAD CEMETERY

On Sunday, 26 April 1992 the new memorial was dedicated at 3 p.m. under a steady downpour; the clergy led the congregation up the main avenue in similar weather to that of 80 years before.

The Anglican, Roman Catholic and Methodist churches joined in the service of remembrance and thanksgiving. Traditional hymns were played by the band of the Salvation Army. Members of the public were joined by Members of Parliament, the Mayor of Southwark and other distinguished guests. The sermon, preached by the Rev. J.E.D. Davies, was one of thanksgiving for those like Sidney Marsh who gave so much to the youngsters of London. The memorial was dedicated by Father Tony Davies, Vicar of St John's, Walworth. Nick Hickman, a Scout Bugler from Dulwich College, the school attended by Sidney Marsh, sounded the Last Post.

At the end of the service an elderly lady stepped forward and laid flowers on the grave. The card read 'In memory of James Skipsey. From the Skipsey family', a moving gesture of remembrance which had spanned 80 years.

MEMORIAL TO 2ND WALWORTH: BRASS PLAQUE RECOVERED – 1997

In 1997 a scrap metal dealer from Deptford, not far from Nunhead, telephoned the archivist of The Scout Association, asking whether the name 'Percy Baden Powell Huxford' meant anything to him and was he related to Lord Baden-Powell. Fortunately the name Huxford was known through researching the Leysdown tragedy. One of the Scouts who drowned in 1912, Huxford was born in 1900 at the time of the Boer War and was given the two middle names of 'Baden Powell' in recognition of the national hero, General Baden-Powell.

The outcome of the conversation led to a visit to the scrap dealer's yard, where a bronze plaque had been uncovered, having been there for over 20 years. The wording on the bronze was stained, but not damaged and fortunately had remained intact. The eight names and dates confirmed that this was the plaque from the Scouts' monument stolen from Nunhead Cemetery in 1969. It was returned to The Scout Association by the dealer who wished to remain anonymous. Without Percy Huxford having been given the middle names of Baden Powell, it is probable that the plaque would not have been recovered.

MEMORIAL TO 2ND WALWORTH, LEYSDOWN – 1995

In *The Walworth Scouts* by Rex Batten, published by FONC in 2003, he wrote:

The *Sheerness Times and Guardian* gave a brief history of the monument in Nunhead Cemetery and then gave the following account of the new memorial at Leysdown:

'In Leysdown, just through the lych-gate, our own memorial is more difficult to destroy. It is a three-ton piece of Kentish ragstone bearing a bronze name plaque commemorating those who died. But it was not put in place until 1995 when the lych-gate memorial at the original entrance to St Clement's Church was dedicated. Until then, the greatest loss of life off the Kentish coast was recorded only in the printed word.'

'The dedication of the stone was an impressive ceremony. The Scouts and local groups took part and representatives of FONC also attended. A cross for each boy was placed around the stone, and it was a very proud moment for Kim Mayo when he was asked to perform the unveiling.'

In the *Sheerness Times & Guardian* of August 1995, its Leysdown correspondent, Ruth Partis, wrote:

The lych gate at the entrance to St Clement's churchyard will be dedicated and officially opened on Sunday at 3 p.m.

At the ceremony, a memorial will also be dedicated to the eight Scouts of the 2nd Walworth Scout Troop who drowned off Leysdown on Sunday 4th August 1912. A young trainee from the training ship *Arethusa* also drowned.

Surrounding the churchyard is windswept open farmland; the church has gone, but the memorial gardens remain, maintained by the local authority.

It is envisaged that a memorial service will be held at Minster, Isle of Sheppey, in 2012 to mark the centenary of the Leysdown Tragedy.

MEMORIAL TO 2ND WALWORTH: REPLICA TO REPLACE BRASS PLAQUE, STOLEN 1969

In May 2003 the nine Scouts were remembered at a special ceremony during Nunhead Cemetery annual Open Day. Among those who attended was 88-year-old Len Filmer, born shortly after his uncles were drowned. Mr Filmer's grandfather, John, was on board the ex-naval cutter when it capsized and two of his 11 children, Noel and Thompson, perished. Len Filmer laid flowers in the Anglican chapel ruins where a replica of the plaque marking the youngsters' deaths in the Leysdown tragedy, which found a new home on the wall, was unveiled. The replacement plaque in fibreglass was most tastefully crafted and was otherwise identical to the brass original.

29 *Plaque set in Kentish ragstone in Leysdown Memorial Gardens, dedicated on 10 August 1995.*

SIDNEY MARSH – POSTSCRIPT

Sidney Marsh was recalled to the Royal Naval Reserve in 1914 as a Paymaster. He survived the Great War 1914-18 and was retired as a Paymaster Lieutenant Commander, RNR, in 1921. His service reports throughout noted that he was an excellent officer. He worked for the Law-Fire Society in Chancery Lane in the City of London throughout his working life, retiring in 1946.

I am fortunate in having permission to quote from the Dulwich College Archives of 1946 the following:

> After 49 years with Law-Fire Insurance Co., a subsidiary of Alliance Assurance Co., Mr S.J. Marsh has retired as Secretary. This week too, he severed another tie with London life. He slept for the last time at Walworth, where he was moving spirit of the Dulwich College Mission Boy Scouts. Mr Marsh is a bachelor, 65 years old. 'You cannot live in a slum and marry', he says. Now he will live in comfort at Ashdown Forest. But he will keep a sympathetic eye on the Scouts he helped start in 1909.

The Dulwich College Archives show that the contents of 46 Brandon Street were handed over to the Boy Scouts Association. This was re-named Lord Somers House in 1946; it closed in 1953 on expiry of the lease and is again a private house. Sidney Marsh was a director of the British Sailors' Society, and Chairman of the Conservators of Ashdown Forest from 1946 to 1967. He then retired, moving to Nutley, Sussex and died on 21 September 1972, leaving an estate of £17,283.55 (around £180,000 today).

Three

Coastwatching Duties, 1914-20

The coastwatching services of the Sea Scouts in the Great War 1914 to 1918 have been seen as their finest hour – lasting four years.

Spies and Invasion

Between 1904 and 1914 Imperial Germany was perceived as a threat to British national security. Invasion theories rolled in and by 1909 people were convinced of this danger, much of it generated by the book *Riddle of the Sands* (1904) by Erskine Childers. Robert Baden-Powell even received a copy of what purported to be the German invasion plan 1908.

German Spies, 1914-16

Eleven German spies caught in the UK during the First World War were shot by firing squad at the Tower of London under Defence of the Realm legislation, and buried at Plaistow, east London, one on 8 November 1914, nine in 1915 and one on 11 April 1916. From contemporaneous accounts, they all 'died well'.

1914

A Committee of Admiralty and War Office Representatives met on 25 February 1914 to discuss coastal defences and the question of coastwatching in the event of war as follows:

a)   'What scale of naval attack the defences proposed for the East Coast Ports would be capable of withstanding.'

b)   'The question of Coast Watch and the responsibility for the maintenance and working of the telephone system.'

c)   They concluded that 84 coastguard stations should be manned on mobilisation.

The Coastguard goes to War

Mobilisation was effected quickly in August 1914. Although the Coastguard Service was an integral part of coastal defences, coastguards packed and moved to naval depots or drafted within hours of receiving telegrams into older reserve ships, enabling vessels to go to sea without the delay of being held in port until crews had been recruited.

The Commissioner of Police, Sir Edward Henry, and the Postmaster General asked Colonel de Burgh, Deputy Chief Commissioner at Scout Headquarters, 'to watch telephone lines between London and Dover.' Patrolling railway lines and guarding bridges was seen as an important duty. The Commissioner of Police at Scotland Yard used 2,000 Scouts to guard the telephone wires. It was believed telephone lines from Dover were being tapped so consistently by foreign spies that the normal telephone from Dover could not be utilised.

Mrs E.K. Wade, B-P's secretary, wrote in her book *27 Years with Baden-Powell* in 1957 that prior to the start of hostilities, 'The Chief Engineer to the Post Office supplied us with secret maps showing where the service telephones were laid. This much-harassed official was greatly relieved when he heard that 5,000 Boy Scouts had been distributed as watchmen along the lines.'

Many smaller coastguard stations were abandoned before the Army took over the buildings, houses, patrols and sentry posts. Civilians were drafted in to help where manpower shortage hampered efficient coast and beach patrols – where the military had insufficient men to staff the stations, Sea Scouts acted as messengers, and if necessary lookouts.

During the four years of war, Scouts were to carry out many public duties, acting as messengers in public offices, helping in hospitals and Red Cross Centres, and later as buglers to sound the 'All Clear' after air raids.

The Mobilisation of Boy Scouts

Sir Robert Baden-Powell, Chief Scout, wrote, 'In this time of national emergency comes the opportunity for the Scouts organisation to show that it can be of material service to the country … Sea Scouts would be watching estuaries and ports, guiding vessels in un-buoyed channels, or

30   *War Service Badge, introduced by the Boys Scouts Association in December 1914 for 28 days' War Service.*

31   *Postcard depicting Coastwatching Sea Scouts in a wrestling bout, 1914.*

showing lights to friendly vessels, etc, and assisting coastguards. It is assumed that they will be excused from school attendance by the Education Committee and from work by their employers.'

August 1914 Bank Holiday – Men of the Second Line

With the European War came the great test for the Scout Movement. The Chief Scout had wired and written out to all Scout County Commissioners on Friday, 31 July, pointing out how Scouts could help the nation.

COASTWATCHING DUTIES: ENGLAND IS WATCHING

Monday, 3 August 1914

The last day of peace was a Bank Holiday which had been extended over four days. The Boy Scouts went to Scout camp in 1914 according to their usual custom for the August holiday.

Long August Bank Holiday, Beaulieu, Hampshire

Boats were provided on the river and excursions around the New Forest were planned for the Sea Scouts. C.V. Swan, Assistant County Commissioner, Northumberland, reported, 'The Tyne Lads in work – 34 of them – saved to go all the way to this camp and back. They left Newcastle on the Saturday evening, travelled all Sunday, and arrived in Camp at two o'clock on the Monday morning after an eight-mile tramp from Brockenhurst.'

War came on Tuesday, 4 August 1914.

32   *Sea Scouts at camp,
early August 1914.*

33   *Sea Scouts at camp,
early August 1914.*

Tuesday, 4 August 1914 – Britain Declares War on Germany

The Tyne Sea Scouts reported that on hearing the Declaration of War they had to break camp on the following Thursday morning (6 August) and return home, immediately taking up duties for the authorities 'mostly at coastguard stations, but also as police patrols on the river, and in other capacities.'

The 1st Mortlake Sea Scouts were also in camp at Beaulieu. To meet the national situation the camp was broken prematurely, and the Sea Scouts returned to Mortlake. They mobilised for special service, and on 13 August a patrol under the command of Scoutmaster James comprising six Scouts, together with ASMs (Assistant Scout Masters) was officially called upon by the Admiralty to serve as coastguards at Felpham near Bognor Regis. The first party was relieved on 19 September by a further patrol from the 1st Mortlake, which continued duties until 3 October, an arrangement which carried on throughout the period of hostilities.

Wednesday, 5 August 1914

Headquarters Gazette, *September 1914*

Vice-Admiral A. Galloway, County Commissioner for Kent, wrote: 'The War Organisation was completed in 1911. In consequence, one telegram from London Headquarters to County Office to mobilise could set the whole Kent machinery in motion.'

Thursday, 6 August 1914

The message sent out was: '1,300 Sea Scouts required by Admiralty to be allotted to coastguard stations for as long as the war lasts.'

August 1914 – the 1st Cambridge Sea Scouts

A contingent of the 1st Cambridge was coastwatching on the Kent Coast at Ramsgate for several weeks. Reporting throughout was covered by wartime restrictions, despite which the available accounts eloquently speak for themselves.

A member of the Cambridge Sea Scouts wrote:

On 4 August I was a member of a Sea Scout Troop in a village on the south coast which must be nameless. On the evening of the 4th the Scoutmaster cycled round to all members of the Troop and told us to be prepared for emergency work. He was unable to say what it would be, but at 5 a.m. the next morning we knew. The coastguards had been called up and we, together with a Troop from a big town, were in sole charge of the two coastguard stations until the military relieved us after ten hectic days. No need to ask if we were thrilled – all of us except the Scoutmaster, who happened to be the village dentist. He felt just as unhappy as the coastguard would have felt faced with a painless extraction!

Our duties during those ten days included the usual work of the station, and a constant patrol along the cliffs and foreshore. We did this in pairs day and night, covering a distance of six miles on each beat; our eyes were ever open for suspicious customers. Needless to say, everyone we met came under that category, but we did actually have our share of spies.

One day we had news that a yellow car was heading for the village from the direction of the port, and that it must be stopped at all costs. It was – by one of our Patrol Leaders hurling his bicycle at the car as it swept over the crossroads, swerved and crashed into a house. The two occupants were only slightly damaged and they were speedily removed by some soldiers who were chasing them in another car.

Another day, five of us were rushed off to guard an aeroplane which had made a forced landing in the heart of the Downs.

But quite the most exciting adventures were the capture of three men who had been flashing messages from a small house on the cliffs. This

34   *A Sea Scout on wartime Coastwatching duties, 1914-18. This included the recording of all shipping movements.*

house happened to be used as the local mortuary, and it had a lantern tower from which there was an uninterrupted view towards the harbour. Our orders were to surround the house and await the military. On no account were we to enter the building, as it was anticipated that the men were armed. The military were over two hours in reaching us – two hours which to us were full of exciting possibilities.

August 1914 – London, 4th Streatham

The 4th Streatham Troop was at camp in Leatherhead, Surrey at the outbreak of the First World War. Each of the Scouts was given a whistle by the local police sergeant and instructed to guard the railway line at the end of the field, although it is questionable whether a youngster of 12 could have resisted an attack during the long night watches. The Territorial Army arrived after three nights, and the 4th Streatham were commended by the officer in charge for their courageous act in helping to defend the country.

The Rev. Everard Digby, Scout Commissioner for East London and Chairman of the Port of London Sea Scouts, wrote, 'on the outbreak of war, we were entrusted with the manning of the coastguard stations on the east coast. The Admiralty gave us a week; we did it in 48 hours. Every Sea Scout in London, over 15,000, went at once. One Patrol at Dover lived on hard biscuits and jam for the first fortnight. Many stuck at the job until they were old enough to join His Majesty's Forces, and many will never come back to us here.'

Sunday, 9 August 1914

Royal Naval Reservists were recalled for duty, leaving coastguard stations unmanned or only partly manned.

Monday, 10 August 1914

Baden-Powell called on Admiral Farquhar about Scouts as coastguards. He also called to see Lord Kitchener about Scouts helping in defence and to offer his services to raise a corps of 'old Scouts' or a battalion of retired South African Constabulary men. Kitchener considered private battalions an irrelevance, and is reported to have advised Baden-Powell to look after the Boy Scouts, as he 'thought it better that old Scouts should be distributed amongst the units of the New Army as leaven'. The mobilisation of the Sea Scouts was the closest Baden-Powell would have to achieving his desire. However, in his capacity of Lieutenant General, he was tasked with inspecting Sea Scouts at the coastguard stations.

Within a week of the outbreak of war the uniform of the Boy Scouts Association, with the fleur-de-lys badge, was recognised by His Majesty's Government as the uniform of a public service non-service body, but special instructions were issued that no Scout or Scout Officers in uniform must on any account carry arms. There is, however, written evidence that a number of Sea Scouts underwent rifle and bayonet training at some coastguard stations.

In August 1914 Baden-Powell suggested a one shilling (5p) ration allowance to boys and to each District 6d. (2½p).

Discussion continued at the Admiralty whether Scouts on coastwatching duties should be paid, or receive an allowance. 10s. 6d. was finally arrived at.

September 1914

Headquarters Gazett*e, September 1914*

Scouts on Coastwatching Duty by Lieutenant L.H. Hordern, RN

> There are nearly 1,300 Scouts out on this work allotted to certain stations by the Admiralty, and they will probably be required as long as the war lasts. It is hoped the Admiralty will make a grant towards the expenses. The boys on this duty receive 1 shilling a day in lieu of rations but no pay for their services, and at present this is costing us nearly £500 a week. As time goes by and the weather gets colder, warm clothing, waterproofs, etc, will be required, and those in tents will have to be billeted in some way. There are bicycle tyres and boots wearing out, and various little claims of that nature in addition to travelling expenses.

October 1914

Owing to the hard weather, the Chief Scout appealed in the press for winter clothes for Scouts engaged in coastguard work.

> They are in much need of warm clothing to enable them to carry out their duties during the winter, and each Scout ought to have the following provided for him:
>
> One great coat, long; one jersey, knitted; one muffler; one pair of stockings

> The response was prompt and liberal, including a consignment from Queen Mary's Guild. The proprietors of the *Daily Graphic* gave most valuable assistance in making known the requirements, and raised a 'handsome' sum for clothing the boys. Queen Alexandra provided a Christmas dinner for those Scouts who were on coastguard duty near Sandringham. Her Majesty's example was generously followed by numerous other ladies living near the coast.

Headquarters Gazette, *October 1914*

At Duty on the Coast

C.V. Swan, Northumberland Assistant Commissioner for Sea Scouts, wrote:

> The boys had responded magnificently to the call made upon them. Life on the coast is full of interest, there being a constant variety of shipping – fishing boats, colliers, cruisers, destroyers, minesweeping trawlers, salvage boats and submarines, to say nothing of the aeroplanes.

> I shall not give away the lad who woke up the PO [Petty Officer] to say he had nothing to report, nor will I go into detail about two Scouts who mistook the comet for an aeroplane or the immediate steps they took in the matter.

> Pay day, with its seven shillings a week for food and wear-and-tear (how much of it is spent on 'wear-and-tear' we need not enquire). Some of the lads here are mill-hands from Lancashire, and they caused a mild sensation one day in the quiet seaside resort where they are quartered by turning out in clogs.

The Chief Scout Robert Baden-Powell inspected as many stations as he could, where he found how reliable the boys proved to be under service conditions.

Headquarters Gazette, *November 1914*
Chief Scout's Clothing Appeal

Some £3,450 [£150,000 today] in money and a considerable quantity of warm clothing has come in. Amongst the latter, the principal are over 200 blankets, 220 jerseys, 2,000 pairs of stockings, 300 shirts, 350 helmets, 150 pairs of gloves, and about 100 overcoats. All these and many other articles in similar quantities have been distributed amongst the 1,300 Scouts on duty.

£1 was needed to spend on each Scout to provide oilskins, sou'westers and boots. Then we should like to provide them each with a blue jersey, blue stockings, and a suit of Scout clothing in blue, together with a thick blue monkey jacket for the cold weather.

11 November 1914 – Walmer Sea Scouts to the Rescue

It was 12.15 p.m. that the gunboat HMS *Niger* was torpedoed by an enemy submarine, off Deal. The Chief Officer at Deal Coastguard Station immediately ordered the coastguard boat to be launched. This was speedily carried out by seven Sea Scouts attached to the station and with them as crew the Chief Officer went off to the assistance of the sinking ship. Several other boats set out, but the one containing the Sea Scouts was the only one under oars.

Their boat encountered very rough seas – half a gale was blowing – and narrowly escaped collision with the number of other ships racing by. The Chief Officer stated in his report that it was only through the discipline and coolness of the Sea Scouts that the boat was saved from disaster. There were many ships nearby saving the survivors but the Sea Scouts were able to render useful service by passing signals from the destroyers. 14 men from HMS *Niger* were lost, and three wounded, of whom one died subsequently.

The return proved difficult as, owing to the strong tide, the crew could not bring the boat back to Deal, and would have had to make for Ramsgate, ten miles off, had not the Kingsdown Lifeboat hailed them and towed the crew back to Deal.

The Scouts had been afloat for around three hours and they arrived back in an exhausted and soaked condition and one Scout had partially collapsed through the cold. They had, nevertheless, proved themselves real sailors and showed courage, coolness and discipline.

They were all members of the Walmer Sea Scout Troop and the Patrol comprised Donald Rose, Fred Rose, Stanley D. Stokes, Albert Foam, Walter Bullen, Alfred Bushell and Bertie Beal who were awarded Certificates of Merit for their actions.

Wednesday, 16 December 1914

The bombardment of Scarborough, Hartlepool and Whitby by the German Navy resulted in 137 civilians being killed and 592 injured.

Extract from the Scouts' Book of Heroes *(Pearson, 1919)*

My Experiences under Fire by King's Scout Rob Miller

The following is a remarkable account of the experiences and bravery under fire of King's Scout Rob Miller during the bombardment of Whitby.

35 *A building in Farringdon Road, London EC, renamed Zeppelin Buildings in 1916, having been bombed by an airship raid on 8 September 1915. The London raids were referred to in Jack Cornwell's letters home.*

> At about 9 o'clock on the morning of 16 December, I was standing with a Territorial in front of the watch house, when two cruisers suddenly hove into sight coming up from the south travelling at great speed. 'Go and fetch your glass, Rob' said my companion, 'Let's see what they are'. I ran into the one of the coastguard's houses for my telescope and watched the cruisers approach.

We thought they belonged to our own Fleet, though we couldn't make out why they were in such a hurry. The operator came out of the house with an ensign and told me to haul it up. I had no sooner done this that there was a terrific bang and a great bit of the cliff fell down. We didn't need any more telling that it was the Germans out at sea, and we didn't wait for the next shell.

The Territorial and I ran towards the houses down the passage. It was like a thunderstorm, very near, and we could see the shells bursting. I was hit by shell splinters in both legs, and hadn't time to think which was the best way to go, as I was just in front of the lookout station, but I followed the others. I managed to keep on through the yards, which were choked with fallen masonry, to the coastguards' houses. When I ran through the building it was full of bricks and slates. We both managed to get into shelter, where we stopped until some other Territorials came up. When they saw I had been hit, a sergeant very kindly bandaged my legs.

The firing stopped, and a Territorial carried me down towards the town. Halfway down, the ambulance met us, and I was taken to the Cottage Hospital. Gangrene set in immediately, and my right leg had to be amputated the following day.

I didn't feel scared in the least by the bombardment, probably because it was so unexpected. If I had known it was coming I should have been scared out of my life. I wouldn't believe they were German boats until they opened fire.

The worst part was when we were lying down in shelter behind the houses, as we could only lie still and listen to the bursting shells, wondering whether we should get hit again. I, of course, was quite helpless and couldn't have moved, whatever had happened.

The Chief Scout telegraphed his sympathy and received a reply from Miller that he was still smiling.

To Officer Commanding Boy Scouts Detachment, Cayton

The Local Secretary at West Hartlepool reports:

> During the bombardment of this town the Scouts behaved splendidly, helping the authorities; but I regret to state we had a Scoutmaster killed at work. [Scoutmaster Ramsey was killed by a piece of shrapnel whilst hurrying from business to report for duty]. I have received a flesh wound on the leg by a splinter of shell but it is nothing very serious. We have had three or four Scouts killed at their homes [three Scouts killed while running messages]. It was horrible while it lasted.

1915

20 & 21 February 1915

In his capacity as a Major General (Inspecting Officer) Robert Baden-Powell carried out coastguard inspections from Folkestone via Dover to Kingsdown, Deal, Ramsgate, Margate, Westgate, Birchington, Reculver and Whitstable. Amongst his remarks he said, 'another good lot' about Canterbury and Folkestone.

April 1915

The Admiralty granted Sea Scout Coastwatchers 18 shillings without rations.

Frederick Ashen's Diary Extracts – 1915-17

The following significant reminiscences of Sea Scout Coastwatching during 1915 and 1916 were compiled over 25 years by the family of Frederick Charles Ashen of Sydney, New South Wales, Australia, who died aged 103 in 2004.

As the day to turn 15 approached Frederick Ashen was to join the Navy as a boy sailor. He had never been to sea, but took a shine to the idea. All the forms were raised and completed on 8 September 1915, to be lodged the next day. The following day however 'Ma' was so distraught at the thought of her Fred going off to war that he was unable to bring himself to lodge the papers. The same day news was received that London had experienced its first air raid by Zeppelins. [30 May 1915 – 7 killed, 35 wounded]'

Frederick gained Ma's approval to do some coastwatching. He transferred from the Scouts to become a Sea Scout, as they were employed as coastwatchers. He set out for the small town of Rottingdean, for many generations a smugglers' community set amidst chalk cliffs on the Sussex coast near Brighton.

After Frederick arrived in Rottingdean on 27 October, he was teamed up with several patriotic lads, some from London with whom relations were usually more belligerent than they ever had chance to become with the enemy. It was from the cliffs near Rottingdean that this highly-motivated team diligently watched the coast in 1916.

One member of this team was Frederick's friend from Bristol Street School, Tubby Kynoch. Sometimes their quest was for firewood to ensure they could keep their lodgings warm. They foraged for food, a quest which rarely met with success, but Frederick became accomplished at placing a baking tin in front of the fire in their lookout hut when he had the night shift, and

36   *Sea Scouts, wearing naval-style rig, reporting on arrival for Coastwatching duties, c.1915.*

would bake a loaf of bread. (Frederick's diary is full of comments, noting at the end of most days how hungry he was.) The lads must have been a hardy bunch, with only their serge Scouts' uniforms, complete with shorts and long socks, to protect them from fresh sea gales. Their duties varied between manning a lookout hut on the cliff and walking along the beach at low tide. On the beach they had to be careful with their timing, otherwise they could have been cut off by the incoming tide.

Leading this team of highly-trained cut-throats was Mr Gale, a tall, bespectacled man who made a habit of learning several new words from the dictionary every day. The lads were often invited to the large house of a local gentleman, apparently a descendant of one of Nelson's captains, who had a fine collection of miniature model ships, with which he would refight Nelson's numerous battles. Other nautical off-watch activities were lessons in splicing ropes and knot-tying. More energetically, some lads began playing hockey in a local competition. Despite such distractions, routine coastwatching continued throughout. The locals threw their rubbish off the cliffs, and sometimes he would look down onto the beaches and see swarms of rats on the move – there was plenty to support a thriving rodent community. The discovery of a British sailor's body on the beach one day, still in his cap with its minesweeper's tally, was a sober reminder of the War.

After five months in Rottingdean, Frederick volunteered for a further period of coastwatching. He was sent to Saltburn-by-Sea on the north-east coast of Yorkshire where lookout patrols continued. Whilst watching from cliff tops his team was supposed to be alert for messages flashed by light from out at sea, but it seemed that no one was clear what sort of messages to expect. As winter approached knees had all the more reason to start knocking; whilst predominantly south-westerly winds weren't too bad, the occasional north-easter was bitterly cold. Some respite was gained when several pairs of thick socks knitted at a nearby girls' school were delivered.

Frederick's duties included delivering messages from Saltburn to Redcar. It was in Redcar, on the evening of 27 August 1916, that he witnessed an unforgettable spectacle. The local racecourse had been put into use as an airfield, from which fighters would take off to offer some resistance to the bombers and Zeppelins which periodically crossed the Channel. On this particular evening a Zeppelin was reported approaching the coast so the fighters took to the darkening sky. Later their engines were heard returning and the oil drums placed along the edge of the impromptu airfield were lit to guide the fighters home. Everyone was surprised when bombs starting screaming down from the night sky.

Frederick recalls that some members of the local constabulary, along with other dark figures, were not slow in diving for cover, but he was so enthralled he just stood watching. The aim was good, and several bombs hit the racecourse, leaving the airfield deeply pockmarked, but the Zeppelin had stirred the locals into action by this stage. The big 9.2-inch Naval guns located upon the cliffs began shooting. Their thunderous roar was followed by bright blue flashes exploding in the clear night sky. Frederick remembers, 'he was still climbing when I saw a blue explosion of a shell exploding just below the tail.' The whole airship was lit up from end to end. It stopped its climb and slowly started to sink. It crumpled in the middle and the inner end of each half sank more rapidly downwards. The whole volume of hydrogen gas burning 'really vividly white' illuminated the whole night almost like day. In the sharp light the tiny figures of some of the Zeppelin's crew could be seen detaching from the inferno and plummeting down: 'terrible it was'. The remains of the Zeppelin were still burning

37   *The AVRO 521A. This machine was considered 'a beast to fly', with a tendency to spin off on right-hand turns. It claimed the life of Lieutenant W.H. Stuart Garnett, scientist-pilot with the Central Flying School Testing Flight.*

brightly when they fell into the sea some miles from the coast. (The Zeppelin concerned was LZ 21, a naval airship with a crew of 24, one of whom survived. A British fighter pilot, from the Cadbury family (the chocolate manufacturers), was credited with the Zeppelin's destruction, but from the ground it seemed to Frederick Ashen that the guns had brought it down.)

At the start of 1917 Frederick finished coastwatching and returned to Birmingham to begin an apprenticeship.

Lieutenant William Herbert Stuart Garnett, RFC, 1882-1916
Leader of 1st Ratcliff Sea Scouts

I am extremely grateful to the Garnett, Jay and Bottomley families, St Paul's School, London, the Royal Cruising Club and Toynbee Hall, all of whom have supplied previously unpublished information about the life of Stuart Garnett.

Today, after a period of many years, Stuart Garnett takes his rightful place, being recognised as a co-founder of Sea Scouting. A most remarkable person who worked as a teacher for a short time at public school, a practical engineer, a barrister, and an author, giving tremendous energies to whatever he undertook.

1882-1916

Born in 1882, Stuart Garnett was the son of distinguished scientist Dr William Garnett, Education Adviser to the London County Council. In my conversation with the late Peggy Jay she remembers him as being a bright, intelligent and amusing child. He attended St Paul's School, but was not recorded as being other than average. He did exceedingly well at Trinity College, Cambridge, graduating in 1903, and was called to the Bar of the Inner Temple in 1905, becoming legal adviser to the newly-created National Insurance Commission.

In 1906 he wrote and illustrated *Turbines*, a textbook to promote the use of turbines in the Royal and Merchant Navies, and was to join the Royal Cruising Club.

In 1909, he ran a boys' club at Toynbee Hall, east London, from which the 1st Ratcliff Sea Scouts, the first Sea Scout Troop in London, eventually emerged, a powerhouse for the spread of Sea Scouting in the metropolis. He was an enthusiastic sailor, strong swimmer and alpine climber. It was through his meeting with Sidney Marsh that the 2nd Walworth acquired a cutter and took up boating activities.

In 1912 he co-wrote *National Insurance*, its preface written by the Chancellor of the Exchequer, David Lloyd George, MP, and in 1913 wrote *Children and the Law*, for the next 40 years one of the main textbooks dealing with young offenders. In 1914 he wrote *Seamanship for Scouts*, which received a wide circulation and which contained a good number of photographs of the 1st Ratcliff Sea Scouts on Stuart Garnett's ketch *Idler*. Before his death he was writing a handbook on the game of whist.

1912-14

Stuart Garnett's obituary in the *Toynbee Record* of 1916 recalled that during 1912/13 he skippered the yacht *Mirror* for The Scout Association in and around the East India Docks. One account of this is as follows:

One awoke one early February morning to find oneself next to Scott's old *Discovery*, and among the incidents of the exciting day that followed was the appearance of Garnett who proceeded, after a brief greeting, to the top of the mast where he sat for two hours shouting strange names of ropes and tackle and then, having decided that, with the help of about three boys, he would rebuild the ship, he departed forthwith to prepare his plans.

The deeds of Garnett and his Troop of the little sportsmen he gathered are tales to be told and not written. His Shadwell friends saw him stick to the East End and come back time and time again, so when War broke out one heard of Garnett commanding a minesweeper with a crew of his old Sea Scouts and flying an admiral's flag, and the odds are that scores of boys in East London thought that the Mr Garnett they knew was now an admiral [in 1915 the yacht *Zarefah* did become Admiral Minesweeping's flagship.]

Stuart Garnett threw himself into national defence with all his accustomed energy. Appointed a member of the Motor Boat Reserve, on 14 August 1914 he borrowed from Mr Steane Price the luxury steam yacht *Zarefah*, which he manned with officers and crewmen, Cambridge graduates and undergraduates, together with older Sea Scouts from East London, and engaged in minesweeping duties. When commanding the yacht, he once swam out to a live mine in the Channel, cut it free and swam back again. He received a commendation from the Parliamentary Recruiting Committee for his actions.

By the summer of 1915, Stuart Garnett had attained the rank of Lieutenant Commander RNR but, because of his ever-increasing interest in aircraft, gave up his naval duties to join the Royal Flying Corps. He was an observer in France for several months where his inventive genius was recognised, and as a result he joined the staff of the Central Flying School, Salisbury Plain, qualifying as a pilot. He is credited with inventing a revolutionary gunsight, but it has not been possible to verify the detail.

In Hampstead in August 1915 he married Sybil Maud Bradley of Streetly, Staffordshire.

In September 1916, whilst Stuart Garnett was flying an AVRO 2351A prototype two-seater experimental aircraft at 1,500 feet above the Central Flying School, an eye witness, Harold Balfour, later Under-Secretary of State, reported that he had attempted to make a right-hand turn. The nose of the aircraft dropped until the AVRO went into a spin, the nose vertical to the ground. The impact was terrific – Stuart Garnett was killed instantly, aged only 34. His possessions – a wallet, a pipe and a motorcycle – were returned to the family.

Headquarters Gazette, *October 1916;* Toynbee Record, *1916;* The Times,
23 September 1916

Death of Lieutenant William Herbert Stuart Garnett, RFC (formerly Lieutenant Commander RNR) – 22 April 1882-21 September 1916

Consulted by Robert Baden-Powell on Sea Scout matters, the following appeared on the death of Stuart Garnett:

We very much regret that, after a full and varied life including good service to [the Scout] Movement, Lieutenant Stuart Garnett was killed at a Flying School on 21 September. He took a very active interest in Sea Scouting and wrote a book on the subject. In order the better to devote himself to work among the boys he lived many years overlooking the docks in Limehouse, East London.

Garnett was primarily a scientist of repute, but also a keen pilot, always anxious to try his hand on our experimental aeroplanes.

16 August-14 December 1916
Diary of a Coastwatching Scout, Hope Cove Sea Scouts
Extracts from the Diary of Patrol Leader A.J.H. Clayton (77th South London/1st Streatham)

A.J.H. Clayton, of East Grinstead, East Sussex, was another of the Scouts who exchanged his Scout shirt for a Sea Scout jersey to take part in coastwatching duties at Hope Cove near Kingsbridge, South Devon. He donated his diary to The Scout Association Archives in 1974.

Wednesday, 16 August 1916

I packed most of my things overnight and after sundry farewells went to Brown's place. We started for the great adventure wondering what it would be like. We left Paddington at 12 o'clock. Mr Golding, the ADC Sea Scouts South Devon, met us nearby and came with us to Kingsbridge.

Friday, 18 August 1916

I was on watch at 4 a.m. being wakened by the CW [coastwatcher] at 3.45 and came off at 8. The morning watch (the 4 to 8 watch) Scout is orderly for the day. I had the job of washing up the crocks, not a nice job but someone had to do it. Brown and I bagged the top bunks of the six but found some fleas had forestalled us – apparently the personal property of the pet kitten of those here before us. We hope to get rid of these in a scientific manner with Keating's Powder and carbolic. Mr Kelly said 'They are fine things in the winter, it keeps you warm rubbing their bites. I found one in the blankets I lent Mr Golding.' The other boys with us are Stockport boys but have been at other places on the coast before.

Sunday, 20 August 1916

Our Station is rather important because (besides the fact I am here of course) the Acting Divisional Officer is here; he a Warrant Officer doing Commissioned Officer work. Besides him there is the Station Officer, Mr Kelly, who is a 1st Class PO Chief Boatsman. All the seven other men who were here before the war have gone back to their ships but their wives and children still live here (Oh those children, we long for the day when they go back to school).

Wednesday, 30 August 1916

Received parcel from mother containing box of cakes and pasties, soup and a balaclava helmet. I asked for a Sea Scout stocking cap which is better because it can be used as a cap and when cold as a helmet right over the head.

Saturday, 2 September 1916

In the afternoon I had to go half way to Bantham to meet the boy from there with a dispatch at a distance of five or six miles. We have to do this when necessary, the arrangements about the time to meet being made on the phone.

Wednesday, 6 September 1916

Len, Slim, Sam and I went out in the boat mackerel fishing in the afternoon, about level with Thurlestone Sands about five miles out. When we started out there was a good deal of water in the boat and we had taken the stern bottom boards out to 'bail out'. We had the jib rigged on an oar and 'your humble' in charge of it; Sam was trying to transfer the sea from inside the boat to outside. Slim Jim was at the tiller and Len pulling.

There was a tide at the mackerel line over the stern and Sam was struggling to haul it in when he kicked out the plug which should be protected by the boards, consequently the water came in (nothing to stop it – it had to come out). Slim Jim stood gaping like a chap who had seen a ghost. Len sprang forward and tried to put the plug in where his fingers were. They rammed the plug in at last after the boat had a good deal of water in. I saw Len dive forward letting go the oars so I grabbed at them myself but missed one. So we held out and got back altogether, except in trying to get a photo of some gulls we ran onto a rock. Went out again with Len and Brown, and learnt to scull over the stern. We also got a fine lot of mackerel (five) in a mooring over by the Bolt.

Wednesday, 13 September 1916

A lot of ships went by today – patrol boats and drifters (auxiliary fishing boats). It is fine to see them steaming in line abreast on the look-out for submarines. Three motor launches (submarine chasers) went by at a great speed in line ahead. All these we have to report. Plenty of sailing boats of all kinds, a three-masted schooner among them cutting along fine. There is also a large two-funnelled three-masted liner or mail boat, besides a number of tramps.

Sunday, 17 September 1916

In the afternoon the watch reported two submarines submerged about 3½ miles out. This was reported along the coast and two destroyers came out to look for them. Greystone then reported these 'submarines' had turned into small sailing boats. Disturbance of the airwaves seen round those destroyers when they found out, leaving the scene.

Wednesday, 20 September 1916

The weather had quite calmed down from wet and SW winds. Out again in the boat. Three drifters pass. They now work on a special stretch of coast, each fleet five or so, patrolling for submarines, mines etc. When we went back they were firing and one of them had the 'powder danger flag' hoisted [showing that a vessel is carrying, loading or discharging explosives or highly inflammable materials]. (Red Burgee letter A to warn other ships off.)

Sunday, 1 October 1916

Today is the day when people change their time back to Greenwich Time and everything is an hour late now. This is also the beginning of the Naval winter season so we start dark caps, put the ensign up later etc.

Friday, 15 October 1916

In the evening I went to Thurlestone Sands with Slim to help get a barrel of something that was washed in. Len and Sam tried with some men and came back later soaked. After waiting, the tide was taking it out again. We found a rope, I took my boots and stockings off, had an oilskin on and waded out to the barrel to get a rope round it. It was some sport – the waves were breaking right over me. I had to give it up in the end and get dry. The tide left it and the others managed to get it up.

Monday, 16 October 1916

On watch this afternoon. We invented a booby trap for our door this afternoon. It is a cup or jug of water arranged on a shelf by the door. Brown and Len were caught fine.

Friday, 27 October 1916

Last night a fierce gale sprang up. In the morning we heard that one ship (the schooner *Western Lass* of Fowey) had gone ashore and another schooner later. We received messages on the coast phone at different times of the day. The Salcombe Lifeboat went out. They say it was a fine sight to see the Cox get over the bar.

The men were rescued from *Western Lass* by LSA (Life Saving Apparatus) and we received the following message from Salcombe at 10.40 a.m.

'Have just received information [lifeboat] has capsized. Our boat could not get out. Later we got from Prawle "Only two men rescued from Salcombe Lifeboat. Lifeboat completely capsized. Have informed … etc."'

In the evening we heard that two had been picked up. The waves were high, dashing against the wall and springing up as high as a house.

The paper reported the tragedy of the Lifeboat Crew: 'It was at Salcombe, the beautiful little Devon village where Tennyson wrote his well-known lines, *Crossing the Bar*, which caused the loss of 13 out of the crew of 15 men on 27 October 1916. During a furious gale the lifeboat was launched to rescue the crew of the schooner *Western Lass* of Plymouth, which was ashore off Prawle Point asking for assistance, but the shipwrecked crew had been rescued by the Prawle lifesaving apparatus. The lifeboat started on its return journey, but was completely capsized when 'crossing the bar'. The two survivors were thrown onto a rock 50 feet from the shore, to which they were able to cling. A line and stimulants were passed to them, and later a stronger line with life buoys, and they were at last rescued in an almost exhausted condition. The Lifeboat Institution, besides defraying the funeral and incidental expenses, contributed to a local fund raised for the benefit of the heroes' families'.

Saturday, 29 October 1916

We got a phone message from Prawle – 'The wreck of the *Western Lass* is beginning to break up.' The seas were still a bit rough and coming over the wall.

Wednesday, 1 November 1916

Three of the crew of the Salcombe lifeboat were buried today and three yesterday. Weather wet and windy. Received letter from home. On telephone duty this afternoon.

Sunday, 5 November 1916

Hope Cove Sea Scouts at Dartmouth

I was on watch at 6 o'clock. As day broke we saw a two-masted top sail schooner riding at anchor about ¾ of a mile off the coastguard station. About 7 o'clock she dragged her anchor and with mizzen and jib she tried to make for the harbour. She had gone half way across the mouth of the harbour when a very large sea struck her broadside and nearly capsized her and tore the jib to ribbons. She was practically helpless and could only run before the wind; she was driven onto the rocky cliffs by Mickleberry Cove and fell to pieces. The telephone seemed to break down and I was ringing up Forcross one way and Brixham the other for the LSA and Lifeboat. The Brixham Lifeboat came out but went back again and the Torcross LSA came but all the LSA in the world would have been useless.

The press reported the awful disaster at Dartmouth, which resulted in the loss of five lives, late on Saturday night and the early hours of Sunday morning. The gale assumed a ferocity which 'almost beggared description'. With her masts and sails gone and probably the rudder there was nothing which could be done to save the brave crew. The schooner was burning flare lights constantly. But as she was a mile out it was impossible to render assistance and she met her doom nine hours later. The bodies later recovered from the rocks were unrecognizable. The Coroner's Inquest concluded that the crew of the *Princess of Thule* died by being cast into the sea as a result of the wrecking of the schooner.

Friday, 10 November 1916

Hope Cove Sea Scouts at Dartmouth

A patrol trawler, the *Benton Castle*, was blown up off the harbour because of a mine. Our CW did not see it, but the weather was very thick. Five of the men were picked up, some dead and some injured. I did the morning watch 2 to 6. We decided to change the watches to take the same way as we did at Hope Cove, because we were awake for 24 hours.

Saturday, 11 November 1916

Hope Cove Sea Scouts at Dartmouth

The harbour is closed to all shipping in or out. It is suspected that the Danish steamer *Elve* has been laying mines off the harbour – one sank the *Benton Castle*.

Sunday, 12 November 1916

Hope Cove Sea Scouts at Dartmouth

It is awful thick today and the Minesweepers have been unable to work.

Thursday, 16 November 1916

Hope Cove Sea Scouts at Dartmouth

I was on afternoon watch. It was cold but very clear – Minesweepers were out again. I saw them through the glass firing at something in the water. This 'something' was a mine for after shelling it 'went up' with a large column of water. Brown and I went to see the Dartmouth pictures. Not much good.

Saturday, 2 December 1916

Hope Cove Sea Scouts at Lincombe

A deceased body observed floating. I went for the Police at 1200.

Sunday, 3 December 1916
Hope Cove Sea Scouts at Lincombe
The body that of a skipper RNR was brought up and put into a coffin in the CG Station. I was acting PL [Patrol Leader], not too successful.

Thursday, 14 December 1916
We returned home soon after this date.

At this point the diary ends.

1917

David Lloyd George, MP, Prime Minister

In 1917 Robert Baden-Powell received a letter from the Prime Minister, David Lloyd George, showing how greatly the work of the Scouts was appreciated.

I do not think I am exaggerating when I say that the young boyhood of our country, represented by the Boy Scouts Association, shares the laurels for having been prepared with the old and trusted British Army and Navy. For both proved their title to make the claim when the Great War broke out upon us like a thief in the night. It is no small matter to be proud that the Association was able within a month of the outbreak of war to give the most energetic and intelligent help in all kinds of service. When the boyhood of a nation can give such practical proofs of its honour, straightness and loyalty, there is not much danger of that action going under, for these boys are in training to render service to their country as leaders in all walks of life in the future.

1918

Headquarters Gazette, *August 1918*

Coastwatching

Vice-Admiral Sir Cecil Thursby, on handing over his appointment as Coastguards and Reserves to Vice-Admiral Sir Dudley de Chair, acknowledges the valuable assistance 'rendered by Sea Scouts employed on Coastwatching, and is impressed by their smartness, intelligence, and keenness in carrying out their important duties.'

The Admiral Commanding furthermore 'brings to notice the very cordial assistance that he has at all times been rendered by Lieutenant W.R. Stanton, and the RNVR.'

Census of Sea Scouts

The first available census of Sea Scouts showed that 2,425 were registered.

1919

The Times, *21 July 1919;* Headquarters Gazette, *August 1919*

Stepping-Stones in our History – the Great Victory Parade

The historical Great Year of Peace set its mark on the history of the Scout Movement. Of the Great Victory Parade, *The Times* reported the Naval contingent was headed by Admiral of the

Fleet Sir David Beatty, who had the Union Flag carried in front of him, followed by his staff and flag officers. Captain Wilmott Nicholson headed selected crews of light cruisers, destroyers, submarines, flying squadrons, Royal Fleet, minesweepers, Royal Naval Reserve and 50 Scouts, accompanied by seven bands.

The Admiralty decided to recognise the valuable service rendered during the war as Coastwatching Scouts, signal boys, cooks, orderlies at Naval flying stations, and in other ways by including in the procession a party of 50 Sea Scouts among the Naval Auxiliary Services. They brought up the rear of the naval units, followed by the Mercantile Marine.

The Scouts were given a place of honour; as a unit in the splendid naval force the Sea Scouts appeared under their own flag, on their own merit. They had been accorded this privilege in recognition of the work they did for the country in carrying out coastwatching duties during the war, most remarkable in being the only boys' organisation taking part in the parade.

As soon as the Sea Scouts passed by they were recognised by their flags and duly honoured. The Scouts' green and yellow distinguishing flag was carried turn and turn about by the Coastwatching Sea Scouts from the east and south coasts. Behind the flag marched Lieutenant W.R. Stanton, RNVR, who had organised the Sea Scouts so splendidly. At the rear of them were two stalwart Sea Scout buglers, wearing their green armlets and bugle presented for air raid services. The four lines of Sea Scouts who marched 12 abreast were drawn from Troops at Portsmouth, Bournemouth, Hanwell, and St Pancras.

The First World War Coastwatching Service
Patrol Leader Derrick Brown, February 1917

> When in years to come we are asked, 'What did you do in the Great War?' we will be able to answer proudly, 'I was only a boy, but I did my bit as a Scout on Coastwatching duties.'

FOUR

JACK CORNWELL VC, 1900-16

BOY FIRST CLASS JOHN TRAVERS CORNWELL, VC –
THE BOY WHO MADE HISTORY

'Jack' Cornwell was a Scout, not a Sea Scout, but is revered in Navy and Sea Scouting circles. It is appropriate he be recognised here. For many years the painting of Jack Cornwell by Robert Baden-Powell was displayed in Sea Scout headquarters throughout the land. He has become one of the most celebrated of all Victoria Cross recipients of both World Wars, and in death achieved the fame he could not have imagined in his very short life. His service career lasted ten months, his final 29 days spent at sea aboard the light cruiser HMS *Chester*.

THE CORNWELL FAMILY

John Travers Cornwell was born on 8 January 1900 at 8, Clyde Cottage, Clyde Place, Leyton, Essex, the son of Eli and Lilly (née King). John, known to his family as Jack, was the second of their four children – they had three boys and a girl – he also had a half-brother and a half-sister. Eli originally came from Cambridge to live in Stratford, and Lilly was born in Bedfordshire. Their home was in a small street in Manor Park, Essex.

SCHOOL DAYS – MAY, 1905-13

From the age of five Jack attended Farmer Road School (later to become George Mitchell School), between May 1905 and July 1910.

In 1910, the family moved to nearby 10 Alverstone Road, Manor Park, Essex, where Jack attended Walton Road School which he left aged 14 at Christmas in 1913. According to the Headmaster of Walton Road School, Mr J.T.C. Gribble, Jack's school work was average. Teachers said they always felt they could depend on him. Quiet and reserved, he seldom caused any trouble. The school taught straightness, truthfulness, and a good character were things that were worthwhile in life, and it was renamed after Jack Cornwell in 1929.

By the age of 14 Jack, fresh-complexioned, was described as short in stature – 4ft 11ins – but stocky in build and had inherited from his mother some of her dour features. On leaving school he was remembered as being a friendly and humorous 14-year-old.

SCOUTING DAYS, 1913-15

During school days in Manor Park between 1910 to 1913, Jack joined the St Mary's Mission (Manor Park) Troop, becoming a keen Scout. He enjoyed boxing, taking part in Troop tournaments. He had gained the Missioners Efficiency Badge, and also the equivalent of his 2nd Class Badge. Jack was a Patrol Second (now Assistant Patrol Leader).

Scoutmaster J.F. Avery, 21st East Ham Troop, wrote 'I knew Cornwell very well. He was what I used to call a "daredevil". He would attempt any task no matter how hard it was. He was just the sort of lad that would meet so glorious and brave an end. I don't think he knew what fear was.'

Accounts state that Jack's Scout Troop closed down shortly after war was declared when the officers enlisted. There is new evidence the older Scouts – the patrol leaders – continued to run the Troop. Jack was a member of the Troop until he joined the Royal Navy in 1915.

38 *A previously-unpublished Troop photograph of St Mary's Mission, Little Ilford Troop, 1915, showing Jack Cornwell (middle row, third from the left) shortly before joining the Royal Navy.*

Employment – June 1914

There are two versions of Jack's work on leaving school – one that he worked as a van boy for the Brooke Bond Tea Company, the other that he was a dray boy at Whitbread's Brewery, Ilford.

In May 1963, *Whitbread News*, the company paper, recorded, 'For a short time in his brief career, Cornwell was a member of this company – a Whitbread dray boy at Manor Park Depot.' It is probable that Jack worked first for Brooke Bond and then at Whitbread's.

No employment records still exist for the period for either company, but Eli Cornwell found Jack work at Brooke Bond at a starting pay of 10/- (£10 in today's money).

Research Sheet issued by the Royal Navy National Museum

The sheet, entitled 'Jack Cornwell, Boy VC', shows that during the years 1913-15 Jack won a special Boy Scout Award for freeing a girl from a drain. Scout Headquarters have no information on this, but local researches mentions the following account of Jack's actions, which circulated for many years. It is, however, not verifiable from any written source.

29 September 1914

The Brooke Bond delivery van was parked for a Friday lunchtime break; the driver was in the cab reading the *Daily Sketch* and Jack was sitting under a nearby tree. A wide grass verge hugged the river close to a house which was accessed from the tree-lined road.

A small dog ran quickly down a steep slope, chased by a young female; both fell into the river. Hearing the girl shout, Jack raced to the scene. A further shout followed and Jack ran on, removing his overalls and boots. On arrival he found a ditch about four feet wide and four feet deep, separating the river from the steep bank. The girl was chest-high in foul-looking water, holding up the dog. The force of Jack jumping into the water caused all three to become submerged, but they re-surfaced and Jack lifted the dog clear of the water. Two friends of the young woman walking nearby took the dog, helping Jack and the girl out of the water.

Jack made no mention of his exploits, but was interviewed by the *Hammersmith Herald* and a small column appeared in the *Evening Standard*.

Later, when Jack arrived at the Church Hall where the 11th East Ham Troop held their meetings, most of the Troop were outside. In the hall the 'Scout Silver Cross Badge of Courage' was pinned upon his shirt. Some accounts put Jack Kipling, son of Rudyard, at the presentation.

When the widow of Jack's brother Ernest, Mrs Irene Cornwell, and his sister, Mrs Alice Payne, presented Jack's VC to the Imperial War Museum in November 1968, she repeated the account of his actions at this incident, which were published in *The Times* newspaper the following day.

4 August 1914 – War declared, War Fever

Jack Cornwell volunteered for the Navy in August 1914 but was rejected on account of his age, 14 years and 7 months. The Royal Navy appealed to Jack, but his parents refused to allow him to join up; his father thought he was too young, and they could not bear the thought of losing him. Jack therefore concentrated his energy on Scouting in Ilford.

The events of the War changed the minds of the family. In March 1915, Eli Cornwell, an old soldier and at 62 well over military age, answered the call of Lord Kitchener and volunteered for the Army. He managed to get back into uniform as a private in the Essex Regiment stationed in Chelmsford. This time with parental permission Jack was allowed to apply for enlistment in the Royal Navy.

RECRUIT TRAINING – BOY SECOND CLASS, SERVICE NUMBER J/42563

Jack attended the local Recruiting Office on 21 July 1915, presented his references and enlisted for 12 years. This period of engagement dated from 8 June 1918 to 1930, as 'Boy Service' was not included in their calculation.

39 *An image of Jack Cornwell, HMS* Vivid, *Devonport, a shore training establishment, c.1915-16, from a photograph displayed at HMS* Raleigh, *Torpoint, Cornwall.*

The recruitment documentation process only took a week – Jack was accepted on 29 July, entering the Royal Navy at Devonport on 31 July as 'Boy Second Class', Service number J/42563. On entry he was shown to be 5ft 2ins tall, with a 31½-inch chest, fresh complexion, brown hair and blue eyes.

BASIC TRAINING – HMS VIVID, 31 JULY 1915

This took place at Keyham Naval Barracks, Devonport, near Plymouth Sound. There were 6,060 young sailors at the land-based Training Establishment – a stone frigate. New-entrant instructors were selected from the older Petty Officers usually for their perceived qualities of patience and humanity.

No misdemeanours were recorded on Jack's service record during his training. He tried hard and behaved well, and was known as a willing and smartly-turned-out boy. While there he was a regular churchgoer attending Church of England services. He sang in the choir, underwent religious instruction, being confirmed whilst in Plymouth. He was advanced to Boy First Class on 19 February 1916.

ROUTE MARCHES AND DRILL

J.T. Cornwell
6 Mess E Block
No. 1247. BTE
RN Barracks
Devonport
Tuesday Eve [January 1916]
Dear Mum,

I was very pleased to get your letter and to hear that all is well as leaves me at present.

I hear that conscription [January 1916] has come out official but I hope they won't nab Ern [Ernest] and tell Lilly that I am sorry she could not get in School but tell her I never got the rats if I could not go she mustn't. I don't suppose it's the school she wants but the Rubies and Violets Cowards. I am very sparing with writing today as we have been on a route march all morning and drill all afternoon so I am pretty tired you can bet and will be glad when turn in goes so will write more later.

> I remain your every loving
> Son Jack
> Remember me to all at home.

HMS *VIVID*, GUNNERY TRAINING – 22 JANUARY 1916

After three months Jack and his messmates started their gunnery course taught by Petty Officers. His instructor, an old Navy man, had been a London Police Sergeant and befriended Jack.

He found seamanship comparatively easy. At HMS *Vivid* for gunnery training the going was more difficult. Quickness of eye and deftness of hand was required to operate the machinery, carrying out orders correctly without hesitation. His instructors spoke well of him, marking him as 'quite good' and willing 'but not as quick as he might be'. On passing out his Certificate of General Efficiency recorded that Jack qualified with 'Gunnery 84%, Seamanship 70%, Physical Training – Good, Swimming – Very Good, and Character – Very Good.' Good marks in these tests helped to speed your rate to Able Seaman, which brought increased pay.

After shore training Jack served on HMS *Lancaster*, a training cruiser moored at Chatham undergoing a refit. For six months he remained with the other 19 recruits in his intake.

After training, Jack spent a few days before Easter 1916 at home with his mother and family, where he expressed the hope that before long he would 'get into action and see the Germans beaten.' Shortly afterwards he was ordered by telegram to join the Grand Fleet at Rosyth, Scotland.

On joining, Jack's height was recorded as 5ft 2ins, on leaving 5ft 3ins. His weight on joining was given as 96lbs (about 6¾ stone), on leaving 108lbs (about 7½ stone); clearly this lifestyle suited him.

40 *Boy Seaman First Class Jack Cornwell, HMS* Lancaster, *a 1902 training ship (cruiser), c.1916.*

JOINING THE FLEET

On Easter Monday, 24 April 1916, few on King's Cross mainline station would have taken any notice of a group of young sailors standing by the Edinburgh-bound train saying goodbye to friends and families – a common sight in wartime. Jack was saying farewell to his family, a tearful mother there dismayed at his sudden departure. 'That's what I signed on for Mum. I have to go.' Jack promised his sister Lilly he would buy her a piano after the War. The train pulled away slowly, Jack waving to his mother, sister Lilly and brother George.

HMS *CHESTER*

On Jack's arrival at Rosyth via Edinburgh and North Queensferry, there was a great array of warships, battleships, cruisers and destroyers, laid out at anchor, an awesome and inspiring sight.

HMS *Chester* was a Birkenhead Class light cruiser. Commissioned by the Greek Navy as the *Lambros Katsonis*, work started on her at Cammel Laird's Yard, Birkenhead, in October 1914. In April 1916 she was commandeered by the British government and underwent her sea trials as HMS *Chester* which were completed in May 1916.

The difference from other British cruisers was the substitution of 5.5-inch guns for 6-inch guns. Firing a lighter shell, the gun was easier to handle in rough weather, but as the gun shield did not reach the deck, gun crews were left vulnerable to enemy shell splinters.

41   *An oil painting by Burgess of HMS* Chester *on which Jack Cornwell served during the Battle of Jutland in 1916. The painting was presented to the City of Chester by the light cruiser's builders, Cammell Laird.*

42   *A 5.5-inch Naval Gun from HMS* Chester, *1916, now permanently displayed at the Imperial War Museum, London.*

2 MAY 1916 – HMS *CHESTER* COMMISSIONED AT LIVERPOOL

HMS *Chester* was adopted by the citizens of Chester and the ship's acceptance trials were carried out in the River Mersey. On the commissioning day of the cruiser, 2 May 1916, Jack Cornwell, Boy Seaman 1st Class, formed part of the complement of the newly-commissioned ship, attached to the 3rd Squadron, commanded by Captain Robert Lawson, RN. Joining as a gunner, Jack was made sight setter on *Chester*'s forward 5.5-inch gun.

15 MAY 1916

Chester joined the battle fleet at Scapa Flow on 15 May and completed her battle training on 29 May, one day before the Battle Fleet, led by Admiral Sir John Jellicoe, sailed from Scapa Flow for Jutland and the bleak vastness of the North Sea.

23 MAY 1916 – LAST LETTER HOME

Jack wrote what was to be his last letter to his parents.

> Dear Dad,
> Just a few lines in answer to your most welcome letter, which we received on Monday – first post of the week. That is why you have not had a letter for a long while. Thanks for your stamps you sent me.

We are up in the *(censored)* somewhere, and they have just put me as sight setter at a gun.

Dear Dad, I have just had to start in pencil, as I have run short of ink but still, I suppose you don't mind so long as you get a letter, and I am sorry to tell you that poor old Ada Lambert is dead, and I dare say by the time you get this letter she will be buried. I have got a lot of letters to send home and about, so I can't afford much more, and we are just about to close up at the gun, so this is all for now; have more next time.

I remain, your ever-loving son,

Jack
x

Tuesday, 30 May 1916, 11.30 p.m.

All formations of the Grand Fleet were at sea proceeding in three columns towards the ordered rendezvous – 152 Royal Naval ships comprising 28 dreadnoughts, 9 battle cruisers, 8 armoured cruisers, 28 light cruisers, 78 destroyers and a mine-layer, also a seaplane.

Wednesday, 31 May 1916 – The Battle of Jutland

Three tense days followed, then on 31 May the British Squadrons and the German High Fleet of 160 ships almost met by accident in the foggy conditions.

The cruisers were too lightly-armoured and lightly-gunned to take their place in the battle line with the heavy ships. HMS *Chester* was stationed as a 'linking ship' to pass signals visually between the armoured cruiser screen to the Battle Fleet and the three ships of the 3rd Battle Squadron. The Executive Officer of *Chester* wrote:

> We got the first news of the enemy about 2.30 p.m. Three hours before we ourselves were in touch with the enemy but were intercepting frequent reports of the action between the naval battle cruiser fleets and were anxiously wondering whether we should arrive in time to share in the scrap. It was a beautifully clear afternoon.

Jack Cornwell's action station was sight setter on the forward 5.5-inch gun which had a crew of ten. He wore earphones and was in direct contact with the gunnery control platform at the masthead where the gunnery officer issued his instructions for range corrections to the gun as required. Jack was ready at his post at the left-hand side of the shield of the forward six-inch gun.

5.30 p.m.
HMS *Chester* sighted gun flashes, two enemy destroyers and a light cruiser.

5.36 p.m.
Two German destroyers of the 2nd Scouting Group, escorting the light cruiser SMS *Frankfurt*, commanded by Konteradmiral [Rear Admiral] Fredric Bödicker were sighted, followed by three

more cruisers, *Pillau, Wiesbaden* and *Elbing* which hove into view almost simultaneously. The four cruisers, with a combined firepower of 32 1,500mm guns, opened fire at a range of 7,000 yards (3.9 miles).

The ranges of the guns of both HMS *Chester* and *Frankfurt* were 8,000 yards (approximately 4.5 miles). The first German salvo landed some 2,000 yards beyond the vessel, but the second salvo gauged the range.

HMS *Chester* did not reply until the Germans had fired their third salvo. The enemy's fourth salvo put HMS *Chester*'s No 1 gun port side out of action, and killed and wounded a large number sailors, resulting in only one gun being left in action. To make observations of the fall of the shots easier, *Wiesbaden* and *Elbing* were ordered to cease fire. At the same time Bödicker followed the fleeing *Chester* at full speed in a north-easterly direction and then ran into the 3rd Battle Squadron.

5.37 p.m.

HMS *Chester* sent her only full salvo of action towards *Frankfurt*, but the third salvo from the German cruiser straddled HMS *Chester*, with direct hits on board, sending jagged fragments of steel sweeping across her decks.

Faithful unto Death

From the minute the battle had begun, the forward gun turret of the *Chester* received the full force of the enemy's fire. A German shell struck the position where Jack Cornwell and the rest of the gun crew waited at action stations.

The forward turret bore the brunt of the combined fire of the German ships. As the first shell burst, five of Jack's comrades fell dead. The second shell fell at the foot of another gun crew member, blowing him to pieces. After the third shell burst there was no one left to instruct Jack. All around him, sailors lay dying, some horribly mutilated by shrapnel. Jack himself was mortally wounded from a shard of steel which had penetrated his chest. It was said that a dying crew member told him to run for it – but he did not. Jack Cornwell remained standing alone at his station for some hours, amid a scene of carnage.

For 19 minutes *Chester* ran before the German guns; 17 or 18 direct hits were received and much splinter damage was sustained by shells exploding on impact in the water close to the vessel. During those 19 minutes one in five of the ship's company became casualties. Two shells burst in the after control position destroying and blowing overboard the range finder, an instrument weighing 7cwt. The occupants of the room were blown overboard with the exception of the Control Officer, who was left perched on his chair in a corner of the floor of the room where it was still attached to the mast. Four of the ship's guns were inoperative and only one figure was left upright amongst the bodies of the crew of the forward 5.5-inch gun, Boy 1st Class Jack Cornwell.

During a lull in the battle Admiral Hood's *Dreadnought* appeared, her heavy guns allowing *Chester* to disengage. Jack was found at his post, his telephone earpieces clamped to his head, standing erect and straight backed, dying on his feet.

Dying Moments

From various official reports, eye witness accounts and books, some of which differ considerably, the forward 5.5-inch gun of HMS *Chester* fired only one shell when the deck received a direct hit, spraying the area around the gun with lethal fragments of shell. Standing by the gun shield, the bodies of the rest of the crew would have probably absorbed most of the shrapnel before Jack Cornwell was hit in the chest.

This has been confirmed by another Boy Seaman standing on the bridge, who is said to have stated that Jack Cornwell's leg was shattered and he picked himself up and supported himself on the gun shield. Within minutes the control room, which passed on instructions to the sight setters, had ceased to exist, so no orders could have been passed to Jack and his injuries did not allow him to move from his post against the gun shield. He remained awaiting further orders until the end of the action.

Lieutenant (later Rear Admiral) H.E. Morse was in control of torpedoes on HMS *Chester*. He said he could do little because the torpedo tubes were out of action, so he was in an excellent position to witness what was happening. He saw a shell land right in the middle of the fo'c'sle gun. And he noticed 'the boy [Jack Cornwell] still sat there, a very gallant deed', which he reported to the ship's Captain.

The Royal Naval Museum mentions other reports, including Jack volunteering to go to the top of the gun turret to wipe the glass so that the rangefinder could line the target. Another report says he managed to ram home one projectile, close the breech and press the firing button and this projectile exploded on the German ship *Wiesbaden*, causing damage which led to her sinking.

Captain Lawson turned to run towards the position of the German Battle Squadron, steering his vessel towards the fall of the German shells in an attempt to upset the accurate range finding of the German light cruiser *Frankfurt*.

5.40 p.m.

Admiral Hood heard the firing and at about 5.40 p.m. the battle cruiser HMS *Chester* was zigzagging through a storm of shell splashes. The pursuers came into view, saw the battle cruisers, and swung around to escape. Twelve-inch salvos were fired into them while HMS *Chester* escaped across the bow of HMS *Invincible*, firing her last shots as she did so.

HMS *Chester* sustained heavy damage with many casualties, one in five of her ship's company. 33 were killed and 42 wounded. Her fire control and half her guns' crews were knocked out. Three out of the ten guns were disabled.

6.05 p.m.

After 19 minutes, HMS *Chester* reached relative safety, and was sighted by British battle cruisers which opened fire with their large guns.

At about 6.05 p.m., *Chester* rejoined the 3rd Battle Squadron. *Chester* was to remain with the fleet until the next day – she did not see action again. An officer aboard HMS *Castor* leading the 11th Destroyer Flotilla recorded a sighting which took place shortly before 6 p.m.:

Down the length of *Chester*'s central ammunition passage were these wounded men – cheerful Cockneys, for she had a Chatham Crew (usually sailors from London) – the bloody stumps of their tourniqueted legs out in front. Mortally injured, Boy Cornwell was among them. An hour or so later most of them were dead.

1 JUNE 1916

At daylight, 2.32 a.m., Rear Admiral Heath, Commanding the 2nd Cruiser Squadron, ordered the badly-damaged HMS *Chester* to Immingham on the Humber, where she arrived at 5 p.m. On entering the estuary, she was met by tugs which took off the wounded including Jack, who was heavily bandaged, and lowered him gently onto a tug from where he was transferred to bed number 3 of the Yarborough Ward of Grimsby District Hospital in Lincolnshire.

Jack was taken into the hands of Admiralty Surgeon Dr C.S. Stephenson [the term 'Admiralty Surgeon' usually denoted that he was a doctor carrying out surgical duties]. When told that nothing could be done for him, by all accounts Jack was wonderfully brave. It is reported that although in great pain Jack's quiet cheerfulness never left him. Although barely conscious he was still able to speak and when the Matron asked him how the battle had gone, he is said to have replied, 'Oh – we carried on all right!' At the end it was reported that Jack said, 'Give mother my love. I know that she is coming.'

Jack's mother received a telegram about his condition and was on her way to see her son but she arrived too late. He died aged just 16 years and five months, 24 hours after his admission.

According to Leading Stoker Albert Horne, who saw Jack when they landed him at Immingham, 'the Captain called to see Jack in hospital but when he got there he was told that the boy had passed away'.

'He was,' said Dr Stephenson, a man inured to tragedy, 'a wonderfully brave boy.' The chairman of the Grimsby Hospital Committee said that when he saw Jack he was impressed with his pluck and cheerfulness despite his terrible injuries.

Jack's Cornwell's death certificate from Grimsby Hospital, as also confirmed by his medical records, show the cause of death to be 'Intestinal perforation due to wounds received in action. Injuries received in the naval battle between the British and German Navies in the North Sea'. Reports that Jack died of 'shrapnel wounds to the chest/heart' are incorrect.

The Captain of HMS *Chester* wrote to Jack's mother:

I know you would wish to hear of the splendid fortitude and courage shown by your son during the action of May 31. His devotion to duty was an example for all of us. The wounds which resulted in his death within a short time were received in the first few minutes of the action. He remained steady at his most exposed post at the gun, waiting for orders. His gun would not bear on the enemy: all but two of the ten crew were killed or wounded, and he was the only one who was in such an exposed position. But he felt he might be needed and, indeed, he might have been, so he stayed there, standing and waiting, under heavy fire, with just his own brave heart and God's help to support him.

I have not failed to bring his name prominently before the Admiral.

'THE FIRST CORNWELL GRAVE' – 2 JUNE 1916

What happened next has been misunderstood for decades; unfortunately this error continues to be repeated. Most versions say, 'After Jack died of the wounds he received at the Battle of Jutland, he was buried in an ordinary war grave at Scartho Road Cemetery, Grimsby', but this was not so.

The Royal Naval Museum correctly states that on 2 June 1916 Jack Cornwell died from his wounds aged 16 years and five months. Later his body was interred in Manor Park Cemetery, Ilford, Essex, a wooden peg No 323 marking his grave.

In July 1916 the *Daily Mail* reported that Sir David Beatty in his despatch on the Battle of Jutland wrote:

> Boy (1st Class) John Travers Cornwell, of the *Chester*, was mortally wounded early in the action. He nevertheless remained standing alone at a most exposed post, quietly awaiting orders till the end of the action, with the gun's crew dead all round him. His age was under 16½ years. I regret that he has since died, but I recommend his case for special recognition of the highest example set by him.

The headline of the *Daily Sketch* of 7 July said 'Boy Hero of The Naval Battle'. Below was a photo montage of Jack Cornwell, wearing the ship's tally of HMS *Lancaster* with a warship featured below. This was followed on the next day with the revelation that Jack had been buried without a headstone in a 'common grave'.

The Jack Cornwell Memorial Committee was set up on 20 July and was registered as a Charity Trust in 1921. Admiral Lord Beresford (Commodore Sea Scouts) announced that finally it had been decided, with the approval of the boy's parents, that a national memorial to Jack Cornwell should go ahead.

Admiral Lord Beresford asked the Government in the House of Lords in early August whether it was proposed to award the Victoria Cross posthumously to John Travers Cornwell, HMS *Chester*, to which the Duke of Devonshire replied that at present no recommendation had been received.

THE FUNERAL AND BURIAL OF A HERO – 29 JULY 1916

The young hero's body was exhumed from its unmarked grave in Manor Park Cemetery and his impressive public funeral, accompanied by full naval honours, took place on a day which dawned with clear blue skies and temperatures rising into the eighties – a sweltering summer's day.

At 3 p.m. the cortège left West Ham Town Hall, its steps smothered with flowers. Mounted police led the funeral procession, followed by a Naval band playing mournful funeral music, and a Naval firing party, drawn from the Royal Naval Division of the Royal Naval Reserve, marched along with measured step, their firearms reversed. The coffin, covered with the Union Flag, Jack's naval cap on top, rested on a gun carriage drawn by 120 boy sailors from the Crystal Palace Naval Depot. There were many floral tributes, including one of lilies and immortelles, whose blooms never fade, from Admiral Sir David Beatty.

Shops closed and a dense crowd of thousands lined the tightly-packed streets of East Ham as Jack's coffin was drawn past on the gun carriage. Scouts lined the route, and a large number also joined the procession.

43   *The funeral of Jack Cornwell, 26 July 1916.*

In one of the carriages sat the bereaved family. Jack's father, Private Eli Cornwell, in the uniform of a reservist of the 10th Essex Regiment, accompanied Mrs Lilly Cornwell and three sons dressed in black, the chief mourners.

Those who followed the coffin on foot were: The Bishop of Barking; The Mayor of East Ham and members of the Borough Council; Sir John Bethell, MP; Dr Macnamara MP, Financial and Parliamentary Secretary representing the Admiralty; Captain R.N. Lawson, HMS *Chester*. Other dignitaries were among those who also attended the funeral.

Crowds stood 16 deep on one side of the tram-lined main road, ten deep on the other side and police officers were posted every ten yards. The gun carriage had chains to the wheel hubs of the limber. Two sailors were positioned at intervals each side of the drag ropes and five 'leading hands' (senior ratings) were each side of the flag-draped coffin; the band followed behind.

Six boy sailors from HMS *Chester* who were at the Battle of Jutland carried floral tributes in the procession. The St Nicholas Boys' Band from East Ham led 80 boys from Walton Road School. There followed local military units, the 2nd Cadet Battalion of the Essex Regiment and Boy Scouts, including those from the 2nd Ilford.

It took two hours for the procession to reach the cemetery where the open grave, lined with flowers, was waiting to receive the coffin. Some small bunches of flowers had been placed there anonymously, others from eminent sources. Large wreaths included those from the Lord Mayor and Sheriffs of London; The Admiralty sent an arrangement in the form of an anchor; another was made from lilies and carnations, and one from Rear-Admiral Sir David Beatty bore the inscription 'With deep respect'.

The coffin, removed from the gun carriage, was carried to the grave by a bearer party of sailors, to the sound of the hymn *Eternal Father Strong to Save*. The burial service was conducted by the Bishop of Barking. The naval firing party fired a volley of three rifle shots over the grave, the *Last Post* sounded and Jack's shipmates placed a final floral tribute in the form of an anchor on his grave. The many attending sang the hymn *O God Our Help in Ages Past*, followed by the National Anthem.

The press reported the funeral in great detail in the Sunday papers with photographs and banner headlines, in the daily papers published on 31 July and for several days afterwards. The funeral of John Travers Cornwell was a talking point throughout Britain. He was accorded a funeral normally given only to a distinguished person of high rank and status.

The Lord Mayor of London called a meeting at Mansion House to establish a Boy Cornwell Memorial to take the form of cottage homes for disabled sailors, marines and their families and the endowment of naval scholarships.

The Grimsby and District Hospital where Jack died decided to endow a special cot in his memory with a tablet recording his deed of glory.

Sir Robert Baden-Powell reproduced and distributed a copy of his own painting in connection with the Scout's Memorial. On the left hand side of each copy was B-P's distinctive handwriting, stating

> With every thanks for your help to the Memorial Fund.
> Robert Baden-Powell, Sept 1916

The *Sunday Pictorial* wrote at the time that it understood

> the Admiralty is taking up the subject of a memorial to the boy hero of HMS *Chester*, John Travers Cornwell, whose bravery in the Battle of Jutland was described in the dispatches of Admiral Sir John Jellicoe.

> 'All the facts are being carefully considered, and it is not likely that a decision will be long delayed' said an Admiralty official yesterday.

PUBLIC MEMORIAL FUND

On 14 September, the fund was launched by the Lord Mayor of London at Mansion House. On the same day, the Boy Scouts Association announced in the *Headquarters Gazette* the introduction of the Cornwell Badge:

44   *'The Great Boy Scout'. Postcard of Jack Cornwell.*

45 *Cigarette card by John Player & Sons depicting a painting of Jack Cornwell at the Battle of Jutland, May 1916.*

It has been decided to commemorate the heroism of Scout 'Jack' Travers Cornwell, who was mortally wounded at the Battle of Horn Reef [Jutland] whilst serving on HMS *Chester*, by the grant of a special badge. Jack's name would then, as now, be perpetuated with the instigation of a new badge for individual Scout bravery.

Subject to conditions, it is given for Scouts, not adult members, who are of good character, showing devotion to duty, courage and endurance while undergoing suffering in a heroic manner.

THE VICTORIA CROSS

The next day came the news that Jack Cornwell had been awarded the Victoria Cross, one of three won at the Battle of Jutland.

The London Gazette of Friday, 15 September 1916 cited:

> The King has been graciously pleased to approve the grant of the Victoria Cross to Boy, First Class, John Travers Cornwell ONJ 42562 (died 2 June 1916) for the conspicuous act of bravery specified below:

> 'Mortally wounded early in the action, Boy, First Class, John Travers Cornwell remained standing alone at a most exposed post, quietly awaiting orders, until the end of the action, with the gun's crew dead and wounded all around him. His age was under sixteen and a half years.'

Jack Cornwell was the youngest person in the Navy to receive the award.

The *Daily Sketch* of Saturday, 25 October recorded that Eli Cornwell, having died of a bronchial infection, was buried in the same grave as his son Jack in Manor Park Cemetery. A few months after he died, a committee was formed to organise a national memorial for Jack Cornwell: £21,849 13s. 11d. was raised – around £940,820 today.

On 17 November, Mrs Cornwell went to Buckingham Palace, where King George V himself presented her with her son's Victoria Cross.

Commemorative stamps were sold in millions. A stained-glass window in Kingston, Ontario, Canada was designed and installed in their City Hall.

A picture of the boy, standing by his gun, with Admiral David Beatty's report of the incident, occupied a position of honour in more than 12,000 schools.

9 FEBRUARY 1917

At Buckingham Palace, Queen Mary received the members of the Jack Cornwell Memorial Fund Committee, who presented the first instalment of the proceeds of the appeal. Admiral Lord Beresford gave an address explaining the objects of the fund and the means adopted to carry it through.

The official picture for the Admiralty of John Travers Cornwell VC of HMS *Chester* at the Battle of Jutland was painted both on board HMS *Chester* and in his studios by the distinguished artist Frank O. Salisbury. The artist used Jack's elder brother Ernest as a model, depicting Jack at his post of duty – a picture reminiscent of that by Sir Edward Poynter, RA, 'Faithful unto Death', showing the Roman sentry at Herculaneum standing at his post amidst the devastation caused by the destruction of the town during the eruption of Vesuvius. The painting was hung in the Royal Academy in Spring 1917. Admiral Beatty described the scene as a 'moving incident on a day of great incidents'.

On 23 March, a large company at Mansion House witnessed the presentation of the painting to Sir Edward Carson, First Lord of the Admiralty, on behalf of the Board of Admiralty. The inscription at the foot of the painting gave details of Jack Cornwell's heroic action.

Captain Lawson, on being asked for a title for the picture, replied he knew of none which was more appropriate than this: 'Thou hast set my feet in a large place' [Psalm 31, Verse 8].

The portrait was hung in HMS *Impregnable*, Devonport until 1928 when it was moved to the Training Establishment HMS *Vincent* at Portsmouth, and most recently in the Anglican Church at HMS *Raleigh*, Torpoint, Cornwall.

After restoration, the Cornwell VC Painting Rededication Ceremony took place at HMS *Raleigh* on 20 March 2009.

IN MEMORIAM

The Times of 8 July 1917 recorded: 'In memory of Jack Cornwell, VC, a brass tablet placed in Walton Road School, Manor Park, by scholars and staff, was yesterday unveiled by Lady Jellicoe. The Battle of Jutland hero was a former pupil of the school'.

Plans were prepared to raise funds, establish scholarships and build homes, all inspired by the name of Jack Cornwell.

On 29 August 1918 Arthur Frederick Cornwell, Jack's step-brother, was killed on active service in France, aged 30. He was buried at Ecousy-St Mein.

Jack's mother, Lilly Cornwell, moved from Stepney as she could not afford the rent. She received 10s. a week (£10.61 in today's money) from the Navy League which just covered the rent of three rooms.

46   *Plaque to Jack Cornwell VC, unveiled by Lady Jellicoe, July 1917. Walton Road School, East London.*

47 *The Jack Cornwell Memorial in Manor Park Cemetery, Ilford, Essex – Eli Cornwell, father of Jack, died aged 63 in HM Forces, 1916.*

Jack's pension from the Navy was 6s. 6d. (£6.89 in today's money) but Lilly Cornwell received no pension for Eli Cornwell. Out of the 16s. 6d. she had to keep herself, her daughter Lilly and younger son George, who was ill and out of work. She was not in the best of health, but was obliged to work 12 hours a day, seven days a week to bring her wage up to 25s. a week. Lilly Cornwell died aged 54 on 31 October 1919.

On 15 August 1919 Lilly Cornwell, Jack's 14-year-old sister, received a birthday present of a piano, brought out of the proceeds of a booklet written on her brother's exploits by Mr J.C. MacCormack of Northampton. Any further proceeds would go to provide for her tuition. It was Jack Cornwell's last promise to his sister that he would buy her a piano after the war.

A memorial to Jack Cornwell, now also carrying the names of his father Eli and step-brother Arthur, was unveiled by Dr Macnamara on 28 December 1920. The sculpted cross and anchor which rises above Jack's grave in the crowded corner of Manor Park Cemetery now called Cornwell Crescent was paid for by the 'scholars and ex-scholars of schools in East Ham'.

THE IMPERIAL WAR MUSEUM, LONDON

The gun from HMS *Chester*, a Mark-1 5.5-inch breech loader, described as the same gun at which Jack Cornwell was mortally wounded, was installed in the Imperial War Museum. It is maintained in pristine condition occupying a prominent position on the ground floor.

In the south transept of Chester Cathedral wooden panels form a roll of honour for those on HMS *Chester* who lost their lives in the battle of Jutland in May 1916.

In the City of London, a memorial cross to Jack Cornwell can be seen in the churchyard of St Botolph without Bishopsgate.

2 MAY 1924 – AT THE ROYAL BRITISH EMPIRE EXHIBITION

Queen Mary expressed curiosity at a battered deck plate on the ground and was informed that it came from HMS *Chester* marking the precise spot where Jack Cornwell stood and died, thus meriting his VC. The Queen was deeply moved.

In 1929 the Walton School was renamed the Jack Cornwell School. It has since been demolished.

31 MAY 1929 – THE MAYOR OF EAST HAM'S APPEAL

The Mayor of East Ham's appeal raised £8,014.92p (approximately £267,877 today) to purchase a plot of land in Hornchurch on which three pairs of cottages were built for disabled sailors and their families, and are still used for their original purpose. The layout is based on a stylised version of the Victoria Cross. The cottages were opened on the 13th anniversary of the Battle of Jutland, 31 May 1929, by Admiral Jellicoe.

REMEMBERING JACK CORNWELL

The London Borough of Newham (successor to East Ham) named a block of flats in Little Ilford 'John Cornwell VC House', and also named Jack Cornwell Street after him. Newham Council's Jack Cornwell Award for bravery was introduced in 2001. A Jack Cornwell Cadet Centre is the base for Newham Sea Cadets. The London Borough of Newham introduced their Award for Bravery for residents of the London Borough of Newham responsible for an act of bravery within the Borough – one award a year.

There is a Jack Cornwell Centre in Jack Cornwell Street, London E14.

Jack Cornwell is still remembered each year by the British Legion and the Sea Cadet Corps in a ceremony at Manor Park Cemetery. Manor Park also has a public house called *The Victoria Cross*, with photographs of the Battle of Jutland on the wall.

Jack Cornwell was featured on one of a series of stamps issued by the Royal Mail in September 2006 which commemorated the 150th anniversary of the Victoria Cross.

JACK'S MEDALS

The Times of 28 November 1968 stated:

48   Inscription on the base of a memorial cross to Jack Cornwell in the churchyard of St Botolph-without-Bishopsgate, London.

49   Memorial cross to Jack Cornwell in the churchyard of St Botolph-without-Bishopsgate, London.

50 *The Jack Cornwell Parade in Romford, London E12 on 2 June 2002: The Royal British Legion, The Royal British Legion's Women's Section, The Royal Naval Association and Sea Cadet Corps parading in honour of Jack Cornwell, VC, on the occasion of the 50th anniversary of the accession to the throne of HM Queen Elizabeth II.*

The Victoria Cross awarded to the boy sailor Jack Cornwell, perhaps the most famous VC of all time, was presented to the Imperial War Museum at a poignant little ceremony in London yesterday.

Mrs Irene Cornwell, widow of his eldest brother Ernest, presented them on 'long loan'. Jack's sister, 78-year-old Mrs Alice Payne, helped her to unveil the museum's latest acquisition by pulling away a large Union Jack [Union Flag] from the neat display of other Cornwell mementoes, where it will rest.

Mrs Payne said he had been a kind gentle boy, ten years her junior, whose acts of bravery and unselfishness were not limited to that memorable end on the deck of the *Chester*. He had once won a Boy Scout award for freeing a girl from a drain.

Two survivors from the *Chester* were at the ceremony, former Leading Stoker Albert Horne, a Welshman, now aged 75, and Rear Admiral H.E. Morse, then Lieutenant in control of torpedoes, who reported Cornwell's courage to the ship's Captain. 'I could do little myself because the torpedo tubes were out of action, so I was in an excellent position to witness what was happening. I saw this shell land right of the middle of the fo'c'sle gun, and then noticed this boy still sat there.' Admiral Morse said. 'It was a very gallant deed.'

The medals can be seen in the VC/GC Room at the museum.

The Scout Association

THE CORNWELL SCOUT BADGE

I have awarded this Badge to

'in recognition of a high standard
of character and devotion to duty
under great suffering.'

Chief Scout

John Travers Cornwell (Jack), a Scout in the St. Mary's Mission Group, Manor Park, London, entered the Royal Navy in 1915.

It was wartime and training was brief, but Jack helped by his days in Scouting adapted quickly.

On May 31, 1916 while serving on HMS Chester, Jack was struck by a shell splinter. Grievously wounded, he stayed at his post awaiting orders until he was relieved at the end of the battle.

On reaching port Jack was transferred to a hospital in Grimsby, and there three days later he died a national hero. For gallantry he was given both the Victoria Cross and the highest Scouting award, the Bronze Cross.

To commemorate the courage shown by Jack, The Scout Association created 'The Cornwell Scout Badge' in his memory.

This Award is presented to Scouts under the age of twenty five who have shown immense courage, either through risking their life to save others or in facing illness, pain or handicap.

This illustration is from a water-colour by 'B.-P.'

51   *Certificate accompanying the award of the Cornwell Scout Badge.*

Decorations
and Awards
of THE SCOUT ASSOCIATION

The Cornwell Scout Badge

Awards for Gallantry

The Chief Scout's
Commendation
for Gallantry

The Gilt Cross   The Silver Cross   The Bronze Cross

Awards for
Meritorious Conduct

The Chief Scout's
Commendation for
Meritorious Conduct

The Certificate of
Meritorious Conduct

The Medal of
Meritorious Conduct

52   *Decorations and Awards – The Scout Association.*

53   *Emma Dovey, Kidderminster Sea Scouts, awarded the Cornwell Scout Badge in 2004, representing the award holders at the unveiling ceremony of the restored Jack Cornwell painting – Emma Dovey is being presented with a copy of the painting at HMS Raleigh on 20 March 2009 by Captain J. Woodcock, OBE, RN, Officer in Command.*

54   *Legend under the Salisbury painting: 'Thou hast set my feet in a large place', from Psalm 31 verse 8, of which Wesley's interpretation was: 'Made way for me to escape, when I was encompassed by them.'*

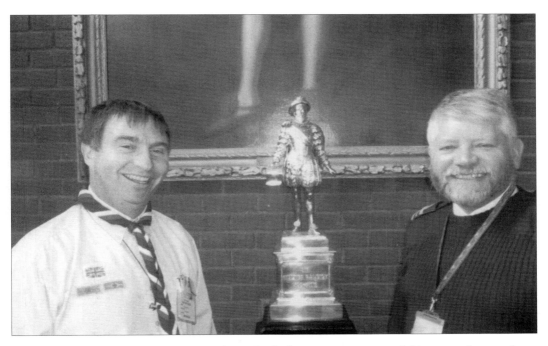

55 *Wayne Bulpitt, Chief Commissioner for England, The Scout Association with Lieutenant Commander David Griffiths, RN (Staff Officer Scouts), at HMS Raleigh, 20 March 2009.*

56 *Inside the Captain's Residence at the reception, HMS Raleigh, 20 March 2009. Barry Sutton, Awards Board, The Scout Association with Wayne Bulpitt, Chief Commissioner for England.*

57   *A painting depicting Jack Cornwell at the forward gun of HMS Chester in 1916. It was painted by Royal Academician Frank Salisbury, who used Jack's younger brother George to represent Jack Cornwell in the painting.*

FIVE

THE INTER-WAR YEARS, 1919-38 – CARRYING ON WITH VIGOUR

1919

The Development of Sea Scouting

A message on 8 February 1919 from King George V was read out at 98 different centres in the United Kingdom by a naval officer deputed by the Admiralty, thanking 250,000 Scouts for the patriotic services rendered at wartime coastwatching duties. At Devonport the Commander-in-Chief, Admiral Thursby, repeated the high appreciation. This was further endorsed by Admiral Sir David Beatty, accepting the post of Chief Sea Scout, and Admiral Jellicoe undertook to inspect Sea Scouts overseas when on his tour of the Empire.

Training Ship Northampton

The ship was acquired in 1919 by the Boy Scouts Association. Writing to Lord Lytton (Civil Lord of the Admiralty) on 30 January 1919, B-P stated: 'The Sea Scouts were becoming a very important Branch [of the Boy Scouts Association] and the Admiralty was well disposed to their efforts, providing coastwatchers boys to replace coastguards during the war.' Developing the Sea Scout Section on practical lines was helping provide young seamen for the Navy and Mercantile Marine. The Admiralty's assistance was asked for in providing a training ship of minesweeper class with tender for this purpose. Lord Lytton replied on 4 February that he would help with this request.

B-P wrote to Lord Lytton again on 24 February about newspaper reports that the surrendered German warships were to be sunk. B-P suggested four of the ships could be used as training ships for Sea Scouts in order to raise crews for the Navy. He saw that the lack of ships and apparatus was holding the Scout Movement back, when the Sea Scouts might have some 30,000 boys in training for the sea.

On 27 February Lord Lytton replied that some 30 British ships of war were now obsolete. He had spoken to the First Sea Lord about placing any of these ships the Chief Scout might require for the training of Sea Scouts.

TS Northampton

HMS *Sharpshooter*, leased by Lord Northampton from the Admiralty in 1904 and renamed TS *Northampton*, was transferred in April 1919 to the Boy Scouts Association to serve as the training ship for Sea Scouting. Sea Scout committees were formed to organise and support the Sea Scout Branch.

September 1919
Admiral Viscount Beresford, GCB, GCVO
10 February 1846-6 September 1919

The *Headquarters Gazette* for October 1919 recorded the death of 'Charlie' Beresford:

> Through the death of Admiral Viscount Beresford the Boy Scout Council loses one of the most valuable and valued members. A great man is dead, and our Movement is very much the poorer through loss of our cheery champion and ex-Chief Sea Scout – Lord Beresford. He was an intense believer in the Scouts, and in any time of difficulty we knew that we had in him an ardent and powerful upholder. Lord Beresford was a typical Scout himself, and set an example for all as a brave, energetic, healthy, good-hearted, able, patriotic, and always a cheery citizen. God rest him.

> Robert Baden-Powell

58   *The Prince of Wales (centre), inspecting Sea Scouts with Captain B.S. Thesiger, Commissioner for Sea Scouts (left) and Lord Baden-Powell (right), 1919.*

59   *Training Ship*
Northampton, *training ship
for Sea Scouts, 1920.*

Admiralty Recognition Scheme

On 25 September 1919 Admiral Commanding Reserves, W.R. de Chair, wrote to the Chief Scout informing him that the Lord Commissioners of the Admiralty had agreed that Sea Scouts could be recognised by the Admiralty on inspection by a naval officer of Sea Scouts' efficiency in seamanship, signalling, etc. In November 1919 the scheme was introduced for Sea Scouts, a significant milestone.

November 1919

The *Headquarters Gazette* reported that Captain Thesiger, CB, CMG, RN, returned from active service to become Commissioner for Sea Scouts. Meanwhile the Sea Scout Branch had been quietly developing all the time, thanks especially to its own good efforts during the war.

1920

Training Ship Northampton – *A Centre for Sea Scouting*

TS *Northampton* opened for instruction on 26 January 1920. On becoming a centre for Sea Scout training, Thames Troops took full advantage, and before long a small fleet of their gigs and whalers was moored around her in addition to the ship's own boats. Owing to an outbreak of influenza on board the ship she closed for the Easter holidays in 1920. Despite this, attendances of 829 Scoutmasters and 5,617 Scouts were recorded.

The use of *Northampton* was directly responsible for starting three Sea Scout Troops at Southwark, Fulham and Forest Hill; Sea Scout Troops were also being formed at Balham, Paddington and Chelsea. There was a large waiting list of boys wishing to join – figures doubled in the course of the year.

The Income and Expenditure Account of The Boy Scouts Association showed an expenditure of £3,347 4s. 1d. for the *Northampton* which, to quote the Chief Scout, 'cost us a heap of money

60   *Scout camping and swimming at the coast returns after the First World War, c.1920. However, coastwatching Sea Scouts were permitted to boat, swim and camp during hostilities.*

[about £71,000 today]'. However if in return they could secure more men willing to be trained as Sea Scoutmasters, as well as boys as eager to learn as those who had up to now used this ship, this money would have been well spent.

Captain Thesiger was recalled to take up Naval Command in October 1920, Vice-Admiral C.S. Hickley acting in his place. Lieutenant Stanton, Secretary of the Sea Scout Committee, retired at the end of the year and Captain Malzard succeeded to his duties.

Sea Scout numbers remained relatively consistent although the training tended to be formal; there were, however, enterprising leaders. One such Sea Scouter was Uffa Fox, the well-known yachtsman and boat designer, who took his Sea Scouts across the channel in the early 1920s. There was a good deal of ropework, rigging of boatswains' chairs, singing of sea shanties and weekends spent aboard floating headquarters. Watches were kept, bells sounded, colours flown and a good scouting and nautical atmosphere prevailed. Many of the well-established Sea Scout Groups of today were formed during the 1920s and 1930s.

Sea Scouting during the 1920s

Scout camping, which was suspended during the war, again became a major activity for both Scouts and Sea Scouts.

61   *Cambridge Sea Scout Drum and Bugle Band, c.1920.*

1921
In 1921 there were 2,704 Sea Scouts.

Warington Baden-Powell
Founder of Sea Scouting, born Oxford 3 February 1847, died Chelsea 24 April 1921.

Headquarters Gazette, *September 1921*
The End of the Line for Northampton
From the 'Sea Scout Editor's Chair', Vice-Admiral Hickley, newly-appointed Chief Sea Scout Commissioner, wrote about his first impressions of Sea Scouting having joined the Movement directly as a Commissioner – he thought that many of the Sea Scouts were too young or too small in stature.

He reported that all Sea Scouts who had visited *Northampton* would be indeed sorry when she was given up: the figures subsequently showed that an average of 620 Scouts and 38 adults per

month had attended for instruction. He had heard it said that it would kill Sea Scouting – 'Don't
believe it'.

Vice-Admiral Hickley said the facts were that *Northampton* was originally intended as a depot
or training ship for all Sea Scouts in the United Kingdom, but only Sea Scouts in London had
materially benefited from the ship, the cost of upkeep being out of all proportion to the numbers
who made use of her. It was too expensive a luxury and one impossible to continue. He hoped
that moorings for boats belonging to Troops would be found; a possibility, if the Port of London
Authority would allow, would be off Lambeth Pier, which was in as central a position as was
possible. *Northampton* would be returned to the Admiralty in November.

On return to the Admiralty, *Northampton's* boats were allotted to some Thames Troops, but the
moorings off the Temple were no longer available for London Sea Scouts, who had to take their
boats to distant points on the river such as the docks. It was said that the London Troops suffered
grievously, some having to be disbanded.

The Captain of the Northampton, Lieutenant G. Malzard, RNR

He said at the time:

> I feel *Northampton* has been of great assistance and has benefited a considerable number of Sea Scout
> Troops. I have specially noticed the very striking way in which a large number of boys have developed
> physically. I am only sorry that more Sea Scout Troops have not formed in the poorer parts of London
> to take advantage of the benefits provided by *Northampton*.

Northampton was doing good work but at a cost the Association could not afford.

Sea Scout Uniform

Writing in Chief Scouts' Outlook in the September 1921 issue of *Headquarters Gazette*, B-P again raised the matter of uniform for leaders:

> One word about Sea Scoutmasters' uniform may not be out of place here. I have never shown myself much in love with that dress, which was invented when I was away at the other end of the world. My main objection to it is that it tends to make Sea Scoutmasters appear on a different footing from other Scoutmasters and from their boys; in other words it tends to suggest that they are an imitation of officers instead of elder brothers.

> Lately a Sea Scoutmaster asked if he might dress 'like a Sea Scout, instead of like a sick-bay steward.' I was full of sympathy with him. I have noted a good many Sea Scoutmasters are now saving tailors' bills and avoiding misconception on the part of the public by dressing as nearly as possible like their Scouts. The latest reason against the present kit is that it would be difficult to protect under the coming Act of Parliament since it is not original or distinctive.

B-P favoured Sea Scoutmasters wearing the round sailor cap instead of a peaked cap, but he was dissuaded from this view by members of the Sea Scout Committee, some of whom were Admirals – who would not wish to wear the round 'ratings' caps.

63   *1st Mortlake Sea Scouts, 1921.*

1922

There were 3,400 Sea Scouts in the United Kingdom.

The Alexandra Palace Rally

600 Sea Scouts attended the 1922 Alexandra Palace Rally. Thames Sea Scouts played a prominent part in the display at the lake, forming part of the crew of the boat in which HRH the Prince of Wales was rowed across the water.

64   *The Alexandra Palace Rally, 1922. The Stadium Commander Rear Admiral B.S. Thesiger, CB, CMG, RN, pictured centre.*

65   (Right) The Alexandra Palace Rally, 1922.

66   (Below) The Imperial Jamboree, Wembley, 1924. Rear Admiral Thesiger with Scout Messengers.

Sidney Dark, Special Press Representative, wrote:

On Saturday 7 October 1922, 20,000 Scouts under the age of 12 packed closely together in one solid mass to welcome the Prince of Wales. Immediately after his reception by the Chief Scout came the inspection of the Sea Scouts who were drawn up beside the lake … The Sea Scouts were, on the whole, rather older than the Land Scouts – splendidly healthy well-set-up lads [ex-coastwatchers]. They were commanded by Admiral Hickley, a typical stocky naval man, and nearly all the Scoutmasters were

67   *Imperial Jamboree, 1924.*

obviously sailors, many of them bearded and middle-aged, all of them of the class that is still the best England can produce. The Prince was much impressed by the Sea Scouts as, indeed, was the Duke of Connaught, who stopped a dozen times and gossiped with the sons and fathers of the sea. Some of the Sea Scouts exhibited their prowess in knot-tying, and rope-splicing, others climbed ropes and performed other feats; the Prince was interested in it all.

The Sea Scouts' display on the lake was excellent fun. Two small boys constructed a raft and paddled it across the water; other boys fell out of boats and gave exhibitions of life saving. There were water

68   *Hong Kong Sea Scouts receiving navigational instruction, 1923.*

tugs-of-war, an exhibition of rescuing from a wreck, Scouts being hauled by a rope stretched across the lake, only escaping a bump on the cement shore as if by a miracle.

The Prince embarked in a boat and was rowed by Sea Scouts to his car, a voyage of at least 30 yards.

1923

Headquarters Gazette became *The Scouter* magazine.

Rear-Admiral Thesiger was reappointed as Headquarters Commissioner for Sea Scouts in February 1923. Sea Scouts continued to flourish with new troops being formed.

1 June 1923

Sea Scout Conference, Imperial Headquarters, London SW1

Rear-Admiral Thesiger reported representatives from most parts of England and Wales attended with many interesting subjects considered. The age of a Sea Scout was again discussed. The Chairman said he did not think it advisable or necessary to lay down any hard and fast rule that the age of joining for a Sea Scout should differ from that of an ordinary Scout. The openings for Sea Scouts who wished to follow the sea as their profession was discussed and many interesting suggestions were received.

Sea Scout uniform met with general approval. The issue of a Sea Scout badge to be worn when Sea Scouts wore blue shirts instead of jerseys would probably be approved. The subject of badges suitable for Sea Scouts was a large one. There was such a large number of badges that was undesirable to increase them, except where necessary.

69   *1st Windermere Sea Scouts crew the* Sea Otter, *a six-oared 26ft-long gig, 1919. Sea Scouting continued to flourish from 1919 onwards.*

The swimming test for Scouts going into boats produced the most varying opinions. Scoutmasters would, on the responsibility of Rear-Admiral Thesiger, allow Scouts to go in boats provided they could swim 50 yards with their clothes on, to consist of shirt, shorts, and stockings as a minimum.

Requests that the Blue Ensign be used by Sea Scout boats were again discussed. This concession was only granted to the *Northampton* as a special privilege. Although it might possibly be granted in the event of a ship once again becoming the central training establishment for Sea Scouting, it would never be allowed to Sea Scout vessels as a whole or to their boats. The use of the Blue Ensign is still rightly most zealously guarded by the Admiralty.

1924

Census returns show 4,409 Sea Scouts.

December 1924

An anonymous donor gave £100 to the Sea Scouts for a boat fund for poor Sea Scout Troops from which grants would be paid for insuring boats, repairing or paying for boat moorings.

1925

Census returns show 4,211 Sea Scouts.

The Scouter, *June 1925*

'For Sea Scouts' by Rear-Admiral E.K. Loring CB

'The Association has lost with the death of Admiral of the Fleet, Sir Doverton Sturdee, a very capable and helpful friend. The money which started the "Sea Scout Boat Fund" was given anonymously, but the fund administration came from Admiral Sturdee.'

Admiral Loring went to Camberley and marched in the funeral procession to Frimley Parish Church, not as an Admiral, but as a Sea Scout.

Generous donors gave six boats, and 12 Troops were assisted with grants from the Sea Scout Boat fund. The fund stood at £150.

Fifty Sea Scouts were invited to play an official part in the ceremony of the opening by King George V of 'Wembley 1925'; the detachment provided by London, Middlesex, and Surrey well upheld the credit of the Sea Scouts.

Lord Beatty's Appeal

The following from The Scout Association Archives gives an insight into how the Chief Scout, the Sea Scout Committee at IHQ and policy interfaced with the HQ secretariat at the time. The Chief Scout, Admiral Beatty and Admiral Loring were on the Sea Scout Committee of 12 members.

The Times, *Tuesday, 20 October 1925*

HMS Implacable – *The Ship that fought HMS* Victory

There appeared in *The Times* an Appeal under the name of Lord Beatty, Admiral of the Fleet and Chief Sea Scout, to preserve HMS *Implacable*, a 74-gun two decker launched in 1789 as the

Duguay-Trouin by the French Navy, which had fought HMS *Victory*, and had been a boys' training ship at Devonport since 1855. The Admiralty could not allocate monies for the ship because it was no longer on the active list. The appeal proposed that the ship could be used as a holiday training vessel for Sea Scouts, Cadets and other training organisations.

This appeal by Admiral of the Fleet, Earl Beatty, to the national press prompted a swift reaction on 22 October from Charles Dymoke Green, Secretary of the Boy Scouts Association, who had been

> requested by my committee to write to your Lordship with reference to your appeal which appeared in Tuesday's press in regard to the saving of *Implacable*. The fact of any announcement appearing over your Lordship's signature as Chief Sea Scout, without previous consultation with either the Chief Scout or any of his representatives, ... is liable to mislead the public ... and has created a situation of considerable embarrassment to the Association ... As a similar scheme in connection with the *Implacable* was ... not approved by the Association some years ago, your Lordship might, in the event of this new appeal proving even partially successful, also be placed in an embarrassing position.

During the next few days there was discussion amongst some members of HQ Sea Scout Committee as to what the position of the Chief Sea Scout was in relation to the Headquarters Commissioner for Sea Scouts and the Chief Scout, and the desirability of the Head of the Navy also being Chief Sea Scout. This resulted in a private letter being sent on 25 October from the Chief Scout to Lord Beatty to the effect that there had been a misunderstanding of the position of Boy Scout Headquarters on the subject of the *Implacable* Fund.

Writing on 31 October to Rear-Admiral Loring, Headquarters Commissioner for Sea Scouts, the Chief Scout said as a matter of principle they would not say they were not in favour of having a holiday training ship. However Beatty should not have expressed his personal views as authoritative without reference to headquarters. By the Annual Meeting of the Council of The Boy Scouts Association held on 1 February 1926 Admiral of the Fleet Earl Beatty, OM, GCB, GCVO, DSO had resigned from the Council – he was displeased that his authority had been questioned.

December 1925

The London Sea Scout Association and the Associations of Middlesex and Surrey amalgamated to form The Upper Thames Association to provide better facilities.

A question often arising was whether Sea Scouts should wear their belts outside or underneath their jerseys. When B-P drew a Sea Scout in a jersey, no belt was shown. Most Troops wore them outside; it was evident that they found it more convenient. The opinion of Admiral Loring was that it was immaterial, provided that all boys in any particular Troop adopted the same fashion. 'With or without belts' continued well into the 1950s.

1926

The census for 1926 showed a total of 4,538 Sea Scouts.

In 1926, the Scouts of the 1st Tyne Troop rescued the crew of a Royal Navy seaplane off Blyth, Northumberland, and were presented with a defaced blue ensign with a fleur-de-lys for their efforts.

1927

The Sea Scout census on 30 September 1927:

British Isles 3,620
British Dominions 1,004
The World 6,108

Kingston-upon-Thames Sea Scouts

During their summer camp at South Cove near Southwold, Suffolk the Kingston-upon-Thames Sea Scouts heard that a fishing vessel (Lowestoft smack LT 250) had gone ashore at Benacre Point, one of her two men having been injured. The Southwold motor lifeboat was unable to render assistance because the vessel was aground. Rough sea was breaking over the ship and a considerable crowd had assembled. It appeared possible the vessel could be hauled further up the beach but the rope broke under the strain at the seaward end.

Without hesitation Robert Marriot of the Kingston-upon-Thames Sea Scouts waded out shoulder deep and scrambled aboard the smack over which the waves were breaking. Rex Davis and another Scout followed Robert into the water, handed him the end of the cable, which he secured to the foot of the mast thereby anchoring the wreck which broke up completely the next day.

1928

How Deep Sea Scouts Began

This account is from papers in The Scout Association Archives:

According to Lieutenant-Colonel H.C. Ware, DSO, Honorary Secretary for Deep Sea Scouts and Sea Scouts writing at the time, 'The Deep Sea Scout Branch was a birthday present to the Chief Scout. On his birthday, 22 February [1928], the Headquarters Commissioner for Sea Scouts (Vice-Admiral Loring) was abroad. He left his Deputy, the Rev. Leonard Spiller, Sea Scout Commissioner for Middlesex, to act for him and attend to correspondence and business whilst he was away.'

'Two papers lay on the Admiral's desk that morning, one an account of the activities of some Rover Scouts in the Royal Navy in the Far East, who were working onshore with the local Scouts under the local Commissioner. The other was a letter from a Scoutmaster saying one of his boys wanted to go to sea, asking if he could be enrolled as a Sea Scout.'

'Here were two problems to be tackled. The Naval Scouts were alright so long as their ship remained on the same station. But when she was ordered home their registration would come to an end. They would probably be sent to different ships.'

'A keen young Scout going to sea wished to keep in touch with Scouting. There was no machinery, no branch of Scouts to which he could be attached.'

'The acting Sea Scout Commissioner, in the absence of the Admiral, had an invitation to lunch with the Chief Scout and the Chief Guide, who were keeping their birthday by entertaining the Headquarters Commissioners of the two Movements. It certainly looked as though the Sea Scouts ought to give the

Chief a birthday present. What could be better than a new branch of the Movement, to meet the need that was already apparent? The thinking cap was put on, and the Chief Scout was presented with a scheme which was the beginning of the Deep Sea Scout Branch.'

'The Rev. Mr Spiller knew nothing of the scheme but, being a parson, he hit on the idea of inviting the co-operation of the Mission to Seamen who, he felt, would be very willing to assist in linking up the Scouts in the ships with Scouts onshore. Hence a scheme for 'Sea Service Scouts' was submitted to the Chief, to Admiral Loring, and to the Headquarters Committee, in principle approved, so that details could be worked out. It was soon discovered that 'Sea Service Scouts' cannot be articulated quickly without a good deal of sibilant splashing. The Admiral and the Padre racked their brains to think of a more pronounceable name, and in a flash of inspiration, it came: "Deep Sea Scouts".'

'The authorities of the Missions to Seamen and the British Sailors Society were approached to help. They gladly agreed, thus another step was assured. But these Societies worked chiefly among the Merchant Service men. What about the Navy?'

'The Parson naturally thought of the Padres, and the Admiral arranged an interview with the Chaplain of the Fleet, who at once promised to do everything in his power to help by bringing the scheme to the notice of the Chaplains.'

'The Chief was asked to draw a picture for a card to be hung in places where sailors would congregate and in July 1928 the scheme was officially launched, since which time the growth of Deep Sea Scouts has been steady.'

The census gave the number of Sea Scouts, including Sea Rovers, on 30 September 1928:

British Isles   3,685
British Empire   1,630

The Annual Report stated there had been a gratifying increase of Sea Scout Troops and patrols on inland waters, and a brisk enrolment for the Deep Sea Scouts had begun.

October 1928

The Prince of Wales responded to the Chief Scout about the launching of the Deep Sea Scouts with the following message:

I feel that the self-discipline, sense of service and cheery loyalty in doing their job, which are the ideals of the Boy Scouts must, when put into practice at sea, tend to make these lads into the best of seamen.

I therefore welcome the step now taken towards keeping these young sailors in touch with their ideals and with each other, and towards giving them good influences and cheery comradeship at their ports of call.

In October Vice-Admiral A.V. Campbell, CB, DSO, MVO was appointed Headquarters Commissioner for Sea Scouts in place of Vice-Admiral Loring, to be assisted by the Rev. Leonard Spiller, appointed Assistant Headquarters Commissioner for Sea Scouts, who had piloted the Deep Sea Scout Branch.

70   *The 1st Mortlake Sea Scouts band in front of Mortlake Postmen's Office, London SW, 27 April 1930. The band was well established and played at various events.*

1929

February 1929

HRH Prince George, Duke of Kent, KG, accepted the position of President/Commodore of the Sea Scout Branch of the Scout Movement.

There was a total of 6,226 Sea Scouts of whom, 4,562 were in the British Isles, and included 200 Deep Sea Scouts.

1930

Do your own Rebuilding

Between October 1929 and May 1930 Leander (Kingston) Sea Scouts purchased the boathouse next door. Every Leander tenderfoot became familiar with the convenience and principles of simple ferro-concrete construction and the use of common materials for shuttering. Most of the work of pouring cement was carried out in drenching rain. Four 6cwt girders provided a splendid opportunity for Scouters to demonstrate the lashing of shear legs. An architect advised they might manage the work after a fashion, particularly with regard to the hanging of two 2cwt doors. Sundry jobs included electrical wiring, fitting the roof, glazing windows and skylights and carpentry.

During the preceding year three Thames Sea Scout Troops had obtained sailing barges for conversion into floating headquarters – great fun and all in the game.

The *Where Are You Now?* slot on Ed Stewart's BBC Radio 2 programme of 14 October 2001 asking for Sea Scouting reminiscences for this book, brought a good response worldwide.

Len Wild, writing from Australia in 2002, recalls joining the 2nd Kingston (Leander) Sea Scouts in 1930 aged 15. A Sea Scout called at his home on a Saturday and asked if he was interested in coming along to Leander that afternoon. Leaving the gardening he rode off with Fred Hallet to Kingston, meeting Skipper Ebbage (E.L. Ebbage, MBE, GSM, Leader 1921-68, and joined up there and then. Len was taught how to scull over the stern, manage the gigs and in about six months had passed his Charge Certificate for vessels under oars upstream of Teddington Lock. The greatest event he recalled was taking part in Ralph Reader's *Boy Scout Review* at the Albert Hall in April 1936, when several hundred Sea Scouts demonstrated the art of bringing a drowning person to safety and performing the Schaffer Method of resuscitation.

Bob Miller, a member of the 16th Blackpool Sea Scouts, recalls camping, hiking, 'wide games', sailing and rowing. On a Saturday evening during the Blackpool illuminations by kind permission of the Corporation Electricity Department the Sea Scouts were allowed to 'man' the Illuminated Lifeboat armed with small fishing nets, making a collection for the RNLI.

Deep Sea Scouts membership was approaching 600, the Royal Navy making most progress in numbers. The committees at the three Naval Home Ports were in operation.

71   *1st Mortlake Sea Scouts Troop photograph, in front of Mortlake Postmen's Office, London SW, 27 April 1930.*

1931

August 1931

A short pamphlet about Sea Scouting, *What Sea Scouts Do*, was published by Headquarters and reprinted in *The Scout* magazine of 15 August 1931:

> It's great fun Sea Scouting, 'Aye, aye, sir! Let's cast a weather eye on the thrilling activities of the "Wet Bobs". They do the ordinary Scout work but their training and games have a nautical setting. All around the sea you will find Sea Scouts but there are Sea Scouts on rivers like the Thames, the Mersey, the Clyde, the Tyne and the Medway. The Chief Scout says, all Scouts ought to know something about how to manage a boat, and he is specially glad when he hears that the number of Sea Scouts has increased.'

The Scout magazine of 17 October 1931 reported that the Hampstead Sea Scouts had obtained a new headquarters, a 105-foot ex-pleasure-steamer with a main saloon of 35 feet by 16 feet – quite spacious.

Deep Sea Scouts

Much progress had been made in the Deep Sea Scouting in the Royal Navy, particularly in the Atlantic, China and the East Indies stations.

1932

In his reminiscences, Harry Hanson wrote in 2002 that he joined the 1st Norwich Group in 1928; they were land Scouts and he transferred to the Sea Scout Section when aged 15. They had their base on Wroxham Broad where they did sailing, rowing, swimming and canoeing. In 1932 they were chosen to represent England at the Sea Scout Jamboree in Poland.

The Rev. Leonard Spiller resigned as Assistant Commissioner for Sea Scouts, replaced by Mr Robert Hole, an experienced Sea Scouter whose handbook *Sea Scouts* had recently been published – at the time this was regarded as the standard work of the branch.

Deep Sea Scout membership increased to over 1,000, more new members being enrolled every month.

31 October 1932 – The London Gang Show

The first *London Gang Show* produced by Ralph Reader was performed at the Scala Theatre, attended by the Duke and Duchess of York, and was to become an annual institution. In 1936 *The Gang Show* film, produced by Herbert Wilcox, was shown throughout the country and provided the opportunity for local Scouts to co-operate in the performance and gain useful publicity. There was always a proportion of Sea Scouts in the cast. The *London Gang Show* had its final call in 1974, but the *Gang Show* tradition and performances continue throughout the Scouting world today.

December 1932

The award of the Silver Cross was made to Deep Sea Scout W. Mullins. He had slept overnight in the 1st Dublin's Headquarters. Hearing that a child had fallen into the river, he rushed to the location, dived in to the rescue, and dragged the unconscious child ashore. She had ceased to breathe, so he started artificial respiration and brought her round. Very shortly afterwards he received serious injury in a marine accident, which resulted in one of his legs being amputated.

Sea Scout Meets during the 1930s

There were successful Sea Scouts Meets at Petersham, Caernarvon, Chatham and on the Isle of Wight. The Meets attracted Sea Scouts from long distances, were extremely popular events and continued to be held for the next 50 years.

Two principle Sea Scout events were the Petersham (Surrey) Sea Scout Whitsuntide Meet in spring and the *Implacable* Sea Scout Meet in August at Portsmouth.

Petersham, 1933

There were 350 in camp at Petersham with Thames Sea Scouts loaning their boats. The first Meet was recorded as being successful.

Groups from overseas attended. Afternoons were given to water activities, there were large numbers of boats of all sizes – some Troops had quite splendid craft. One activity was 'blockade running', in which pulling boats, gigs and whalers, etc, were stationed at various points on the river and Sea Scouts attempted to intercept the blockade runners – canoes and kayaks – each of which carried a cargo of lemonade or ginger beer. These could be intercepted by throwing a line across the blockade runners and, if successful, payment in bottles could be demanded.

Douglas Robertson was a member of the 22nd Walthamstow Sea Scouts and recalls several Petersham Sea Scout camps in the 1930s. An active yachtsman, he said he still practised what he learnt from those events.

British Scout Kayak

After a number of experiments a kayak was designed to meet the requirements of a Sea Scout Troop with the Scout Shop selling full-sized plans of *How to Build the British Kayak* – 327 copies were sold in the first year.

Isle of Wight, 1933

A successful Sea Scout Meet took place on 8 and 9 July at Newtown Harbour on the north coast of the Isle of Wight. The numbers of craft at anchorage and the large number of Scouts who came long distances to Newtown bore witness to the popularity of such an event – the one complaint was that it was not long enough. The crews had a good 'dusting' getting out of harbour on the outward journey before reaching home.

Petersham and Ham, 1934 & 1935

The 1934 National Sea Scout Meet at Petersham and Ham Sea Scouts riverside headquarters was advertised as the 'Big' Sea Scout Meet – a record number attended at 4s. a head. The 1st Mortlake

Sea Scouts attended, towing their whaler and *Heron*, the Troop's 16-ft sailing dinghy. The Thames Sea Scouts moored their boats close in to the bank within 100 yards of the camp.

In his report to the Committee of the Council on 8 June Admiral A.V. Campbell, Headquarters Commissioner for Sea Scouts, said the Meet at Whitsun was well attended with about 350 Sea Scouts present. Some came from Liverpool, Falmouth and Bournemouth with the majority of Sea Scouts from the Thames. General Godfrey-Faussett inspected the camp on the Sunday morning and Lord Hampton addressed the Meet after Scouts' Own [short Scouts' service] that day.

It is recorded that the River Superintendent of the Port of London Authority was very helpful in allowing them to lay down moorings for the boats and sending off his boats to keep the river clear during the water games.

Admiral Campbell said he hoped to make it possible to have Liaison Officers at seaport towns where yachts lay up and to purchase old yachts and boats as reductions in the Navy had made it difficult to get sufficient Naval boats to meet requirements.

At Whitsuntide 1935 the by-now regular Petersham Meet took place – a total muster of 430. Many Troops lent their boats for the use of those attending.

Implacable, *Portsmouth – 1933-6*

On board *Implacable* were 80 Sea Scouts from 11 different Groups. There were many sailing and pulling activities under the instructional staff of the ship, swimming contests, games and visits to ships of the Home Fleet and HMS *Victory*. The Chief Scout visited during the week.

Writing on his visit to the *Foudroyant* and *Implacable* in August 1934, the Chief Scout (B-P) said:

Here on board the old-time frigate you see boys cheerily imbibing ship discipline and the tradition of the sea under the sympathetic guidance of Colonel Wyllie, the Commander, and his very able staff of instructors. I call it 'guidance' rather than 'orders', since the staff are not only good seamen but understand the boys' enthusiasm, and direct them into the right channels by means that really appeal. Thus the lads, while revelling in their swimming, boat-sailing and other activities, are unconsciously picking up all the health and handiness that pertain to seamanship. Then parties are taken ashore daily on excursions to visit the Dockyard, HMS *Victory*, the modern battleships and other Royal Naval craft, thereby opening up their minds to the magnitude of Britain's sea power. A pleasing feature of this part of their training is the fact the boys are received and shown over the ships by their elder brothers, the Deep Sea Scouts.

Reporting on the visit, Robert Hole, Assistant Headquarters Commissioner for Sea Scouts said:

There was a wonderful spirit right through the trip; The Chief [Scout] sensed it and was satisfied. Accompanied by his two daughters, he was pulled up to the ship (nearly two miles) by a picked gig crew, and taken back by another. He gave a splendid informal talk to the boys on the upper deck, seated most shockingly on a gun!

B-P was by then aged 77, and following a long illness this was his first appearance in uniform in the United Kingdom – a fascinating insight into how B-P visualised Sea Scouting in 1934.

During the first week in August 1935, 112 Sea Scouts spent Sea Scout Week on board the *Foudroyant*, part of the establishment of *Implacable*. The art of ropework was practised and later the Troops went away by boat by themselves on voyages of exploration and discovery. The week coincided with Navy Week, and two visits to dockyards formed part of the programme. The Sea Scouts were given the special opportunity of going over HMS *Royal Sovereign*, seeing her engine room, boiler room, fighting tops, mess decks and bakeries, besides complicated electrical and hydraulic machinery connected with the gunnery.

Sea Scout week 1-8 August 1936 was spent aboard *Implacable* and *Foudroyant* with Sea Scout Commissioner Captain Hordern in charge, assisted by the Rev. Pat Spiller and the Rev. G.T. Waldegrave. The week afforded a great chance of improving their boatwork, *Implacable* bringing new life to the event. Navy Week running at the same time provided an additional attraction.

Sea Scouts came from Fulham, York, Stepney, Walsingham, Hillingdon, Paddington, Chorleywood, Chalkwell Bay, Cuddington, Medway, Ampleforth, Bournemouth, Brussels and Paris. Half went to *Implacable* and half to *Foudroyant*, being allocated to ship's quartermasters, duty Petty Officers and emergency crews, then port and starboard messes. Hammocks were slung at 8.30 p.m. and Divisions [ships' company parades] held on Sunday morning.

There was boat pulling and many fine bursts of sailing throughout the week. Swimming and bathing were discounted because of the lack of sun but Swimmer's, Rescuer's and Oarsman's badges were not discouraged. Pulling races were organised on Wednesday and a visit to the Dockyard on Thursday.

22nd Walthamstow Sea Scouts

Douglas Robertson wrote:

> The 22nd Walthamstow was a large Troop affiliated to St Mary's parish church. It was fortunate in its officers, who had educational or service backgrounds, and a large Rover section, some of whom had sea-going experience. Sadly the War took many of these chaps. I have been greatly indebted to my Scout experiences, which served me well in war and peace.

> The 22nd Walthamstow had an ex-naval whaler which was rowed from our moorings on the River Lea at Tottenham, down the river to Bow Creek, through the lock into the Thames, then up-river to Petersham. I recollect being towed behind a small fleet of rubbish barges pulled by a tug, a somewhat hazardous procedure as the tug would only slow slightly and a barge-hand would catch our line and make it fast and off we would go at about six knots. The return of our boat would take place a few weeks later when weather and times would suit. I recollect breaking a 14ft ash sweep [oar] and knocking myself out on the thwart [seat] forward of me in a furious attempt to catch up with a London tug.

February 1934 – Ship Ashore

Sea Scouts of Rose Hill School, Tunbridge Wells, Kent, received their training on a ship *The Scouter*. The ship was 50 feet long, equipped with funnel, masts and rigging and was built on the school lawn. Rose Hill School was the preparatory school Robert Baden-Powell attended. The land ship was a local landmark for many years. A swimming pool was later put in its place.

72   *Sea Scouts of Rose Hill School, Tunbridge Wells, Kent (B-P was at the prep school in 1868) with their 50ft long land-ship headquarters, with mast, riggings and navigation lights, constructed on the school lawn, 1934. The land-based ship was a well-known landmark for many years before it was dismantled in the 1950s.*

1935

In the United Kingdom census were 4,534 Sea Scouts and Sea Rovers.

March 1935

Sea Pie, a colourful instructional booklet written by 'Gilcraft' and published by the London Geographical Institute contained coloured diagrams depicting the various types of national and signal flags, knots, bends and hitches, constellations, ships buoys, sea birds, etc – an indispensable book for Sea Scouts. It was advertised as 'a book which makes Scouting a real live exciting thing, and we want more of them'. Unusually for Scout publications of the time the front cover had an Art Nouveau-style design.

November 1935 – A Percy F. Westerman Treat

Robert Hole writing in *The Scouter* said,

> The appearance of another Percy F. Westerman Sea Scout story was always an occasion for rejoicing. Personally, I've much to thank PFW for; it was reading one of his books that originally brought me into the Movement. He has re-published three of the old ones, *Sea Scouts All*, *Sea Scouts Abroad* and *Sea Scouts up Channel*, as a Percy F. Westerman Omnibus.

The Scouter, *December 1935*

Earl Jellicoe, 1859-1935

'The passing to Higher Service on 20 November of Admiral of the Fleet Earl Jellicoe removes one who had given his best to Scouting in New Zealand, London and the Isle of Wight. He was County Commissioner for London from 1925 to 1928.'

Admiral Philpotts, County Commissioner for London, wrote:

> I met Lord Jellicoe first 44 years ago when he was a Lieutenant, and in 1912 I was his personal assistant at the Admiralty when he was Second Sea Lord. I was with him for a couple of years in the Grand Fleet, and then became his assistant again when he returned to the Admiralty when he became First Sea Lord. All the time I was in close contact with him, and came to admire him more than any man I have ever known …

> He became Commissioner for London at a time of great stress and difficulty, and the results of his patient work and the influence of his personality live on still. His life was devoted to the service of his country and the good of his fellow men.

Cornwell Scout Decoration – Sea Scout W.D. Davidson

Sea Scout W.D. Davidson, 1st Carshalton Group, was awarded The Cornwell Scout Decoration for 'courage, capability and character having borne long illness and suffering in a heroic manner. Called to Higher Service soon after he had been told he had been awarded the Decoration which was placed on his grave.'

1936

20 January 1936

Death of King George V; Accession of King Edward VIII

In the annual Report of the Association, the Chief Scout wrote, 'The past year has seen two momentous pages turned in our national history, first the death of the sovereign King George V, followed a few months later by the renunciation of the Crown by his successor, King Edward.' (10 December 1936).

11 March 1936

David Beatty, First Earl Beatty, was born 17 January 1871 and died 11 March 1936, aged 65. He was promoted Admiral of the Fleet in 1919 and served as First Sea Lord until 1927. He was the second Chief Sea Scout and held the appointment from 1919 to 1925.

Bronze Cross

The decoration of the Bronze Cross, the highest award of the Association for gallantry, was awarded posthumously to Patrol Leader D.S. Watson, aged 17, of the 33rd Fulham (Sea Scout) Group who sacrificed his own life to save that of a brother Scout, Allen Arnold, when their Kayak upset in the Thames off Chelsea Embankment on Sunday, 15 March 1936. The two Scouts had paddled from their Troop Headquarters to a barge moored just off the Chelsea Embankment. On their return journey the Kayak overturned. Watson told Arnold to hold on to him and they started for the bank. The boys were making good progress in the water. Scout Cook swam out and brought Arnold to the shore, and Watson was still swimming. Suddenly, when near to the shore, Watson disappeared. Scoutmaster Nicholson and Assistant Scoutmaster Monk dived to find Watson, but to no avail.

2nd City of London Sea Scouts

Louis Heren, to become Deputy Editor and Foreign Editor of *The Times* in 1981, recalled his time with the 2nd City of London Sea Scouts in the 1930s in his book *Growing Up Poor in London*. Mr Thomas, the Scoutmaster, remained in the background to attend to business requiring the attendance of an adult; otherwise the Troop was run by the members. The Troop of about 20 came from all over London and were aged between 12 and 18. The headquarters was a derelict office building at 12 Crutched Friars and Mr Higgins, the Assistant Scoutmaster, lived in West Garden Buildings opposite. The Troop magazine was the *Red Duster*, a cyclostyled four-page magazine which came out at infrequent intervals. They had become Sea Scouts because there was no other way of getting near a boat. Mr Thomas owned a converted ship's lifeboat, the *Molly*, kept in a mud berth at Benfleet, which they visited once a month at weekends, to keep her in good trim.

The 2nd City of London also went to Greenhithe down-river on the Kent shore, a three-hour cycle ride from the City. The Troop had a connection there with the *Worcester*, a training ship for Merchant Navy cadets, and were allowed to camp on ground owned by the ship above the village. The local cement factories coated the village with fine, grey-white dust. *Worcester* had a small fleet of naval whalers which the Sea Scouts were allowed to use when the ship was closed for the summer holidays. The whalers were seaworthy and almost non-capsizable. They were 20 feet overall, double-ended and equipped with a centreboard, but heavy for five boys to row, and could not sail close to the wind. The knowledge that all Royal Naval ships carried whalers had a powerful effect on the Troop, always galvanised into displays of disciplined crewmanship when aboard. Visits to Greenhithe became less frequent around 1937 when the Troop moved from Crutched Friars to Scott's *Discovery* moored at the Thames Embankment.

73   *Funeral procession to St Paul's Cathedral of Earl Beatty, second Chief Sea Scout, on 16 March 1936. The new Lord Beatty and his brother, the Hon. Peter Beatty, escort the coffin, followed by the Duke of York representing King George V, and the Duke of Kent, at that time Commodore of Sea Scouts.*

Deep Sea Scouts

Considerable development of the Deep Sea Scouts in training establishments of HMS *Ganges*, Harwich and HMS *St Vincent*, Gosport. Malta had become the centre of the Deep Sea Scouts in the Mediterranean.

1937

12 May 1937

Coronation of HM King George VI

King George's Jubilee Trust invited the Boy Scouts Association to sell the official Coronation programme at all Coronation festivities. There were 7,000 Scout volunteer programme sellers and 52 programme depots along the route. The London Scouts sold 166,000 copies in three hours, while the waterborne Sea Scouts sold programmes from their boats. The total sum collected and handed over to the King George's Jubilee Trust was £37,000.

SEARCHLIGHT DISPLAY BY HOME FLEET AT PLYMOUTH.

74 *Postcard of a searchlight display by the Home Fleet at Plymouth. Stuart Garnett's tender to the yacht* Idler *is among the small boats on the left of the picture, 1936.*

The Rhodesian contingent to the Coronation were the first Scouts to be televised. Scout Headquarters publicity recorded: 'Sir Percy Everett, Deputy Chief Commissioner, was the first Headquarters Commissioner "to endure this new form of public torture."'

The Royal Navy assembled many ships for the Coronation Review which presented the opportunity both for a Deep Sea Scouts conference at IHQ and a weekend conference for Royal Naval Deep Sea Scouts at Portsmouth.

The Mission to Seamen organised the first Merchant Navy Week at Southampton, providing an opportunity for many thousands of the public to learn about Deep Sea Scouting and Sea Scouting through the Deep Sea Scouts from HMS *Revenge*, who staffed a stall at the Southampton exhibition.

Able Seaman Richard Torr, Deep Sea Scout – 1938

'RB', a serving Naval officer, wrote in the June 1938 issue of *The Scouter* magazine about Deep Sea Scout Able Seaman Richard Torr:

I had known Able Seaman Torr as a Sea Scout. When he had the chance he was away from the ship hiking with other Sea Scouts. I was second-in-command of HMS *B* ...; at the time we were half-way through a two-and-a-half-year commission on the Africa station, enjoying a spell at Simonstown [South Africa]. That evening there was half a gale, but nothing to stop the motor launch running as usual, and she was sent to bring off a 'hiking party' at 10 p.m. Johnston, the stern-sheet man who balanced astride the tiller with the boat rolling, lost his footing when she gave a heavy lurch. He was in oilskins and sou'wester. Torr scrambled out of the stern sheets and dived into the darkness. The boat was turned, and thanks to the coolness of the midshipman in charge, and the aid of a flashed message which brought the ship' searchlights to bear on the spot, both men were soon recovered. But Torr had a severe, freely-bleeding head wound; he must have hit the moving blade of the propeller as he dived in, but he had not allowed the pain to stop his saving a life, which he undoubtedly did. Once on board every care was bestowed on him, but I had a bad report next morning and went forward to the sick-bay to see for myself. Torr's eyes opened very slowly as I stood by his cot, and I murmured a few words of admiration of his gallantry. 'Well, I've done my good turn for the day, sir, anyway,' was all he whispered; that afternoon he died.

We buried him next evening just before sunset in the little sandswept cemetery close to the shore of Fis Hoek Bay, protected from the swirling sand by the tamarisk trees, where many sailors have their last resting place. Such a fine sailor and shipmate, only 22 years of life. I took special care when the cross was erected to mark his grave; I urged that the inscription should read 'Richard Torr, Able Seaman, Royal Navy, and Rover Scout of HMS *B* ...' I felt he would have wished that.

Talk of War

By 1938 once more there were rumours of war, the public's worries being well founded.

In June IHQ issued a general statement that the nucleus of an organisation was to be established. A sub-committee of the Imperial Defence Committee had been formed in 1935 to consider the situation. A system that would give protection against air raids was called Air Raid Precautions (ARP), later renamed Civil Defence.

In October 1938 Lord Somers, Deputy Chief Scout, wrote to all Commissioners giving details of what the Movement should do in the event of national emergency. Scout Groups were to be maintained at a high standard, with proper liaison with the local authority.

In November 1938 Scout Headquarters Notices announced that an ARP armlet had been approved for wear by Scouts when engaged on ARP duties.

The Committee of the Council of The Scout Association had formed an emergency committee during the 'crisis period' to deal with emergency measures. It was decided that enquiries should be made to establish the exact forms of service required of Scouts by various Government departments in case of emergency, in particular with regard to coastwatching duties.

Coastwatching

In the November 1938 issue of *The Scouter*, Robert Hole wrote on what could be expected:

Scouts as coastwatchers, Scouts acting as signallers and runners at lifeboat stations, Scouts manning the life-saving apparatus, Scout Groups affiliated to coastguard stations for special times in emergency – these are all possible for Groups that are prepared to train.

In 1938 the Port of London Authority set up the Thames River Emergency Service.

Memories of the 2nd Wallasey Sea Scouts

Dick Jones recalls the period:

In 1938 the European situation had a profound effect on the Troop. When Neville Chamberlain returned from Berlin [30 March 1938] waving a piece of paper declaring 'Peace in our time', events proved otherwise. Shortly afterwards the ARP moved in and took part of our HQ for storage, etc. I remember evenings assembling gas masks for eventual distribution. The prospect of moving from HQ was depressing. Nothing could replace to a young Cub or Scout the subterranean mystery and magic of

75   *An oil painting on canvas of Poole Sea Scout Patrol Leader Bruce Horne, 1939.*

the Concert Hall basement. The fun-packed events which spanned the whole week, including Scouts' Own on Sundays, were a magnet to us all. Even the 'bogey hole' had its hair-raising excitement. There was a Parade Room, which served for games, whist drives, and tea after boating on Saturday afternoons. There was a room for billiards, table tennis and leisure activities. We had a tuck shop at the far end of the stage, which was used to enact plays and concerts. Slide shows were held on Saturday nights. 'The Cabin' was Skipper's Den and badge room; the Rover Den and George's workshop were where Tom Hird built a dinghy. You could have it all for a modest sub, and an odd bottle of 'Sweet Nell' from the tuck shop – it did not cost a penny; just as well, as nobody had a penny. All that was under threat.

Six

RRS *Discovery*/HMS *Discovery*, 1901-2009

A Brief History of RRS *Discovery*, 1900-36

Royal Research Ship *Discovery*, built in 1901 for the Royal Geographical Society for its British National Antarctic Expedition, is the ship on which Captain (then Commander) Robert Falcon Scott, RN, made his first expedition to the Ross Sea. Sea Scouts received a great boost in October 1937 when the ship was transferred from the Colonial Office to the Boy Scouts Association for their Sea Scout Training Ship – a memorial to Captain Scott and other Polar explorers. *Discovery* became the sole survivor of Dundee's shipbuilding tradition.

Construction of *Discovery* started on 16 March 1900. One of the last wooden three-masted sailing ships, she was built by the Dundee Ship Building Company at a total cost of £44,322 out of a total budget for the expedition of £92,000 [£5¼m today]. She is 179 feet (54.56 metres) long, 34 feet (10.36 metres) broad, and her sides are 26 inches (0.66 metres) thick. Her engine was a 450 horsepower triple expansion engine. Officers and scientists slept in ten individual cabins, the sailors slept in hammocks; bunks were added during a 1924 refit.

Discovery was launched on 21 March 1901 by Lady Markham, wife of Sir Clements Markham FRS, promoter of Polar exploration. She sailed to Cape Town and New Zealand, and finally crossed the Antarctic Circle on 3 January 1902. She became solidly iced in for two winters, though her crew under Captain Scott carried out their scientific surveys. She arrived back in the United Kingdom at Spithead near Portsmouth on 10 September 1904 to a hero's welcome.

By 1905 the Royal Geographical Society was in financial difficulties so it sold *Discovery* to the Hudson's Bay Company. She was converted into a cargo ship – fur-trading between 1905 and 1911. She was laid up in the West India Docks from 1912-15 after which she was chartered to run supplies from Brest in France to Archangel in war-torn Russia. She was again laid up in London's West India Docks, and in February 1922 the Hudson's Bay Company granted

Discovery to the 16th Stepney Sea Scouts as a temporary headquarters.

In March 1923 *Discovery* was bought by the Crown Agents for the Colonies for the purpose of scientific research in the South Seas. In 1925 she sailed for the Falkland Islands, and until 1928 she worked as a Royal Research Ship on scientific studies. She returned to the UK on 29 September having travelled 37,000 miles.

Between 1929 and 1931 she was lent by the British Government to Sir Douglas Mawson to lead the British, Australian and New Zealand Antarctic Research Expedition (BANZARE), arriving back in London on 1 August 1931. She was laid up at the East India Dock between 1931 and 1936 – dates vary between accounts.

While laid up, she was regularly inspected and maintained. Miss B.M. Borley and Miss W.J. Hope, who were employed by the Crown Agents for the Colonies, heard that *Discovery* might be sold and started to collect funds to secure her for the National Maritime Museum at Greenwich, to pay for *Discovery*'s upkeep as national asset and to preserve her for the Nation.

76   RS Discovery *engaged on oceanographic expeditions. She was sold to the Crown Agents and refitted by Vospers, c.1925.*

Sir John Middleton, a member of the 'Discovery Committee', approached the Boy Scouts Association with the suggestion that the ship should become a training ship and hostel for Sea Scouts; she was eventually offered in October 1936 to the Boy Scouts Association in this capacity. The offer of the ship delighted Lord Baden-Powell, who wrote to Lady Houston, an English benefactress, philanthropist, adventuress and patriot, sending her a sketch of *Discovery*, the result of which was a £30,000 Trust Fund for expenses. An agreement was drawn up between Lady Houston and the Boy Scouts Association enabling the vessel to be used as Sea Scout Headquarters. Most importantly it was specified that *Discovery* would serve as a living memorial to Scott, Oates, Shackleton and other heroes of the Antarctic expedition. The acceptance was contingent upon the need for the Boy Scouts Association to raise sufficient money to ensure her proper upkeep.

The British Government tried hard but without success to sell the ship to Commonwealth governments. The Falkland Islands, where the ship was registered, agreed to the project, and the necessary money was subscribed. The Port of London Authority allotted her suitable moorings easily accessible to the boys who were to use her. The Pilgrim Trust also contributed £1,000 to build the pier connecting ship to shore.

1937-9

In January 1937, the Colonial Office made the official announcement of the gift of *Discovery*, and this was repeated in most newspapers and broadcast from all stations of the BBC.

In June 1937 King George VI, through the Home Office, sanctioned the retention of the title 'Royal Research Ship' which was a significant honour for the Sea Scouts, custodians of the ship.

The national press were effusive in their praise for the future use of the ship. Mr H. de Winton Wigley, author and correspondent of the *News Chronicle* of 27 July 1937, reported:

> Near HMS *President*, alongside the Victoria Embankment, one the most famous old ships in the world has come to rest. She is the old *Discovery*, the ship in which Captain Scott made his first expedition in 1901. From now on she will lie in the Thames tideway, hard by the heart of the City of London. She has been presented to the Boy Scouts Association, which will fit and maintain her as a memorial to Captain Scott and as a centre for Sea Scouts. Yesterday morning, she cast off for the last time and, with two tugs, came to her moorings, less than a mile from the Houses of Parliament – a lasting memorial to British courage and endurance.

Mr Joe Miller, the original sailmaker and Mr A. Letter, an engineer from Captain Scott's ship, also visited the vessel, now moored by Victoria Embankment. Jonk's cartoon of Joe Miller appearing in the November 1937 issue of *The Scouter* magazine, said he 'was on nodding acquaintance with the best polar bears and penguins'. Other Jonk cartoons said the cabin ventilators enabled Sea Scouts to acquire a rolling gait. As *Discovery* had no portholes, brass mushroom vents providing light and air – nicknamed 'ankle bashers' for obvious reasons – were let into her deck. There were two ships' wheels – jokingly said to be one for Scouts and one for Cubs! This joke was still being re-told 20 years later.

A timber jetty was built to provide access from the Embankment, with two levels and steps between. A short gangway had to be adjusted every hour with the tide. Downstream of the jetty were three sets of buoyed moorings on which were kept two 27-foot Montague whalers which were in constant use for training Sea Scouts.

7 October 1937 – the Handover Ceremony

Discovery looked trim and neat, as did the Sea Scouts who manned her. At 3 o'clock, HRH the Duke of Kent, in the uniform of Commodore of Sea Scouts, arrived on board, and the brief ceremony of the 'handover' began. The Rt Hon. W.G. Ormsby-Gore, Secretary of State for the Colonies, outlined the history of *Discovery* and announced that the Boy Scouts had received generous assistance from Lady Houston and the Pilgrim Trust towards the cost of the vessel's maintenance and endowment. Sir Herbert Henniker-Heaton, Governor of the Falkland Islands, formally handed over the ship to the Duke of Kent to serve as a training ship for Sea Scouts, and as a memorial to Captain Scott and all those who in her had played a part in the work of Antarctic research.

The Duke stressed the very fine tradition *Discovery* bore and that if he had been of an age to be trained on board he would feel not only very thrilled, but somewhat overawed, at being so closely associated with the ship.

77   Discovery, *neat and trim, 1937.*

78   RS Discovery – *journey south, 1902.*

Short speeches were made by Captain Armitage, who sailed in the *Discovery*, and Commander Shanklin of the Port of London Authority, followed by the Chief Scout thanking The Duke of Kent and all who had helped with the gift.

Also present were distinguished guests, together with six men who had sailed on the original expedition, and those who had a direct connection with *Discovery* – Lady Kennet, widow of Captain Scott, Mrs Wilson, widow of Dr Wilson and Lady Royds, widow of Lieutenant Charles W.R. Royds; also among them was (Scout) Marr who had accompanied Shackleton on his last expedition.

The Duke of Kent spent a considerable time on board and seemed very pleased with what he saw. After his departure B-P came on board again to have a word with the Sea Scouts. It was a remarkable sight to see the Sea Scouts gathered around the Chief, and within a few seconds the rigging was swarming with Sea Scouts; looking down from the bridge the Chief seemed to be standing in a framework of Sea Scouts.

The London Zoo provided a husky dog as ship's mascot. The Sea Scouts were called to take part in a television broadcast in connection with the opening ceremony; they were promised further chances at Alexandra Palace for Sea Scouts showing viewers what they did.

In 1937 there was a paid crew of three – the Master, the Chief Engineer and the Bo'sun. Lieutenant-Commander E. Nicholas, OBE, RN, a formidable-looking Master Mariner, took little part in the Sea Scout side, while Bo'sun Miller was skilled in the arts of sea, sailing and instruction, which he would pass on to the Sea Scouts.

Discovery became a familiar landmark for Londoners, lying in her berth on the Embankment. A small museum and shop were set up on board for visitors, providing a modest income for the ship. Members of the public were admitted between Tuesday and Saturday, adults 6d., children 3d., Scouts and Guides in uniform free.

The star Sea Scout performer on a Sunday afternoon was the smallest member of the Service Crew, who would sit on the main trunk with the spike of the lightning conductor between his legs. The watching public were often clearly concerned for his safety, but what they did not know was that during the week he earned his living as a riveter's mate, catching red-hot rivets in a bucket of sand, whilst standing on high girders.

Reminiscences of Discovery *as a Sea Scout Training Ship*

'Dusty' Miller recalls he joined the 201st North London Troop around 1934-5. The Troop subsequently started a Sea Scout Patrol, and the arrival of RRS *Discovery* at the Embankment gave them a Headquarters. They would cycle to the Embankment once a week for their period of instruction and history. They were ceded the port side of the sail locker, and the Hampstead Sea Scouts became their mentors. Their Sea Scouting knowledge expanded to 'boxing the compass' from eight points to 32, rowing a whaler on the Thames at all states of the tide, ship recognition by day and night and techniques of avoiding them. Then the Second World War came and they were called up into the services, some to return, others not.

The late noted journalist, foreign correspondent and author, Louis Heren, formerly of the 2nd City of London Sea Scouts, recalled that the Troop moved from Crutched Friars to Scott's *Discovery*, which they were allowed to use as a Headquarters. They had called on a retired Admiral at Christmas for permission to use the ship. They were supposed only to use the main cabin, but quickly came to terms with the two naval pensioners who were the caretakers. They worked hard, doing much of the cleaning and polishing for the naval pensioners who paid them accordingly, but it was worthwhile. In turn they were taught to splice and much else. One of the naval pensioners was good with small boats, and taught them how to handle the boats safely on the fast tides. They got to know the Thames River Police, who would occasionally tow them back to *Discovery*'s moorings when they had misjudged the tide.

He recalled that, amazingly, the independence of the Troop remained unimpaired by their new surroundings. Whichever authority was responsible for *Discovery* left them alone. The main cabin was the area of the ship where members of Scott's expedition had been quartered, largely filled by a big table and bolted-down chairs. To port and starboard were sleeping cabins, each with built-in bunk and furniture. The woodwork was solid and beautifully constructed and the paintwork was spick and span.

The best evenings were when the tide was just on the turn, when they would go up river to Chelsea Bridge and beyond, or down to the Tower or Shadwell New Park. They came to learn almost every inch of the river and to be expert, when necessary, in working against five- or six-knot currents. Without a word of

79   *Sea Scouts alongside RRS* Discovery *taking part in Y-Scheme Instruction, 1944.*

command from the man at the tiller they would work their way under the bridges or into the dead water behind the moored lighters or piers. Louis Heren remembered the final accolade when the River Police became less enquiring and tugboat men would take a line from them – they belonged; the river and the City was theirs. He later qualified this by saying 'silly, of course' – they did not own the boat they rowed and could have been asked to leave *Discovery* at any time without redress.

Louis Heren eventually went to Goldsmiths' College in New Cross, south-east London, where he attended evening classes on the art of writing. One of his first efforts, on Sea Scouting, was published by *The Times* house journal circulated to staff of the paper. Thus he drifted away from the 2nd City of London Sea Scouts, and then the War came.

1939-45

War intervened but *Discovery* continued to be used every weekend for the purposes of Sea Scout training.

Sunday, 3 September 1939

Extract from the Paddington Sea Scouts Service Crew Log, RRS Discovery

6 a.m.	Glorious morning, hands turned to.
7 a.m.	Washing down.
8 a.m.	Morning papers, work stopped to read the news.
9 a.m.	*Discovery* became headquarters and control station of Sea Scout signallers in the River Emergency Service ARP Organisation of the Port of London.
10 a.m.	Four Paddington hands enrolled in the River Emergency Service.
11 a.m.	The Master, ship's company, River Emergency Service, and service crew gathered to hear the British Prime Minister [Mr Neville Chamberlain] speak to the world.

It is thus that the Paddington service crew learned of the expired British ultimatum to Germany. Gathered in the galley on that strange Sabbath morning at a quarter past eleven, they heard those quiet words: 'It is the evil thing that we shall be fighting against, brute force, bad faith, injustice, oppression and persecution.'

It was the Paddington service crew that prepared *Discovery* against all eventualities when the terrible wails of the first air-raid warning startled London. Battening down the hatches, making the wardroom gas proof, wondering what was going to happen. Many thoughts can disturb the mind at such times, thoughts of the good old days, thoughts of how the future had been planned, thoughts of what the future might probably be.

80 *Work in the engine room, RRS* Discovery, *1943. Fine triple expansion engines and boiler were later removed and broken up for scrap as part of the war effort.*

81   *Sea Scouts undergo instruction in sail recognition, RRS* Discovery, *c.1944.*

Our ideals would carry our crew on to even happier days than those that had passed, even greater achievements than those we had fondly hoped for in the era that had so suddenly closed.

One hundred Sea Scouts aided the PLA as signallers and in Air Raid Precaution duties. An account of this part of the Home Defence organisation is given in Chapter 7.

Pre-Naval Entry courses were held on board during this period attended by 2,500 Sea Scouts, one in four gaining a commission.

1946-50

When the War ended in 1945 *Discovery* returned to her peacetime role as a Sea Scout training ship. By June 1946, courses for Sea Scouters commenced, designed to give instruction in the care and repair of boats, boat orders, discipline and boat handling up to the standard required for Charge Certificates. The Discovery Committee administered and arranged the courses, assisted by the Discovery Service Crew. During 1948 all activities ceased while the ship underwent a major refit, when much of the deterioration of the war years was arrested and repaired.

Brian Ewart was a Senior Sea Scout in the 16th Ilford West formed in 1945, which became the 1st Ilford North. They became heavily involved with RRS *Discovery* when the Master was Mr Punchard, followed by Eric Evans. 'Tiny' Mathews was First Mate and Mr Cole was the Bo'sun. Brian Ewart and his friends were recruited to spend most weekends bringing *Discovery* into commission as a Sea Scout Headquarters after its wartime role as HQ of the Thames Defence Force. The 1st Ilford North considered themselves the 'cats whiskers' and their rivals in all things were the 35th Westminster Sea Scouts.

82 *(Left) Instruction Signal Lamp on board* RRS Discovery. *Behind the massive substructure were 26 inches of solid wood.*

83 *(Below Left) Eric Evans, Master RRS* Discovery, *instructing Sea Scout leaders in seamanship, c.1950*

84 *(Right) RRS* Discovery – *Sea Scouts climbing the rigging.*

85 *The* Discovery, *1948 – its timeless beauty matched against the ever-changing City of London skyline.*

Brian was a member of *Discovery* ship's company for about eight months between 1947 and 1948. He recalls the strong smell of tar and ropes below decks and in the Bosun's store, forward under the Pool starboard side. The sound of the trams running along the embankment could be heard below the waterline, from the port bunker used as an occasional mess deck and classroom. The scraping of the gangplank along the deck was heard as the ship rose and fell when large craft passed by. The Thames was busy in those days.

Brian recalled the succession of 'slightly-mad' cooks (chefs), many of whom were said to have had previous sea service, who were employed to provide meals for weekend courses. One was known to throw cleavers and knives at people who were late responding to the 'Cooks to the Galley' pipe.

The game of Pirates was played both on deck and on the after-mess deck (old engine room). Participants had to get from aft to the fo'c'sle without stepping on the wooden deck, a sort of gymnastic British Bulldog, as they were pursued by a picked team of slipper-wielding enthusiasts. The route was from the roof of one of the small lazaret-type structures (storage spaces between the decks of the ship), aft by the tiller flat, up and along the sea plane deck, aft of the funnel, by a rope to the bridge across one of two bulks of timber between the bridge and the forward mess deck companionway housing, and along the rail capping onto the poop!

Some Pre-War traditions continued, reminders of the small crowds which formed on the Embankment whenever someone climbed to the 'barrel' (crow's nest) [110 feet high – over 30 metres]. If the individual then climbed out of the barrel and stood upside down on his hands with his feet in the air, the crowd became three deep! Brain Ewart said it should be noted that he did not have a head for heights and could not get higher than the lower crosstree grating on the mainmast. The foremast and mizzen were out of bounds due to dry rot.

While boating, one of the evolutions was sweeping round the anchor chains and pulling up against the tide to come alongside the ship. They always carried a life ring in a whaler in case they came across someone else in trouble. They did not wear life jackets or buoyancy aids, as they thought themselves immortal. Games of Smugglers and Excise Men were played with the River Police and their searchlights at night, at

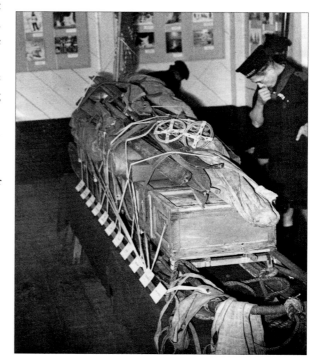

86 *An exploration sledge – Polar Exhibition on RRS* Discovery.

87   *Polar tableau from Ealing Studios, RRS* Discovery. *Several polar exhibitions were held from 1949 to 1951.*

slack water, off Cherry Garden Pier amongst the barge rows in the Pool of London. Afterwards, hot chocolate was dispensed (with a little something added) in the River Police Station. Those were the days, said Brian Ewart. *Discovery* had a 14ft inboard motor boat called the *John Burchell* which had been built by students of the Wivenhoe Evening Institute.

For a candidate being tested for a Charge Certificate, rowing as a member of a whaler's crew was always made into a memorable event. The crew were all briefed beforehand to pretend to lose an oar or to start a fight, while the examiner unscrewed the bottle screws of the yoke lines to the rudder which would make the boat unsteerable, all at the *moment critique* – 'if you can keep your head when all around are losing theirs' was the order of the day. The examination for a Charge Certificate holder was rigorous because the holder had to be seen as a reliable hand.

Brian well recalls being drilled on the flat roof of Temple Underground Station opposite, and dressed in full uniform with a black 'Peramoid' oilskin coat, as guard of honour for the opening of the film *Scott of the Antarctic* at the Odeon, Leicester Square. He recollects being marched to the Odeon and back, having been inspected by Peter Scott. As part of a six-man team, Brian dragged a sledge along the road to the Odeon, Leicester Square for part of the Antarctic Exhibition at the cinema. He sat in a tent wearing full Antarctic gear, writing a log by the light of a Pemmican lamp, not moving until only one person was staring at him. He then scratched his nose and observed the shock and surprise of the member of the public who could not get anyone else to believe that he was a real person and not made of wax.

Parts of the daily routine were the constant phone calls from 'crusty' old Naval officers every time their Polar flag (plain white) at the mainmast of *Discovery* fouled its halyard.

One unusual event was catching a tourist carving his name on the rail capping down aft by the Ensign staff. Brian and another crew member marched the unfortunate malefactor to the Master's cabin, where he was given a tongue-lashing and sent ashore. Fair and firm, Eric Evans did not suffer fools gladly.

Eric Evans once told me that when he was Master of the ship an official was due to visit to carry out an inspection of the fabric of the ship. On arrival, the inspector demanded an alcoholic drink, which was difficult as the ship was dry. He persisted, so the inventive Eric, unbeknown to the

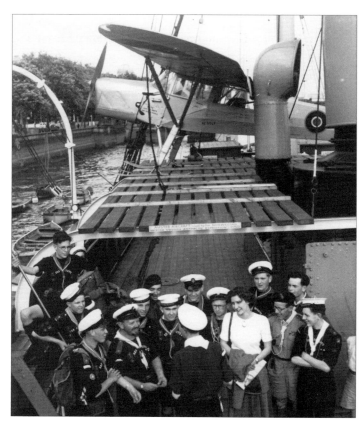

88 *A sea plane on the deck of RRS* Discovery *– Antarctic Exploration – Polar Exhibition, which included a section on the Norwegian/British/Swedish Antarctic Expedition, 1949.*

89 *Pulling boats alongside RRS* Discovery, *c.1950.*

official, poured some orange juice into a glass which he laced with raw alcohol, normally used for cleaning purposes. The recipient drank the contents down in one gulp, passed no comment and carried out the inspection.

1951-5

Douglas Myers visited *Discovery* with his Sea Scout Group one weekend. There were three officers on board – the Master who lived ashore, the First Officer Mr Dick Coles and the Purser Mr Martin – one carpenter lived on board and one carpenter lived ashore, plus three crew boys who lived and worked on board. He applied for a position when there was a vacancy, and on 20 May 1951 he became a pantry boy which entailed looking after the wardroom, serving the ship's officers and guests who slept in the cabins of Captain Scott's officers around the wardroom, serving meals, clearing away, washing up, scrubbing the floor, making the beds and polishing the brasswork. When this work was done he could go on deck to help with the maintenance of the ship, or the training boats alongside. In addition he was responsible for opening the shop and serving in it. In time he made the position of Head Boy. When Marshal Josef Tito arrived by sea from Yugoslavia in the naval vessel *Galeb* (*Seagull*), he was brought up the Thames under Royal Navy escort, and Douglas recalled he had the duty of dipping *Discovery*'s ensign as the ship passed by. Part of his duties were to escort important visitors around London.

The Great Tide

On 31 January 1953 a devastating tidal surge rushed up the River Thames. Sea levels were three metres above normal, causing the river to burst its banks in places. Douglas Myers reported that the river washed over the parapet, across the Embankment and into Temple Underground Station, and clearly recollects that *Discovery* was in danger of breaking loose from her moorings. 58 people died when Canvey Island, Essex, on the Thames estuary, was flooded, so the Port of London Authority took *Discovery*'s whalers and gigs to the island to help evacuate the people there. After the floods had subsided, the First Officer and Douglas took one of the motor boats to bring *Discovery*'s boats back. It was a foggy day and they did not get very far, having to spend the night alongside a line of barges; then they had breakfast with a Barge Watch Keeper. They continued on their way, picking up the boats from Greenhithe Sea Scouts Motor Torpedo Boat Headquarters, spent the night on board and then returned to *Discovery*, after which the boys of the crew had to spend some time clearing the rubbish from the jetty brought down by the floods. It had been a long journey.

A visitor to *Discovery* at that time was Duncan Carse who made his mark as a polar explorer but was principally known as a professional radio broadcaster and actor – one of the rôles he played was Dick Barton, Special Agent, which in its heyday attracted 15 million listeners. Duncan Carse, who died aged 90 in 2004, would have wished to be remembered for his work in mapping the island of South Georgia between 1951 and 1957. He held the coveted Polar Medal awarded to him in 1939, with two clasps awarded in 1992.

Douglas was sorry to leave the ship when called up for his National Service in 1953.

90 *Sea Scouts receiving splicing instructions on RRS* Discovery, *c.1950.*

JACOB'S LADDER

Mike Cudmore from Bexhill was a Sea Scout in the early 1950s. He had joined for a week's course at the end of one December.

He recalled: 'The Thames was in full flood, with water near the top of the Embankment walls. The ship was moored just offshore and there was a fixed walkway out to her. This was under water and only the sides of the hand rails were visible.'

Hoisting his kitbag onto his left shoulder, he worked his way along a handrail to the ship, to the bottom of a short Jacob's ladder up the ship's side. He then climbed the ladder, single-handed, the other hand holding his kit bag. He progressed up one step, leaving go with the right hand, the other holding his kit bag. Up one more step, again leaving go with the right hand and grasping the next rope up above, each foot board, etc, until he got to the top.

He went up the last step, let go with the right hand and reached over to grasp the top of the bulwark. Being an Antarctic ship, the top rail was over a foot wide and he clawed vainly for a hold. Nature took its course and he fell over backwards into the water, kit bag and all, fortunately within the handrails of the walkway below. They fished him out with (to him) inappropriate merriment, and so he had joined his first ship. He was later to become a Commander RN.

Transfer of the Discovery

By the early 1950s the cost of *Discovery*'s upkeep had become a great a drain on the funds of the Boy Scouts Association and decisions needed to be made about her future.

In Admiralty papers on HMS *Discovery* held at The National Archives at Kew, recently released under the Freedom of Information Act, the following document headed 'Historical Note – Transfer of The *Discovery* to the RN 1953' can be found; this covers the period 1953 to 1955:

> By May 1953, the London Division, RNVR [Royal Naval Volunteer Reserve] had expanded to 600 officers and 2,000 ratings and it became evident that the accommodation available in [HMS] *President* and [HMS] *Chrysanthemum* was proving inadequate for the administration and training of such large numbers, many of whom were pre-National Service ratings who were given a guarantee of National Service in the Royal Navy in exchange for undertaking RNVR training prior to call-up.
>
> While searching for additional accommodation, Admiral Commanding Reserves heard that the Boy Scouts Association was finding the expense of maintaining *Discovery* as a training ship for Sea Scouts beyond the financial capacity of the ship's endowment and their other funds.
>
> After inspecting the ship, Admiral Commanding Reserves proposed to the [Admiralty] Board that *Discovery* should be acquired for the Naval service as an additional Drill ship for the London Division to meet their requirements for additional accommodation. The Boy Scouts Association welcomed the proposal and at first offered the ship as an unconditional gift, but it was later decided that to legalise the transfer it would be necessary for the Admiralty to purchase the ship for a nominal sum and £1 was eventually paid.
>
> Before the Board agreed to take the ship over she was docked and surveyed. The cost of her refit and conversion to naval use was estimated as:

	£	
Initial docking and survey	2,000)	
Repairs	15,000)	Actual cost £45,795
Alterations and Additions	25,000)	
Provision of Dolphins	6,000)	
Provision of Pontoon	5,000)	Actual cost not known
Repairs to moorings	250)	
	£63, 250	[£1.1m today]

In September 1953, Mr Peter Scott heard of the proposals to transfer his father's ship to the Admiralty and raised certain objections, mainly on the questions of alterations to the ship and public access. He formed a Discovery Committee with the aim of raising sufficient money to keep the ship for youth training and a national memorial to his father. Although the committee had a reasonable chance of raising the money they required, Mr Scott eventually withdrew his claim after receiving further assurances from the First Sea Lord on the question of public access.

The Admiralty also agreed to ensure custody of the Scott relics, the property of the Boy Scouts Association, which were to remain in the ship, and they accepted financial responsibility up to £500.

Peter Scott was to write in his book *The Eye of the Wind* in 1961:

> For many years *Discovery* had belonged to the Boy Scouts Association, on the council of which I now sat. Thousands of people each year came to see her … The Wardroom and Officers' cabins were beautifully maintained and there was a collection of Antarctic relics connected with my father. But the maintenance was costly and in due course it became necessary to find some plan. There were rumours that the Admiralty were prepared to take her on but proposed to use her 'for storage of files'. This seemed a sad waste of a ship whose history and tradition could surely still be used to fire the imagination especially of young people. I decided to ask a number of eminent men, among them Admiral of the Fleet Lord Cunningham, Lord Alanbrooke, the Bishop of Portsmouth, Sir Edmund Hillary, Sir Raymond Priestley and Sir Michael Balcon to join the Committee to examine the proposals.

> A Discovery Trust was considered but never formed because the first Lord of the Admiralty came back with an entirely new plan for using the ship for training pre-National Service men and allowing Scout and other youth training to continue at weekends. My big guns had been trained but it was never necessary to fire them. Quite recently the questions of re-rigging the old ship had been raised in Parliament by David James, an old wartime friend [of Peter Scott] who had also been in Coastal Forces. He proposed that the yards should be restored to *Discovery* so that she could become again a square-rigged ship instead of what he described as a 'bastard schooner'.

On the day of the RNVR Jubilee Review on 12 June 1954, the Admiralty announced that the Royal Research Ship was to be taken over from the Boy Scouts Association, and used as an additional drill ship for the London Division of the RNVR and the flagship of the Admiral Commanding Reserves.

Treasury objections to the expenditure were finally overcome, the work was completed and the transfer ceremony and commissioning of *Discovery* as an HM Ship took place on 20 July 1955.

In accepting the Boy Scouts' original offer the [Admiralty] Board undertook to leave the original ward room and cabins in their present condition and allow the Sea Scouts facilities for week-end training and mooring of their boats.

The Sea Scouts were permitted to berth up to 12 boats alongside the ship, access for training on Saturday and Sunday, storage for their equipment and accommodation for up to two officers and 20 cadets (Sea Scouts) on Saturday nights. In November 1958 these facilities were extended to the Sea Cadet Corps.

The question of public access was the subject of lengthy discussions, but it was finally agreed that the ship should be open to the public every afternoon from 1300-1645, and access allowed to Scott's Cabin, the Wardroom, upper deck and bridge.

After repairs and alterations at Blackwall Graving Dock lasting 12 months, the Royal Research Ship was on 20 July 1955 commissioned as naval vessel HMS *Discovery*, and was returned to her moorings at Victoria Embankment. In 1956, 300,000 visited the ship. During this period a valuable chart locker vanished. The Ministry of Defence (MoD) files disclose that an inconclusive investigation was carried out.

When she was taken into naval service, heads of RNVR Departments were given the use of the wooden cabins bearing the names of the leading members of Scott's Expedition which were grouped around her wardroom. There was keen competition for these cabins, which were in fact not those which had been used by Scott – the original cabins had been removed in the early 1920s when the ship was converted for use as a store-ship for the Hudson's Bay Company, the former wardroom having become a hold; *Discovery*'s original charthouse also did not survive. The myth about the 'Scott' cabins seems to have arisen in 1937 – and still persists – when, I was told, 'Sea Scouts' painted the names of Scott and other members to the cabin doors.

1955-76

Discovery wore the flag of Admiral Commanding Reserves from 1955 until 1976. The ship was chiefly used by the London Division RNVR for members who were completing pre-National Service training. When National Service was abolished in 1960, *Discovery*'s role became much reduced. During the later period she was used as a recruiting centre in London, for new entry training for the Naval Reserve, and to substitute for HMS *President*, the Headquarters Ship of the London Division Royal Naval Reserve (RNR) when the latter was under refit.

During the next ten years the use of HMS *Discovery* as a training centre for Scouts and Sea Scouts was steadily developed to accommodate the naval administration of the ship. She was used during the week by the London Division of the RNR as an additional drill ship, and at weekends she continued to be used fully for residential training for Scouts and Sea Scouts. David Clayton, the Honorary Secretary of the Discovery Committee, writing in the September 1966 issue of *The Scouter* magazine, reported that the use of the ship had expanded rather more than 250 per cent. Facilities included accommodation for up to 45 and the use of four RNR whalers, two Home Counties gigs and four Coypu sailing dinghies.

Deterioration in the condition of *Discovery* and the need for extensive repairs almost led to her demise in the late 1970s – the Ministry of Defence, as a result of spending reductions, found the cost of upkeep difficult to justify.

1978-9

Disposal of HMS Discovery

On 4 March 1978, *The Times* carried an article saying that the MoD was looking for a new owner for HMS *Discovery* – with the reduction of the RNR, she was no longer needed. Although the wooden hull was sound, it was said there was extensive rotting in the inner shell (although some conservationists disputed this). Neither the cost of a refit, likely to exceed £500,000, nor the annual maintenance cost of £40,000 could be borne on the pared-down Defence votes (budget).

MoD files held at The National Archives and recently released reveal that lengthy discussions took place over the future of HMS *Discovery*, broadly summarised as follows. Some officials, particularly naval officers, thought that the ship should be preserved for the nation, while other officials thought such cost would be prohibitive. The MoD wished to avoid the type of publicity generated in the early 1950s when it was first proposed that the ship should be scrapped. During that period the First Sea Lord had given firm undertakings to Peter Scott about the future of the ship, and the MoD (Navy) did not wish it to appear that they had gone back on the word of the First Sea Lord. Tenders for the purchase of the ship were invited which produced a limited number of enquiries, including one to turn the ship into a floating restaurant.

Because of the ship's history, the MoD decided that, rather than scrap her, they would gladly give her to anyone who seemed responsible and capable of preserving her. The Maritime Trust had expressed interest in the future of the ship and its preservation, and were subsequently chosen. Part of the discussions at the time was about what equipment should be handed over with the ship, items which now appear to have been missing from the inventory. It is interesting to note that at the end of the file the last few pages have been redacted (blacked out), from which it appears some criticisms were raised at the final stages by the Maritime Trust.

Six months later, *The Times* of 19 October 1978 confirmed that *Discovery's* future was assured, having been handed over to her new owners, the Maritime Trust, on 18 October at a ceremony on board, attended by the sons of the famous men who had sailed in her.

Sir Peter Scott, son of Captain Scott, and Lord Shackleton, son of Sir Ernest, were among the guests who crowded into the cramped quarters below decks to hear Admiral Sir Terence Lewin, Chief of Naval Staff and First Sea Lord, announce that the Secretary of State for Defence had approved the free transfer of ownership to the Maritime Trust from 2 April 1979, the Trust having to restore and preserve *Discovery* exclusively for use as a museum.

Further Memories of Discovery

One Sunday in 1975, 'Chalky' White and I, of the 4th Streatham Sea Scouts, took our Charge Certificate examinations at HMS *Discovery*, the test conducted by a kindly Sea Scouter Seymour Burt from Fulham Sea Scouts. The first part of the examination was to take charge of one of *Discovery's* whalers and pull away. As soon as the whaler got under way, things became the stuff of nightmares. Rowing under the anchor chains of HMS *Discovery*, our experienced crew feigned deafness. In the middle of the Thames, 'man overboard' occurred and we had to rescue the lifebuoy representing the casualty, by which time we were in danger of being drawn under Waterloo Bridge. Having completed various evolutions (exercises) we eventually moored up, rowing against the tide. By now the small crowd which had gathered alongside the Embankment were offering gratuitous advice, particularly a man in a raincoat. We rowed back to Putney, where there followed an examination on rules of the road, buoyage, navigation lights and signals. Chalky and I both passed, being awarded the coveted Charge Certificate, endorsed for the River Thames down to the Nore, for boats up to 32 feet under oars.

Farewell

On 19 March 1979 as a farewell, the national press carried an evocative picture of the 14th Richmond Sea Scouts. Having been to say farewell to Captain Scott's Antarctic ship, in which

Scouts had trained since 1937, the picture shows the Sea Scouts pulling a whaler away from *Discovery* and the Embankment. The London Division of the RNR gave up the use of the ship on 2 April 1979 when she was handed over to the Maritime Trust for preservation, and once again she became a Royal Research Ship.

During 17/18 April 1979 the *Discovery* (Sea Scout) crew removed all their equipment and property from the ship, and held their farewell party attended by more than 100 past and present members of the crew. The evening was tinged with sadness but all stated their intention to support the new Dockland Scout Project which was later to be established in East London.

1980-6

The Maritime Trust spent 1980 searching for a new berth so that she could be dry docked and turned into a museum ship. Mr Basil Greenhill, Director of the National Maritime Museum, said that, when funds could be found, RRS *Discovery* would become a gallery of exploration with displays telling the story of man's exploration of the seas.

A national appeal for £850,000 to restore the ship to her 1923 condition realised £430,000 and promises included an offer by the Greater London Council of £1 for every £4 given, up to a maximum of £100,000.

In 1985 a new home in Dundee was offered to *Discovery* by Dundee Heritage Trust in partnership with the Scottish Development Agency.

To enable *Discovery* to leave London, St Katherine's Dock had to be dredged. She then headed away from her berth on 27 March 1986; a Sea Scout team of volunteers from the Sea Scout

91   *'Home to Dundee'.*

Discovery Team manned the ropes and warps as she passed through the dock. On Easter Sunday, 30 March 1986, on the peak of a spring tide, with the narrow lock gates open at both ends, she was moved into the Thames above Tower Bridge and docked safely into the floating dock ship *Happy Mariner*, which belonged to a Dutch shipping company operating regularly out of Dundee.

On leaving *Discovery* in London someone had chalked:

RRS *DISCOVERY*
1937-79

WHEN IT BECAME HMS
WE CREPT ON BOARD –
AND SPENT SEVERAL MORE
HAPPY YEARS THERE; TILL
SHE WENT TO HER FINAL
RESTING PLACE IN DUNDEE,

IT WAS THEN WE JOINED
THE
LOCAL SEA SCOUTS
IN DOCKLAND

OUT OF SMALL ACORNS GREAT OAKS GROW

On 3 April 1986, as she approached the River Tay after a 500-mile journey home to the town where she was built, *Discovery* was met by the Tay Pilot cutter, the lifeboat *Spirit of Tayside* and the *Coral Star* carrying sightseers. Crowds lined the estuary to cheer her, while a flypast by a wartime Shackleton Bomber from Lossiemouth and three RAF Phantom fighters from Leuchars welcomed the old ship home. *Discovery* seems to have had a hand in her final berthing, in that she became jammed in the hold of the *Happy Mariner*. She finally reached Victoria Dock on the midnight tide of 3rd/4th April. The crowds by then had gone home, but an RNR piper on board the wooden fighting ship, the frigate *Unicorn*, saluted her arrival.

1992 TO DATE

In 1992 she was moved to her custom-built dock to become an integral part of Discovery Point, Dundee's flagship tourist attraction. The Maritime Trust continued to own *Discovery* until 1995 when she was transferred to Dundee Heritage Trust and the Scottish Development Agency on 29 November 1995 for the sum of £1 – a one-pound note dating from 1901, the year of the launch of *Discovery*, was handed over to conclude the transfer.

After the signing of the Agreement, detailed planning began on a £2.6 million restoration project. I visited RRS *Discovery* in Dundee on 16 October 2005 to discuss putting together a history for

92   *RRS* Discovery's *ship's wheel, Dundee City of Discovery, 2005.*

Dundee Heritage of *Discovery* when it was a Sea Scout Training Ship during the years 1937-55. Standing by the ship's wheel I felt nostalgia for the old ship. After being shown around by a guide

93   *RRS* Discovery's *ship's bell inscribed in bold letters 'London 1901', Dundee City of Discovery, 2005.*

I asked him if he could tell me any unusual tales about the ship. He said the previous year (2004) a ladies' group were having Christmas lunch in the wardroom, after which one of the ladies complained about the rudeness of one of the ship's staff, who had remarked to her that 'ladies were not welcome on the ship'. A check was made, and it was found that there was no staff there at the time. I asked the tour guide what his view was – he said it was a good story.

Ships that go Bump in the Night

Debbie Burton from Discovery Point is on record as having said that there had been strange goings-on on board the ship.

Earlier this year a guest at one of the dinner functions said they saw someone. She said she had conversed with him all the evening. But rather eerily no-one else could see whom she was talking to.

94 *RRS* Discovery *mast, re-rigged.*

95   *RRS* Discovery, 2005.

A surprising number of visitors refuse to go into some of the rooms on board, and some years ago electricians were brought in to find out why the bulb over Shackleton's bunk kept blowing, but no earthly reason could be found. It is also said that ghostly footsteps continue to be heard on the ship, with opinion split as to whether they are those of Shackleton, who did not wish to leave the ship, or those of another sailor, Charles Bonner, who fell to his death in 1901.

Charles Bonner's death took place on *Discovery*'s maiden voyage. On 21 December 1901 at Leyton, New Zealand, Scott wrote that they had been visited by some Maori ladies who were served with lunch on board. In the excitement of the ship's departure, the crew waved from the rigging. Perched on the highest mainstay, the Able Seaman climbed above the crow's nest to the top of the mainmast. He tripped and fell, letting out a wild cry, his body cartwheeling down through the rigging, cracking his skull on the corner of an iron deckhouse, a fatal injury. The loss of this smart young seaman was greatly felt by the crew. Charles Bonner was buried with full naval honours two days later at Port Chalmers, the main port of Dunedin, New Zealand.

Another death during the expedition was that of Able Seaman George Vince, born in Blandford Forum, Dorset on 20 September 1880. He died falling over an ice cliff into the sea at Ross Island on 11 March 1902. It was rumoured that he was pushed.

The restoration of RRS *Discovery* and the opening of Discovery Point in 1993 were the culmination of many years' effort by Dundee Heritage Trust, formed in January 1985.

96   *RRS* Discovery, *2009.*

SEVEN

THE SECOND WORLD WAR, 1939-45

This chapter covers the participation of the Sea Scouts in the River Thames Emergency Service (RES) during the Second World War, and other war services. Most RES records were destroyed for reasons of confidentiality shortly after the War.

1938

The Formation of the River Thames Emergency Service

In 1938 the Port of London Authority (PLA) set up 'The River Thames Emergency Service' (RES) where yachtsmen were encouraged to join, to be called upon to do patrol work in their own boats on the Thames.

1939

On 23 April, the PLA held a large-scale exercise to test the readiness of the RES should war come. Sea Scouts were sent to various piers locations, prepared to receive and convey by telephone messages sent from vessels on the river.

3rd Hillingdon Sea Scouts – RES

Douglas Francis recalls that prior to the Second World War they trained for work to be undertaken should war come. Douglas Francis was stationed on Cherry Garden Pier on 23 April, the day an RES exercise took place.

The Sea Scout Signals Group of 60 trained for the purpose of RES communications. At the outbreak of war they were based aboard the Training Ship *Worcester*, moored off Greenwich. Several were billeted in the *Ship Hotel*, Greenwich, later destroyed by enemy bombing. With no enemy appearing they were sent home and back to school.

The Thames Sea Scout Committee undertook to supply volunteer Sea Scout Signallers to the RES. Douglas and several members of the Troop volunteered and spent several weekends brushing up their Morse and semaphore at training sessions at the HQ of Petersham and Ham Sea Scouts on the Thames. The following instructions were issued:

TO SEA SCOUTS AND OFFICERS ENGAGED IN PORT OF LONDON DEFENCE

The Chief has sent us the following cable:

'Congratulations on Practical Sea Scout Training for National Service. Best Wishes.

BADEN-POWELL.'

In the event of a national call for ARP workers to report all sea scouts and officers who have volunteered will report at the station to which they were posted at their last exercise. If in doubt report to the *Discovery.*

Late Instructions
Bring 24 hours food, kit, and gasmasks. You will be fed, billeted and paid.

DO YOUR BEST TO DO YOUR DUTY TO GOD AND THE KING.

RONALD COLLIER [Hon. Secretary]

Douglas Francis had received instructions from the Thames Sea Scout Committee to supply volunteer Sea Scout signallers to the RES. Several weekends were spent brushing up Morse and semaphore; they reported to RRS *Discovery* on 3 September 1939, the first day of the War.

They were allocated cabins which surrounded the wardroom and detailed a watch on Westminster Pier. The Troop were sent in pairs to various piers including Lambeth, West India Dock and Greenwich. They would walk or cycle to their duty, often in the blackout, and worked alongside Sea Scouts from other Troops, enjoying rowing in off-duty periods. Mr Waley-Cohen, later a Lord Mayor of London, was an officer in the RES, and Douglas remembers rowing him across the river to check stores held a barge.

1st Mortlake Sea Scouts

The 1st Mortlake Sea Scouts received instructions from the PLA for their pinnace *Minotaur* to be held in readiness for the RES, and on 1 September she proceeded to the mustering point. *Minotaur* was based on the Putney Station of the RES at the Thames Rowing Club boathouse and manned by Rover Sea Scouts. Work consisted of practices combined with regular river patrols.

After six weeks the pinnace was stood down and returned to the Troop, whilst her crews were re-mustered to other craft.

John Weeden of the 1st Mortlake had enrolled in the Royal Naval Volunteer Supplementary Reserve (London Division) on 19 October 1937 and was mobilised for War Service as a Probationary

Temporary Sub Lieutenant on 20 October 1939. Later appointed Lieutenant Commander, John Weeden was awarded the Distinguished Service Cross for Gallantry, Skill and Endurance while serving in HM Torpedo Boats.

3 September 1939 – Outbreak of War
22nd Walthamstow Sea Scouts

Douglas Robertson joined the 22nd Walthamstow Sea Scouts around 1930 and was an active Rover Scout at the beginning of the war. Shortly after the start of hostilities he found himself out of work – he was always told that he could be called up soon. He was advised that the Royal Navy had a recruiting scheme for Sea Scouts with some basic knowledge of signalling. It seemed the answer to his uncertain future.

Within days Douglas was on RRS *Discovery* on the Thames Embankment. His training took place in the cabin working at the great table, an atmosphere he would never forget. For six weeks the group of 20 were on an intensive course of signalling procedure, general instruction on flags and lights for inter-ship communications, by the end of which they could send and receive signals to the satisfaction of the two Petty Officers training them. They were told to stay at home, and within a few days they would be instructed to report to the naval authorities at HMS *Royal Arthur* located at the requisitioned Butlin's holiday camp at Skegness in Lincolnshire.

On 7 December 1939, when he had been at home for about two days, his Army call-up papers landed on the doormat with a four-shilling postal order (about £6 today), a railway warrant and instructions on what clothing to pack. Dismayed, he leapt on his motorcycle and rode to the recruiting office. He was greeted by an 'old-time' Petty Officer who said he 'didn't know anything about it, his officer was up in London and wouldn't be back this week, and what was more if he didn't report for duty he would have the Red Caps [Military Police] hammering on the door and he would be in serious trouble.'

By 15 December 1939, at the age of 20 Douglas found himself in the Army, wearing size 11 boots, two sizes too big, with two pairs of socks to take the slack, and that was that for the best part of seven years.

Despite his initial disappointment Douglas Robertson came to recognise that army service may well have saved his life. He saw later when he was being transported in convoy that Sea Scouts carried out inter-ship bridge-to-bridge signals on merchant vessels, duties performed in a very exposed environment.

1st Tyne Sea Scouts

The 1st Tyne Sea Scouts Boat Station became part of HMS *Elfin*, an operational submarine base. The Sea Scouts were issued with special passes to enable them to continue to use the harbour areas.

3rd Chalkwell Bay Sea Scouts

When War broke out the 3rd Chalkwell Sea Scouts were ready to do their bit. Peter Daws presented himself at the *Lobster Smack Inn* at Canvey Island, where the PLA were operating the RES. He told them, 'I have a group of trained Sea Scout signallers whom you cannot do without.' They responded, 'Right – you're on'- or words to that effect.

Peter Daws was promoted to 'Signals Officer' and told to round up his flock of would-be-heroes, the unknown stalwarts of the 3rd Chalkwell Bay Sea Scouts, who they say were the youngest 'combat' force in the UK at the time. The Sea Scouts took refresher courses on RRS *Discovery* then returned to Hole Haven or Cliffe Fort in Kent for duty. Training was to a high standard and relay signal courses were organised to improve speeds; at table one would even ask for the salt by tapping Morse code on the table. They wore naval bell-bottomed trousers, Sea Scout jersey, navy blue donkey jacket or bridge jacket, matelot's hat and a white *Discovery* scarf tied with the *Discovery* knot – still worn today.

The Scouts were assigned to vessels attached to their station. The vessels included commandeered yachts, fishing boats and a London tug. All vessels were armed with a machine gun, and had special buoys which were used for mine spotting, dropped by enemy aircraft into the estuary at night. During air raids the crews watched from their positions at anti-aircraft (Ack-Ack) guns located on barges moored in the Thames estuary.

Other duties involved monitoring shipping and keeping watch on vessels, especially sailing barges, off the Blythe Sands which were heavily mined. Those who served at Hole Haven and Cliffe Fort included Skipper Peter Daws, Peter West, Ginger Lowen, Frank and Stan Bentley, Bolton, Snow and Campbell (3rd Chalkwell Bay) who were all in the Navy by the years 1941/2.

The *PLA Monthly* magazine reported:

> The war did not immediately take the course that was anticipated, but the work of the small launches in assisting the Admiralty soon brought them under notice. One incident must suffice to indicate the valuable nature of their work.

> On the night of 24 November 1939, [enemy] mine-laying aircraft appeared over the Estuary. One plane flying at 50 feet was observed by the RES personnel at one of the Section Headquarters. The limitations of civil defence were fully exposed, for had they been armed they could not have missed the plane. The plane veered south-west after passing over the watchers and dropped mines close to three fully-laden tankers anchored in the river. The position of the tankers was highly dangerous as, with the change of tide, one of them would swing over the mine. It was hazardous to move at all until the tide had turned. A fast launch proceeded to the spot where it remained and watched until the tide changed. When it was found the tankers were just clear of the mine, the ships were instructed by the RES crew to move their position, which they accomplished without further incident. A cool quarter of a million sterling [over £7 million today], it has been estimated, was saved by the prompt action of this crew.

1940

On 14 May the BBC Nine O'Clock News broadcast an official announcement:

> The Admiralty have made an order requesting all owners of self-propelled pleasure craft between thirty and one hundred feet in length to send all particulars to the Admiralty within fourteen days from today, if they have not already been requisitioned.

The Admiralty gave no specific reason for registration.

26 May-4 June 1940 – The Epic of Dunkirk

'Operation Dynamo' was masterminded by Vice Admiral Bertram Ramsey, who was given less than a week to prepare. He directed and inspired a small staff, about 27, who had the awesome task of planning the evacuation from Dunkirk, under constant attack, of up to 400,000 British and French troops constantly assembling there.

A secret cipher telegram message was sent by the War Office to the Admiralty stating emergency evacuation was required.

Admiralty signal Dover 'Operation Dynamo is to commence.'

Admiral Ramsey had under his direction 129 vessels comprising ferries, coasters, scoots (Dutch coasters) and small boats which had for some days been in the course of assembly at various locations.

Monday, 27 May 1940 – 10.30 a.m.

On the Upper Thames between Teddington Lock and Oxford many boats were to be found. Because of the war comparatively few remained in use and were laid up ashore.

The Admiralty Small Vessels Pool telephoned Teddington and the action of acquiring flotillas became on-going.

A family member at Tough's Boat Yard recalls a telephone call being made to the yard by a senior naval officer. There was no formal paperwork involved other than a list of the names of boats being

97   Sundowner, *Ramsgate, Kent, which took part in the 1940 evacuation of troops from Dunkirk. A Sea Scout, Gerald Ashcroft, was a member of the crew.*

written down in pencil on a scrap of paper, and the boats were collected. This historic list is still preserved in the boatyard's records.

The boatyard selected to act as a clearing house for the small boats was Tough Brothers, Boat Builders of Teddington, where the tidal Thames ends; Mr Douglas Tough's family had been on the river for three generations. He and Mr Ron Lenthal, accompanied by a naval officer, progressed along the upper reaches of the Thames, collecting and requisitioning suitable motor cruisers.

Admiralty officers searched the numerous boatyards down river from Teddington to Brightlingsea on the Essex coast, which yielded up to 40 serviceable motor boats or launches; these were assembled at Sheerness, Isle of Sheppey, the following day. Most owners co-operated, some joining the volunteer crews assembled at Tough's Yard to take the vessels to Sheerness. There a Royal Naval crew took over, each craft being chartered to the Ministry of Shipping.

Friday, 31 May 1940

The BBC broadcast a second appeal for volunteer mariners and all small boat owners to come to the help of the Royal Navy, since only boats of shallow draught could draw up to the beaches at Dunkirk. Applications came in by telephone and members of the PLA Emergency Service were sent to Teddington to act as runner crews.

1st Mortlake Sea Scouts

In May 1940 the 1st Mortlake Sea Scouts' 45-foot motor picket boat *Minotaur* was back on her moorings during which time Tom Towndrow was active in refitting and skippering their pinnace. He was seen by a Royal Naval Commander and two Petty Officers on 29 May, who instructed *Minotaur* to proceed to Sheerness. He contacted the Town Clerk of Barnes Borough Council, for whom he worked, obtaining a few days leave. At 11 p.m., the Admiralty issued instructions for *Minotaur* to report to a down-river destination as early as possible. By midnight the crew was found, by 8.30 a.m. the next morning they were underway downriver, refuelling and taking on stores and water as they went. Three other Sea Scouts from the 1st Mortlake crewed boats from Chiswick which were short of crews.

In the hands of Rover Sea Scouts Tom Towndrow and F. Jackson she set out for Sheerness. In the absence of a naval crew they continued to Ramsgate which they reached at 8 p.m. the following day. They took on stores, fuel and two naval ratings armed with two .303 rifles and 600 rounds of ammunition, after which they received detailed operational instructions to get underway for the French coast.

Their voyage started at 10.45 a.m. on 31 May. Tom Towndrow recalls,

> The whole of Dunkirk was still very much in our hands, but we did not know this. The crossing took six hours and was by no means uneventful. Destroyers raced past, almost cutting the water from beneath us, threatening to overturn us with their wave.

> We approached the beach with great caution at Dunkirk because of the wrecks. We found things fairly quiet and got on with our allotted job of towing small open ships' boats laden with soldiers to troop transporters anchored in deep water, or loading our ship from the open boats and proceeding out to the transports.

We were working about a quarter of a mile away from six destroyers. Suddenly all their anti-aircraft guns opened fire. At the same time we heard the roar of 25 Nazi planes overhead. Their objective was the crowded beach and the destroyers. One plane made persistent circles round us. Another Nazi plane was brought down in flames far too close for our liking! I had to restrain a crew member from engaging a fighter plane with his rifle.

By the time the action finished, one enemy aircraft had been destroyed for the tragic loss of two destroyers sunk; in addition, there were heavy losses on the beach. Eventually our fuel ran low and the engine made ominous noises, so we were relieved. We took our final load to a trawler, returned to our east coast base, refuelled and turned in for a few hours' sleep. We were then told to stand by, as fast boats were making the next crossing. We shipped aboard another motor boat as crew, and left before it got dark under convoy of a large seagoing tug. Our job this time was to work from the Mole at Dunkirk Harbour in conjunction with the tug. The operation was supposed to be carried out under cover of darkness, but with the petrol and oil tanks on fire it might have been daytime. Having loaded the tug we came away barely in time. As we left the Mole the Germans got its range and a shell demolished the end of it.

On the way back we Scouts [1st Mortlake] transferred to a naval cutter, full of troops which were making the return journey. The officer in charge had lost his charts. Knowing the course back we were able to take over. After a nine-hour crossing we made our east coast base once more. German aircraft constantly followed all small boats out to sea, gunning the crews and troops on board.

On completion of Operation Dynamo, instructions were received for *Minotaur* to leave Ramsgate and proceed to Sheerness. There she was inspected by Captain Wharton, RN, who stated she would be repaired for Admiralty service, and the opportunity presented itself for members of the crew to sign on for the duration of the Patrol Service.

Commissioned into the Royal Naval Reserve, Tom Towndrow held various postings including secretary to the Captain of the French battleship *Paris* in Plymouth, before being appointed as Royal Navy Liaison Officer on the Free French submarine, *La Sultane*, based at Oran, Algeria. For his service to the French Navy Tom Towndrow was awarded the Croix de Guerre. After the War he qualified as a solicitor and carried on Sea Scouting; he died aged 91 on 4 September 2006.

The crews of the RES were greatly disappointed that only a few were allowed to take their craft over towards Dunkirk, but as an integral part of the Home Defence system they could not be spared. They were able to render valuable help by piloting many pleasure vessels and private yachts into the lower reaches of the Thames, and assisting at Tilbury in fuelling and provisioning.

3rd Hillingdon Sea Scouts

Douglas Francis remembers the upheaval which took place during the Dunkirk evacuation. He assumed that would take part in bringing back the troops, but the RES was to stay on the Thames to help repel any invasion attempt. To this end boats were fitted with a machine gun and issued with some old Ross rifles of First World War vintage. The arming of the RES was carried out by making the Service a Home Guard Unit afloat. The Royal Navy became disturbed 'that the defence of the Thames was in the hands of this motley bunch of amateurs'. Whilst all of those under the age of 18 were sent home the adults, who had hitherto all worn officer-type uniforms, were incorporated into the Royal Naval Volunteer Reserve (RNVR).

Percy F. Westerman

Percy Westerman, well-known writer of adventure stories featuring Sea Scouts, wrote a fictionalised account, *Sea Scouts at Dunkirk*, in 1941, reissued in 1954, which proved to be popular reading.

June 1940 – 2nd Wallasey Sea Scouts

By mid-1940 in Scout Troops throughout the country it was 'Scouting for Boys' again, young leaders aged between 15 and 17 years running the sections, their former leaders having been called up.

The wartime conditions caused great changes. Owing to blackouts, Troop meetings of the 2nd Wallasey were held on Saturday afternoons. More than once they were trapped all night in the air-raid shelter in the cellars of their Headquarters. Rationing and the absence of lighting were problems also to be overcome.

Tents were camouflaged, and their summer camp at Brynbach, North Wales, extended to three weeks because of air raids. About 400 French boys in camp there had been evacuated from France. One day they were visited by one Colonel de Gaulle, and the British Scouts had to act as guards on the approach lanes to the site as after Dunkirk no troops were available to perform this service. Later that evening, standing on a nearby hill, it was very moving to hear those French boys singing *La Marseillaise*. The French Scouts had no idea when and if they would see France again.

Many of the Sea Scouts aged 14 and 15 put their ages as 16 to join the Home Defence services, the ARP, the AFS [Auxiliary Fire Service] and the HES [Hospital Emergency Service] as messengers, fire fighters, stretchers bearers, and later the Home Guard, before joining the services.

The minimum age was 16 but nobody asked too many questions.

As messengers, when the sirens sounded they grabbed their tin hats and gas masks and cycled to their allotted posts. It was a good way to get out of school, until the Headmaster realised that it took five minutes to get to their posts; and wondered why it took them 45 minutes to get back after the all clear. He soon sorted that out.

Sea Scouts crewed boats on patrol and manned various stations on land. The most important of these were Coalhouse Fort and Cliffe Fort in the Thames Estuary where Sea Scouts were continuously on duty. They had once formed part of the Thames defences and commanded two long reaches of the river. It had been manned before, in 1914, also by Scouts and reportedly was haunted.

August 1940 – 3rd Chalkwell Bay Sea Scouts

On 24 August 1940 Sea Scouts from the 3rd Chalkwell Bay assisted in the firefighting caused by German bombing attacks on the petrol storage depot at Thameshaven, Essex, on the Thames. Patrol Leader Ginger Lowen, signaller and crew were commended by the Admiralty for their part during and after the raid.

Liverpool Sea Scouts

Cliff Adamson and his brother Peter joined the Sea Scouts in Liverpool at the beginning of the war; Liverpool suffered badly from the Blitz during 1940 and 1941 and they were glad to be in uniform to enjoy the camaraderie of the Sea Scouts.

The Sea Scouts met in a wooden hut in the local church grounds. At band practice the hut reverberated, not from the bombs but from the noise of the band. Cliff recalls they quickly learned to play the bugle, blowing hard; Peter took to the drum and on Sundays they marched around the district after Church Parade. Cliff quickly became Troop Leader and Peter a Patrol Leader. Soon there were over 60 Sea Scouts, two Troops – Port and Starboard Watch.

A relative of Sir Stafford Cripps, MP came to see the bomb damage and report back to the Government, also to visit Captain Walker, the Commander of the Royal Naval Escort Group, Liverpool. The two Troop Leaders, Ernest Nicholson of Starboard and Cliff Adamson of Port Watch, were selected to take part in the visit. Captain Frederick John Walker was not aboard his ship but Cliff recalls they were well entertained by the officers and crew.

The party repaired to a restaurant for lunch. Ernie and Cliff picked up their trays, had two mugs of tea and about a dozen cakes apiece! Cliff recalls 'His Lordship', the distinguished visitor, paid up but that he looked absolutely shocked. As he left for the train, he asked for Cliff's name. Ernie replied, 'Oh, that is Clifford Falcon Theodore Marmaduke Bartholomew Adamson', and gave himself a similar name. Cliff thought their guest was glad to leave Liverpool.

Cliff Adamson recalls his Scouting days when camping with camouflaged tents in Llangollen. By the age of 16, Cliff was in the Merchant Navy. Peter Adamson became an actor, appearing on television as Len Fairclough in 1,797 episodes of *Coronation Street*. When fundraising through Scout Bob-a-Job week started in April 1949, a young Wolf Cub by the name of Paul McCartney, later Sir Paul McCartney, singer and composer, who lived close by, called at the Adamson house seeking any Bob-a-Jobs.

September 1940 – 3rd Osterley Sea Scouts

The bombing of the London 'Blitz' (Blitzkrieg – Lightning War) started on 7 September 1940. Hugh Lauman of the 3rd Osterley Sea Scout Group, Middlesex, recalls during the Blitz the Pool of London was heavily bombed and a number of riverside warehouses were set alight. One warehouse was full of candles which melted, and molten wax ran into the river where it solidified, forming very large shapes resembling small icebergs. These floated up and down the river on the tide causing a hazard to boats and barges. The Sea Scouts were charged with capturing these obstructions, and with securing or beaching them. Some were too big to manhandle and the Scouts would drive a spike into them and tow them to safety with their whaler.

September 1940 – RRS Discovery

A.P. Luscombe Whyte, the writer, reported in *Strand Magazine* on the Sea Scouts on the *Discovery*, the Thames HQ of the River Scouts, from the first the most important of the RES. With their knowledge of seamanship and their quickness of message-carriers, they were invaluable.

100 Sea Scouts from Putney to the Nore aided the PLA as signallers and in ARP duties. Despite the air raids no Sea Scouts failed to turn up for the eight-hour watch. The rate of pay was 12s. 6d. per week (about £18 today) with free board, billeting, uniform and leave of one day in four. Sea Rangers also served with the Thames Emergency Service. Many of the Sea Scouts aged between 16 and 19 lived aboard *Discovery* which by this time had a gymnasium, class-room, canteen, recreation room and hot showers. They slept on board in cabins named after Scott, Shackleton and their comrades.

1941

For the rest of the war RRS *Discovery* was a Parachute Mine Station. Sea Scouts kept a round-the-clock watch for falling parachute mines and, upon sighting them, telephoned a compass bearing through to RN Headquarters.

In March 1941 A.E. Mackenzie wrote in *The Scouter* under the heading 'Sea Scouting in War Time':

> The variety of jobs they undertook makes fine reading: Sea Scouts at Dunkirk in uniform; Sea Scouts doing that fine job of work under fire; Sea Scouts in 'The Blitz' in a Dock working an important switchboard with real 'muck' falling all around – almost everything on fire – the line finally cut, the fellows having to be removed by speedboat from the burning pier – their only exit.

Morrison Shelters

Morrison Table Shelters were introduced in March 1941 for families not prepared to leave their homes for an air-raid shelter. They could spend a night under the protection of their Morrison Shelter.

Peter Wilcox recalls 'the work was quite straightforward using the kit of parts delivered to the houses. The Sea Scouts were often sustained with a drink, a biscuit, cake, etc, and sometimes a small donation towards Group funds.' It was an interest – or shock – to the boys to see how differently some families lived.

5,000,000 Morrisons were distributed and post-war information records they saved many lives. One young Sea Scout recalled that instead of using a Morrison Shelter his parents would put books under the legs of the family bed to make it higher, and sleep underneath the bed during air raids!

7th East Ham Sea Scouts

When George Mence of the 7th East Ham Sea Scouts left school he worked at Barking Power Station. He carried out fire-watching duties and joined the Power Station Home Guard Unit. At 17 he volunteered for the Royal Navy and was posted to the Fleet Air Arm 836 Squadron which manned merchant ships. He was given £2 10s. (about £72 today), told to buy a 'civvy' suit and officially became a deckhand with the Anglo Saxon Line on MV *Empire MacCabe*, a tanker ferrying oil across the Atlantic which carried three Swordfish aircraft used to protect the convoy. He vividly recalls his 'whaler' days in the Sea Scouts which brought back memories when he helped to lower similar types of boat into the Atlantic and sliding down the lowering rope.

2nd Wallasey Sea Scouts

From 1941 to 1943, Easter to October, the Sea Scouts led by their Patrol Leaders were camping most weekends, Friday to Sunday. Camps cost two shillings per Scout (nearly £3 today). When air raids occurred they sheltered in the toilets, and more than once returned to find shrapnel had gone through their tents. All but one of their boats were destroyed on the docks but they were given permission, and loan of boats, to continue water activities on the local marine lake. Rarely an evening or weekend passed without some Scouting activities which were often shared with other Wallasey Troops; with the female members from the 3rd Wallasey Sea Rangers with long-term results – one couple are now grandparents.

1942

2nd Wallasey Sea Scouts

Fire-fighting for the Group became routine for the Sea Scouts. The heaviest raids had mainly ceased in 1941, but lone planes were dropping mines in the River Mersey. There were three lookout – Gladstone Dock, Toxteth Dock and Woodside landing stage. At night two Sea Scouts manned these posts and during raids looked out for mines dropped into the river, take a bearing and estimating the distance. Plotting mines added interest; it was hoped with three observations and the bearings, the minesweepers had some idea of where to operate. By 1944/5, the 2nd Wallasey Sea Scouts were also going to sea on minesweepers and balloon barrage vessels in the Mersey.

Ipswich Sea Scouts

Mr Ivan Hazelton, born in Ipswich in 1929, grew up in the dockland area and was a Sea Scout in the 21st (Holy Trinity) from 1940 to 1943. He was keenly interested in spritsail sailing barges operated by a crew of two; his father sailed in one. They were a sea-going family, his grandfather having been lost at sea on a square rigger.

Ivan picked up knowledge about the hulls and rigs of sail craft by exploring the dockland with friends and got into a number of scrapes due to their youthful exuberance. Ivan had set his heart on going to sea but found that at around 13 the nearest he was going to get was to join the Sea Scouts, which he never regretted. He was forever grateful to Mr Hawkes, skipper of the 21st Holy Trinity, for the effort he put into teaching Sea Scouting, only repaid by their determination to succeed.

After joining the Sea Scouts, Ivan progressed through the basics, ensuring he could swim 25 yards and undress in the water, a condition which had to be met before he could go afloat. He soon found out the only way he was going to get afloat was to volunteer for their ship's working party.

Their home on the water was an old de-rigged Thames barge, the *Quest*. They boarded the vessel, which was moored to a buoy in the main channel by a mud flat. There was water down the creek where they used to push, pull and carry a dinghy around the rocks.

Ivan saw his only way forward was to offer his services to the Skipper to work in the galley. He was taught the elements of cooking, especially how to use a coal range. After six months he began to enjoy galley work, considering the experiences valuable.

98   *The 3rd Tyne Sea Scouts sailing on ketch* Warspite, 1952. *There was no private sailing allowed during the Second World War.*

The day came when Ivan mastered the crew's favourite – sultana duff – plus roast joints and other recipes. Between cooking duties there was plenty of sailing and rowing.

Ivan was a Patrol Leader by the age of 14 in 1943. His first full-time job was Third Hand on the sailing barge *Jock*, which meant cook, deckhand and general dogsbody, for which the pay was £1 10s. a week (about £40 today). The cost of food was shared equally between the three members of the crew, his one-third share being about £1 a week (£26 today).

Ivan Hazleton served as Third Hand, through to Mate and Master in coastal shipping from sail to power, for a period of 22 years, his way being paved by being a Sea Scout which he detailed to me in a letter I received in late October 2001. He had looked forward to a long retirement, sailing his yacht. He wrote his book *Time Before The Mast* but died in 2001 shortly before publication. His daughter Pam Hazleton, writing in the new 2003 edition of his book, said 'The pages penned by him are a testimony to his lifelong love of the sea.'

1942-5 – Derby Sea Scouts

Doug Godlington was a Scout in Derby between 1937 and 1942 but the Troop closed because the Senior Scouts and Patrol Leaders were called up. He got the urge to mess about in boats after reading various boys' adventure books, one in particular about Sea Scouts' adventures in the Brightlingsea area on the Essex coast. This was Percy Westerman's *Sea Scouts Alert* written in 1939, about Sea Scouts up against international criminals and sabotage organisations.

This got him so keen he wrote to Scouting HQ who told him to contact the 1st Dunkirk Derby Sea Scouts – only 15 minutes' cycle ride from home. Sixteen Sea Scouts were in two patrols and spent most of their time on knots, ropework, badges and reading the *Naval Manual of Seamanship*.

There was a scarcity of equipment and Doug Godlington recalls that his uniform was second-hand. Rowing was practised by sitting in upturned bench-forms using brooms for oars. When it came to taking badges for boat handling, tests were carried out in the local park on the River Derwent where the park rowing boats were used. He remembers the Bosun was very critical of his performance – particularly his feather action, and coming alongside the river-side wooden platform was pretty ropey. The examiner passed him, but reluctantly.

There was an offer from the National Fire Service of a cabin cruiser for the Troop, but it had sunk in the canal with only the upper part of the cabin above water. Out of the blue it was found that there were lifeboats for the taking on a Liverpool dock, salvaged from war-damaged ships. The snag was that they were about 20 feet long and weighed a ton apiece. One of the Scouts' fathers worked in the LMS Railway offices and was able to get two of these wooden lifeboats transported by rail to a field site next to the River Trent, south of Derby. The boats' cost of £5 and £7 (£145 and £200 today) made a large hole in the Troop funds.

The river had a strong current which necessitated having to row the 'monsters', and enthusiasm waned. A large mast was stepped in the boats with sail-hoisting arrangement. Even with the sail set, it required a fair amount of rowing output to stem the river current, let alone get moving upstream, which was the only way they could safely go, as downstream round the bend was the A6 road bridge – not to be tangled with at any cost.

The two boats were wrecked in 1947 after the spring thaws of that severe winter; the Trent flooded, the boats were dragged off their moorings and jammed under the arches of the A6 bridge, and the Troop closed shortly afterwards.

Doug Godlington concluded that wartime was hard going for many young people; he missed a year's schooling because of teacher shortages. His interest in sailing continued, and he became a sailing instructor and Commodore of his local sailing club.

99 *A memorial plaque to The Cockleshell Heroes at Southsea, Hampshire. Ten Royal Marines embarked on a raid on German shipping in Bordeaux docks in 1942, of whom only two returned. Lieutenant John Mackinnon, RM, Scoutmaster (Glasgow), was executed by the Gestapo in Paris in 1943.*

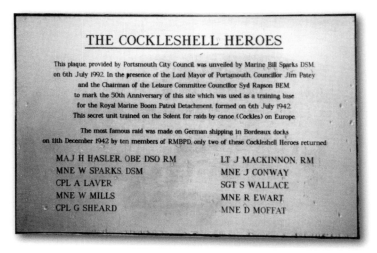

THE COCKLESHELL HEROES

This plaque, provided by Portsmouth City Council, was unveiled by Marine Bill Sparks DSM on 6th July 1992. In the presence of the Lord Mayor of Portsmouth, Councillor Jim Patey and the Chairman of the Leisure Committee Councillor Syd Rapson BEM to mark the 50th Anniversary of this site which was used as a training base for the Royal Marine Boom Patrol Detachment, formed on 6th July 1942. This secret unit trained on the Solent for raids by canoe (Cockles) on Europe.

The most famous raid was made on German shipping in Bordeaux docks on 11th December 1942 by ten members of RMBPD, only two of these Cockleshell Heroes returned.

MAJ H HASLER, OBE DSO RM	LT J MACKINNON, RM
MNE W SPARKS, DSM	MNE J CONWAY
CPL A LAVER	SGT S WALLACE
MNE W MILLS	MNE R EWART
CPL G SHEARD	MNE D MOFFAT

1943

71st Reading Sea Scouts

In his book *Three Flag Hoist – A History of Sea Scouts in Reading* (2004), Vic Rolfe wrote: 'During the War RRS *Discovery* was used for training courses both by the Royal Navy and Sea Scouts. In December 1943 three Patrol Leaders from the 71st Reading (Les Burt, Ray Knott and Vic Rolfe) embarked on RRS *Discovery* for a Patrol Leaders' training course, together with Sea Scouts from other parts of the country.'

The Master of RRS *Discovery*, Mr A.V. Mackenzie, interviewed each Scout, completing his record card as he went. The course was intensive; 'Mac' lectured on 'What Sea Scouting Is', 'How to start and run a Sea Scout Patrol', and 'The Art of Leadership – Know your Man'. Sub-Lieutenant Radford, RNVR, and Mr Nash gave instruction on 'Parts of a Ship'. 'Rule of the Road at Sea' and 'Buoyage' were also covered. They had sessions on signalling, bends and hitches; squad drill took place on top of Temple Underground Station, and there was boating every day. Speakers included Lieutenant Commander Rossetter, RNR, and General Sir John Shea, Scout County Commissioner for London (1936-48).

On the starboard side of the ship, nearest the Embankment, was a primitive floating landing stage where a couple of whalers were moored. Sub-Lieutenant Radford was Boating Officer (also Mines Officer for the River Thames). On the first boating trip in one of the whalers he took a quick look at their badges. The lads from Cornwall were assigned to the oars, the Berkshire lads finished up as passengers. Getting out against the ebb tide was a challenge – they finished broadside onto the pier, with the yoke knocked off the rudder. Sub-Lieutenant Radford enquired of the Reading lads how they could get out of this predicament. Based on their experience with a ship's lifeboat, about twice the weight of a whaler, they explained how to use the stern painter as a 'spring' to launch the boat forward against the tide and clear the landing stage. It worked, and later the Boating Officer stood them a meal at Daly's near the Strand.

In Mac's book Sea Scouts were the elite. Scouts had to learn about the three flags of St George, St Andrew and St Patrick; he made sure Sea Scouts also understood the meaning of three further flags – the Red, White and Blue Ensigns, who flies (or wears) which and where. When used, these must be hoisted not broken. The most important lesson regarding flags for the Sea Scout was not only which way to fly the Union Flag, but when it could be called the Union Jack – it is only known as a Union Jack when it is flown from the Jack staff (at the bows) of a warship; at all other times it is a Union Flag.

In addition to knots, compass, semaphore, Morse, and International Code (flags) instruction, other skills learnt were line throwing – the secret is in the coiling – and 'heaving the lead' to take soundings. Practice would be done from the chains, facing forward, when a ship approached shallow water. As the ship was moored on the port side furthest from the Embankment they 'heaved' the lead from there. This would have been all right if you were left-handed, but if you were right-handed (on *Discovery*) you faced the stern which could result in breaking the port navigation light.

RRS *Discovery* escaped bomb damage during the Blitz, but a trailing cable from a barrage balloon snagged her rigging, ripping off one of the yard-arms, an incident later denied. It was found that the yard-arms were rotten and so they were removed. The Admiralty ordered *Discovery*'s engines and boilers be removed for scrap, an action some conservationists still blame on The Scout Association. When *Discovery* went up for sale the MoD tried to obtain a similar engine but none could be found.

1944

2nd Wallasey Sea Scouts

In 1944 Peter Wilcox spent several days in the Liverpool Bay area, in a crew of 20 aboard an operational Royal Navy minesweeper, one of a small fleet sweeping the shipping channels into Liverpool in case a U-Boat or aircraft had managed to sneak in to lay mines. He recalls carrying out spells of an hour at a time as the sole helmsman at the ship's wheel following a given compass course. Another duty was distributing meals from the galley to various parts of the ship. On one occasion a violent wave threw him against the gunwale and the dinner was propelled from the plate overboard, which required him to return for a replacement! With the ship's motion it was more comfortable to lie down than to stand up.

To detonate magnetic mines, the boat towed a long, thick, insulated black cable which was powered by a special generator. Sometimes paravanes (a form of towed underwater glider) were streamed to cut the anchoring/mooring cables of any mine, although no cables were cut during Peter's trip.

He performed another duty, reloading empty used Lewis machine-gun drums. The Lewis Gun was the lightest armament of the minesweeper, used against attacking aircraft or to explode a released floating mine. There was also a heavier gun with a calibre of about one inch fed from a clip of six shells. The Lewis Gun fired .303-inch rifle-sized bullets. Peter was given several metal boxes, each containing a clip of one type of the bullets: simple ball shot as used in a rifle (bullet-shaped but known as a ball), armour piercing (AP) incendiary (I) and red tracer (T). His task was to refill the drums with their various calibres of bullet.

The food on board was good, and he could always get warm watching the engines from the galley. Peter wrote that his Scouting gave him considerable confidence throughout his life.

National Sea Scout Exhibition – 10-19 April 1944
London Scottish Drill Hall, Buckingham Gate, London, SW1

This was the first national exclusively Sea Scout exhibition. Cost of admission was 1s. 6d. (about £2 today) which included a visit to RRS *Discovery* where Sea Scout boatwork was being demonstrated. Opened on Easter Monday, 10 April by the Mayor of Westminster, a prominent person attended each day. On the first day the Mayor presided with either a Sea Scout or a Sea Ranger, selecting at random, acting as chairman of the exhibition.

The opening ceremony was on a ship's bridge specially constructed for the purpose within the Drill Hall. It looked impossible to get onto the bridge – the funnel was actually a door at the head of a staircase; all the naval speakers were amused at boarding a ship in this way. One very distinguished guest managed to become locked behind the door and it was 45 minutes before the key could be found to effect her release.

HRH Princess Elizabeth, escorted by Sir Percy Everett, Deputy Chief Scout, and Mr P. Denham Christie, Headquarters Commissioner for Sea Scouts, visited the exhibition on 18 April, a few days short of her 18th birthday. The Chief Scout, Lord Somers, was an enthusiastic supporter of the exhibition, but was unable to attend due to ill health; he died in July 1944. At the time Princess Elizabeth was the 'Bosun' of a crew of Sea Rangers recruited from her friends and daughters of Buckingham Palace staff.

The organiser of the exhibition, Mr John Thurman of Scout Headquarters, said:

Its chief value was in giving Sea Scouting new ideas, and interesting other Scouts in Sea Scouting. Providing a nautical atmosphere gave several headaches, but the replica of a ship's bridge at the far end of the hall caught the eye at once, with the mast fitted with signal halyards. A pool in the middle of the hall with model ships afloat on it was built of brick and concrete on sheets of greaseproof paper so no part of the pool came into contact with the main structure of the building. Sea Scouts produced between 300 and 400 models from galleons to destroyers and submarines, including an electronic semaphore instructor.

Boat building was the most popular display, by the Leander Sea Scouts who were building small dinghies especially suitable for sailing on inland waters at a cost of under £5 each (£130 today).

Thirteen thousand people visited the exhibition; all the stewards were Sea Scouts from the main centres of Sea Scouting in the country. John Thurman was asked what the most popular part of the exhibition was for the Sea Scouts and replied that it was the (female) Sea Rangers.

100 *(Left) A visit by Lord Rowallan, who became Chief Scout in 1945, to the 1st Sutton Coldfield Sea Scouts, at Powell's Pool, Sutton Park, Warwickshire, 1944.*

101 *Group photograph taken on the occasion of the visit by Lord Rowallan to the 1st Sutton Coldfield Sea Scouts, Sutton Park, Warwickshire, 1944.*

Sea Scout Sunday, 16 April 1944

This was linked to the exhibition. 1,300 Sea Scouts assembled at the London Scottish Drill Hall at 2 p.m., marched through central London led by the band of the Royal Marines, Chatham Division, to Trafalgar Square and St Martin-in-the-Fields, where a Service of Thanksgiving was held. At the service the speaker, Edward Michael Gresford Jones, Bishop of Willesden, was a Scout.

The Sea Scouts marched back to the exhibition, passing Buckingham Palace and Scout Headquarters on the way. In *The Scouter* magazine it was described 'A most memorable day in the long history of Sea Scouting'. During the march the rain was torrential.

102   *A visit by Lord Rowallan (Chief Scout, 1945) to the 1st Sutton Coldfield Sea Scouts at Powell's Pool, Sutton Park, Warwickshire, 1944.*

1945

Deep Sea Scouts

Jason (Jay) Outhwaite was a Sea Scout in Bradford, Yorkshire, and in 1940 joined the Royal Navy as a telegraphist and was sent for training to HMS *Collingwood*. He found out about Deep Sea Scouts, joined and was issued with a wrist strap with their Scout badge on it. After training he was posted to West Africa and took passage on a Troop Ship. On board were Ralph Reader and his *Gang Show*, all Air Force personnel. During the voyage Ralph saw Jay was wearing a Deep Sea Scout badge, enquired about his Scouting activities and asked if he had appeared in any of his shows. Jay had not and admitted that he could not sing a note.

Although Ralph Reader was a Squadron Leader, everyone called him 'Chief'. He and the RAF *Gang Show* subsequently went on to entertain in North Africa in 1943, the Indian sub-continent and Burma, returning to London before visiting France and Belgium.

1945

Easter 1945 – Minesweeping

A notice appeared in the December 1941 issue of *The Scouter* calling for young men of 17 years of age and over to volunteer to enter the Royal Navy and the Royal Marines under the Admiralty's 'Y' Scheme. A candidate accepted would become a member of the Navy but placed on an unpaid reserve until he was called up for Service.

Geof Simons of the 2nd Wallasey recollected that their Troop was inspected each year by the Admiralty for inclusion in the 'Y' Scheme. They had to show that they were providing adequate basic instruction and training. It was possible during the War for individual Sea Scouts to volunteer to join a minesweeper for a five-day voyage – their own trip actually took ten days. Their parents signed a legal disclaimer over a 5s. stamp (£6.50 today) against all undesirable contingencies.

His account is as follows:

Day 1 Departure:

They reported to the minesweeper base near Four Bridges and went aboard their allocated boats – there was a flotilla of three boats from Merseyside. They passed through the lock gates and sailed down the Mersey on the evening tide. It was with some little apprehension that the Sea Scouts settled down for the night in a seamen's tiny mess in the fo'c'sle. Although the war in Europe was coming to an end, they had seen plenty of damaged Navy ships when rowing around the docks.

The motor minesweepers were small, constructed of timber so as not to activate magnetic mines. Each crew comprised two officers and 14 men in two messes – with insufficient room to swing the proverbial cat (never mind the lead – which sailors are apt to do). The diesel engine was in a tiny, noisy compartment aft. On the quarter-deck was various paraphernalia for the paravanes, hammer, floats, dan-buoys, etc; they were armed with two 1914 machine guns on the bridge and a few rifles.

Day 2 Navigation:

The flotilla sailed up the north-west coast bound for Workington. All was peaceful until hills appeared quite close ahead, and this was a surprise; with much flashing of signal lamps they all did a quick about

103   *The day the Second World War ended. Wolf Cubs, Urswick Sea Scouts, 1945.*

turn. It seemed each boat was following another, including their boat which was supposed to be the flotilla leader. Eventually Workington was found, and as darkness came they tied up alongside. Instead of entering Workington in line ahead with just one pilot, there was a pilot on each boat; such was the confidence of the harbour authorities.

Day 3 Workington, Provision Ship:

This entailed going to the local shops and carrying back supplies. Their boat tied up alongside a Norwegian iron-ore carrier whose crew, who had just sailed from South America, kindly gave them a supply of tinned fruit – a luxury they had not seen for a long time. To get ashore they climbed a long timber ladder fixed at the top of the side of the freighter and at the bottom to their bridge. The fact that the iron ore was being unloaded was forgotten. The ship came gradually higher and higher out of the water, and the ladder was stronger than their bridge … you would know where the damage was done! In the evening all the crews went for a run ashore, taking advantage of the Sea Scouts to act 'duty watch'.

Days 4, 5, 6:

This was off the north-west coast and involved: trailing paravanes on each side of the bow to bring to the surface any contact mines; putting the 'hammer' over the side, which sent out strong sounds and impulses to explode acoustic mines ahead of the boat – unless the mine had a devilish plan of a delay mechanism; the double-L sweep where two long cables were towed behind and a large electric current passed to explode any magnetic mines astern.

On board, the Sea Scouts had the opportunity of a variety of experiences – general seamanship, lookout, steering, knots, splices, peeling potatoes and more potatoes, engine room duties, help with minesweeping gear, etc.

Day 7 Change of Orders:

Much to the dismay of the crews, orders were received to sail for Belfast – they had only expected to be away for five days.

Day 8 Belfast:

The Sea Scouts were sent ashore but when they came to return on board, they were stopped by the police at the dockyard gate, as they had no passes – who ever heard of Sea Scouts sailing on minesweepers? Eventually they were identified by some crew members and allowed through.

Day 9 Homeward:

To get the Sea Scouts home they transferred to a LST (Landing Ship: Tank) to take passage in convoy to Holyhead, Wales. There was a distinct change in the attitudes on board compared with the smaller sweepers. They were considered as Boy Sailors and had their own mess. They were shown over the ship, but spent most of the voyage scraping and painting the Captain's personal sailing dinghy. This was on the upper deck and under his watchful eye from the bridge. The LST had a peculiar and sick-making movement in the sea. The sharp angle of the bow with its bow doors caused it to rise and fall in a series of steps – as if going downstairs; it also developed quite a roll. The minesweepers had the most natural movements of any small boats.

104 *Urswick Sea Scouts – cutter, dressed overall the day war ended.*

Day 10 Back to School:

The Sea Scouts took the train from Holyhead to home, and back to school. The whole adventure, including the tales and vocabulary of the crew, gave a good induction into aspects of Royal Navy life. The friendliness and help from all was remembered as being superb.

As with their Sea Scout predecessors of the 1914-18 War, their proud history in 1939-45 has been mostly overlooked. In a recent exhibition in London about the Thames Emergency Service, etc, there was no mention of the Sea Scouts.

Thus Sea Scouts had continued to do their duty during six long years of war. By 1945 ambitious plans were being made for the future of Sea Scouting.

Petersham and Ham Sea Scouts met continuously throughout the First and Second World Wars. In 1946 they also had an Air Scout Section. It is said they were given a Spitfire aircraft which they buried in the grounds of their Headquarters – both the Group and 'treasure hunters' have been looking for it ever since.

Eight

Sea Scouting, 1946-2009

1946-7

Uniform and equipment were difficult to obtain and expensive, so there followed a period of down-to-earth planning.

1948

XIVth Olympiad

The War over, a postal vote of International Olympic Committee members selected London to host the Olympics, with the sailing events at Torbay, Devon. The War had left Britain with rationing of food, clothing, and housing was in short supply, the 1948 celebrations were known as the 'Austerity Games'.

Lieutenant Commander Horace Taylor, GC, Travelling Commissioner for Sea Scouts, wrote in *The Scouter* magazine, October 1948:

> This was a marvellous opportunity for Sea Scouts to show what they could do. They would have to maintain a crew of 200 Senior Sea Scouts for a fortnight, comprising 50 from the Torbay area, and 150 from the rest of the country, plus a dozen Sea Scouters. The Torquay Local [Scout] Association turned their

105 *Bob-a-Job Week – a Sea Scout combing the dog, Easter 1949.*

106 *Sea Scout signallers' display, London, sending semaphore letter 'C' (ready/ acknowledge), 1947.*

107 *Sea Scout cyclists' Patrol day out, 1950s.*

108   *Senior Sea Scout, c.1950.*

newly-acquired Headquarters into a hotel. The office was like a naval regulating office, Scouts continually signing in and checking out, according to the number of days they could stay (with their ration cards, coupons and points, and fees).

The Sea Scouts were divided into Port and Starboard Watches, each capable of handling a full range of activities. The watches changed over each day after lunch, so there were always at least 90 Scouts on duty.

As soon as the full crew had assembled at Torquay they were called to a dress rehearsal of the Opening Ceremony, when the Torch would be lit at Torre Abbey. They were to muster the National flags and to carry the name boards which preceded the Olympic competitors. The Torchbearers arrived before an audience of 50,000 people, Sea Scouts were prominent everywhere as markers, stewards, flagbearers, and leaders of the parade. The full complement of 200 was on duty, dressed in full uniform, white caps, white scarves, and white gym shoes.

The duty-boys had two main commitments – the Harbour and Marine Spa (the Games HQ). The former involved the ferrying of the competitors, their gear and bags of sails, and their immediate supporters to and fro between the yachts, launches, and jetties; the rigging and launching each day of 27 Fireflies (one-man 14-foot sailing dinghies); also the supervision of the moorings. As their crews became confident in our competence, they were trusted with more work on their precious boats until, eventually, we were out on them alone. One note was dominant throughout, however, 'Scoot, Sea Scoot!'

The harbour parties provided crews for the rescue launches. In one race, three miles out to sea, 19 boats went over. The Paignton Sea Scouts provided a launch which was privileged to wear the official Olympic Flag, which meant that they could be at sea whilst racing was in progress. Their main job was to carry members of the International Jury, whose responsibility was to patrol the bay and keep an eye on the racing.

The Marine Spa party provided messengers, four motor-cycle dispatch riders and interpreters, all at the disposal of Commander Peter Scott's office, the Press, the Sailing Committee, the Information Bureau, and the VIPs. They also issued weather communiqués, having first reduced the Admiralty and Air force signals into language which foreign competitors could understand. During the racing a Scout, armed with a large telescope, broadcast a running commentary to the general public through a system of loudspeakers along the waterfront.

At peak periods they handled assignments at the rate of ten per minute. Some of these were of a short distance, as to the Royal Yacht *Norge* or the battleship HMS *Anson*. Others involved 500 miles travelling to find missing sails. A foreign crew were in a flat spin because the sails of their boat were missing. It was known that they were in England, and that was all. Two Torquay Scouts were sent to Southampton where a search was of no avail, so they went to Portsmouth, then to Cowes where they were successful. They telephoned the distressed crew to set their minds at rest and returned the next day with the sails. It was remarked that the Sea Scouts were the oil within the wheels of the Olympic organisation.

Protests were entered by the competitors for consideration by the Sailing Committee and International Jury. Each protest had to be signalled by International Code from prominent places to the harbour. The Sea Scouts were required to set up and maintain a signal station at the Marine Spa, but ran out of numerals and had to borrow sets of flags from ships in the harbour, and finally radio-telephoned HMS *Anson* to reinforce flag supplies.

It was necessary to collect the witnesses who were required to support the protests. Many had left, so the Sea Scouts had to search all the ships in harbour, the storehouses and workshops, telephoning the hotels of Paignton and Torquay until the missing witnesses were found. The Post Office asked the Sea Scouts to find an American, 'Hawkins', for whom they had a telegram. The Sea Scouts carried out the search routine but in vain. They discovered where William Hawkins was: she was a ship which had been reported as being in difficulty in the English Channel.

What happened to the off-duty watch? Every day 18 of them were aboard the naval patrol vessels, getting a front-seat view of the racing and a good deal of seamanship and coxing experience. Another six were aboard Brixham trawlers, fishing over towards France from 05.00 in the morning until dusk. There were swimming parades and free seats at the Pavilion Theatre. The Captain of HMS *Anson* invited the Scouts to non-public inspections of the ships, and sent launches on separate days so that both watches would be able to go. Another party were invited for a cruise abroad the Swedish training ships, a pair of topsail schooners which were in Torbay for the Games.

The Sea Scouts officiated at the closing ceremony. The Americans won the yachting events; their spokesman, who had won the Gold Medal, devoted much of his speech of acknowledgement to an appreciation of the Sea Scouts to applause from over 1,000 guests.

Crown Prince Olaf of Norway, when expressing his appreciation of the Sea Scouts' work, said that what impressed him most was the eagerly-willing and efficient way in which it was done.

1949/1950

December 1949 – RRS Discovery

This was the busiest year since *Discovery* was presented to the Boy Scouts Association in 1937. In conjunction with the Falkland Island Dependencies Survey, a second large-scale exhibition was opened on 14 December by Lieutenant Commander Peter Scott, MBE, DSC. The distinguished company present at the opening made many appreciative remarks concerning the smartness of the ship.

1950

A Mortlake Tragedy

In August the 1st Mortlake experienced the most tragic incident since formation. On 11 August, the whaler *Wangle III* left Mortlake for a channel cruise in the charge of the Group Scoutmaster John Weeden, with a crew composed of District Commissioner Kenneth Black, Bernard Bell,

109 *The 1st Mortlake Sea Scouts' motor pinnace Minotaur mooring up, c.1947.*

Donald Amos, Peter White, William Towndrow, Brian Peters, Maurice Percival, Robert Walford and William Woods. On 16 August she arrived at Calais, and left port again the following Saturday, at 9.30 a.m.

Wangle III was reported missing, and there followed a most extensive search by aircraft of Coastal Command, and all available shipping for information on the missing Sea Scout whaler. In addition an aircraft was chartered privately by the Boy Scouts Association carrying Mr Sydney Black, brother of District Commissioner Kenneth Black and Mr Scott-Chard of the Admiralty.

The search was abandoned on 26 August without, at that stage, any trace of the missing Scout craft being found.

A service of remembrance for the crew of *Wangle III* was held at St Mary's Parish Church, Mortlake, on Sunday, 10 September. The address was given by the Bishop of Kingston, and the service was attended by Lord Rowallan, Chief Scout, the Mayor and Mayoress, representatives of Boy Scouts Association, the Admiral Commanding Reserves and HMS *President*, and the County Commissioners for Surrey, London, and Middlesex.

French Newspaper Coverage

I visited Calais in 2002 to research further the loss of *Wangle III*. The Central Reference Library in Calais was extremely helpful in making available the original newspapers of the time and providing copies. These reports have not been used or referred to before and provide an account in some detail into the loss of *Wangle III* presenting the tragedy from the perspective of the French press.

Thursday, 24 and Friday, 25 August 1950

VOIX du NORD (Calais) *[Newspaper]*

The editorial carried the information that nine English Scouts and their leader had left at 9.30 a.m. aboard a whaler and were expected on Wednesday afternoon in the Thames Estuary. The Admiralty had sent several reconnaissance boats and several planes for their search.

Concerning the disappearance of the English Scouts, all the Calais correspondents of English newspapers were in a state of alert on Wednesday afternoon concerning the disappearance of a group of young English Scouts and a Naval Officer after listening to the weather forecasts.

On Friday 25 August five planes patrolled above the Channel in the hope of finding the whaler *Wangle III* lost between Calais and the Thames estuary. On take-off the pilot of a tourist plane believed he had spotted a boat that could have been *Wangle III* off Selsey Bill [Sussex]. The pilot, who was flying very low, confirmed he had seen six people aboard the boat who seemed to be heading towards the Atlantic Ocean.

According to a radio message from Ostend, *Wangle III* left Calais on Sunday, and was spotted for the last time on Tuesday off the coast of Denmark. The British and French Admiralties asked all the ships that were in the area to be on the lookout concerning the disappearance of the English Scouts. They were heading for Ramsgate, and since then they have not been seen.

During the evening many requests for news came from London and Paris newspapers and agencies.

Three hypotheses could explain the disappearance of the English Scouts.

The first one would be that they had a tragic end after spending a happy holiday on the continent. The embarkation was questionable and misadventure cannot be written off.

The second hypothesis is that the team, being in difficulty, could have been picked up by a merchant ship without a radio on board.

Third and last hypothesis. – the group changed their mind and instead of heading towards Ramsgate, they set sail towards another harbour without thinking that their long silence would raise concern.

The editorial concluded by saying:

Let us pray that we don't have a drama on our hands, but that it will be a lesson to all young people who don't hesitate to take risks abroad, with inadequate knowledge about navigation, who sail on lakes and rivers and the treacherous North Sea.

Tuesday, 29 August 1950
VOIX du NORD (Calais)

THE BODY OF ONE OF THE TEN ENGLISH SCOUTS HAS BEEN
SPOTTED FLOATING IN THE SEA

Disembarking from the liner *Indictor* from Dover, which moored in the naval harbour of Calais, was Mr Michael Andrew from the Imperial Headquarters of The Scout Association, accompanied by Mrs Weeden, the wife of the officer from the Royal Navy who disappeared in the North Sea with nine Sea Scouts.

Mrs Weeden still hopes that the boat will be found eventually. She went to the Harbour Office with Mr Andrew to talk to the officer.

They still had to go to the quay again in order to have an interview with the owners of the fishing boat close to where the whaler was moored.

Wednesday, 30 August 1950

VOIX Du NORD (Calais) *Editorial*

TEN DAYS LATER STILL NO NEWS FROM THE SCOUTS

We are still without any news concerning the young English Scouts sailing in the whaler and heading towards Ramsgate on Saturday, 19 August. Scout Leaders came to Calais to investigate the circumstances concerning the departure of the young navigators, and the Naval Officer who was in charge.

They tried to discover what more information they could, but no precise details were ever established. No bodies have been found, neither on the seashore nor at sea, and there has been no trace of the whaler.

They left none the wiser. In the meantime Mr Michael Andrew, from Scout Headquarters, went to Gravelines and Dunkirk in order to question the sailors from those two harbours.

Tuesday, 12 September 1950

Shipwreck, English Channel – House of Commons Debate

Commander Pursey asked the Minister of Transport whether he had any statement to make on the loss of ten lives in the Sea Scouts' whaler *Wangle III* on 20 August. The Minister of Transport (Mr Barnes) replied that a preliminary inquiry under the Merchant Shipping Acts into the loss of the whaler would be held.

Sunday, 24 September 1950

VOIX du NORD (Calais)

Captain Lewis, representing the Royal Navy [Ministry of Transport], investigated the facts concerning the disappearance in the Straits [of Dover] of the whaler *Wangle III* with the English Scouts.

Captain Lewis said that at the British Consulate in Calais he had questioned M. Deplanq who was the watchman of the Courgain building [fishermen's quarters] being erected at Calais Harbour, where the Scouts slept during their stay.

Another unexpected witness was M. Eugene Menard, a Calais ships' chandler, who had spotted the Scouts when they came out of the building with their luggage and cooking utensils. He said the young sailors pushed off the boat with the help of oars towards the Paul-Devot Quay and then two of them who had remained on the wharf climbed on board the whaler which moved off. After a few moments they brought the oars on board, the sail was hoisted and then the whaler went towards the jetty.

1951

The Ministry of Transport felt that as there was such a serious loss of life and a great deal of publicity it was advisable to hold an Inquiry.

19-22 February 1951

Court of Inquiry – The Merchant Shipping Act, 1894

Report of Court (No. 7969)

The findings of the Court of Inquiry were delivered on 19 March 1951.

These can be summarised as follows:

- Whether for use on the river or at sea there was a need for permanent buoyancy tanks and lifelines; improved lifebelts of the kapok type should also be provided.

- The Court thought that a crew of ten was too many, and should not exceed seven or eight. *Wangle* was structurally seaworthy but being an open un-ballasted boat she was not the ideal craft for a channel cruise.

- The Court said it would be desirable that the Policy Organisation and Rules of the Boy Scout Association should contain more detailed instructions on sea cruises to destinations outside the United Kingdom.

- The Court was of the opinion that closer touch should be kept on intended movements and routes of cruises outside the United Kingdom.

- Such trips are essentially different from trips on land and it is considered desirable that a maximum number of crew should be laid down; restrictions in the age of the crew should be laid down as well as minimum equipment, space, and proper distress signals.

- Closer touch should be kept but insistence on 'departure' reports would be impracticable.

Use of Whalers for Cross-Channel Cruising

The Court took the view that such vessels are open and un-ballasted, and if they do encounter a cross sea, e.g., where the wind is against the tide, that is one of the worst conditions even when manned by a seasoned and experienced crew. Such seas are dependent on the state of the weather with a wind not more than force 3 to 4.

Cause of the Disaster

What caused the disaster remained a matter of speculation.

It might have been run down by a larger vessel, or it was possible that it might have struck submerged wreckage.

In the conditions of good visibility, it was unlikely that the whaler was run down by another vessel.

The possibility that the whaler came into contact with a moored or floating mine was also remote but this could not be entirely excluded.

In all probability the boat was overwhelmed in a confused cross-sea, caused by a high wind against a contrary tide. *Wangle III* might have capsized which in fact was the most probable cause of the loss.

Sympathy for Relatives of the Crew

The *News Chronicle* reported, 'They had the spirit of adventure which is the essence of their Movement, but they were not rash. They formed a trained crew under skilled command.'

Geoff Preshner today recalls attending post-war Sea Scout Courses on RRS *Discovery* where John Weeden instructed him on navigation – 'He was fair but firm'. John Weeden was awarded the Distinguished Service Cross (DSC) in 1942 for gallantry, skill and endurance while serving in HM Torpedo Boats.

The 1st Mortlake Sea Scouts closed in 2001 and the Scout Headquarters building in Alder Road became a crèche. The colours and one remaining fragment from the stern of the whaler were transferred to the continuing safe keeping at Texel Scout Headquarters.

Sunday, 20 February 2005
Rededication of Wangle III Memorial Plaque
St Mary the Virgin, Mortlake High Street

It was decided that the bronze memorial plaque (24" x 14") bearing the names of the crew of *Wangle III* which had been placed in the Mortlake Scout Headquarters should be moved and rededicated in the parish church of St Mary's, Mortlake, close by.

IN HONOURED MEMORY
OF THE CREW OF THE
1ST MORTLAKE WHALER
WANGLE III LOST IN
THE ENGLISH CHANNEL
RETURNING FROM CALAIS
19TH AUGUST 1950

J. WEEDEN, D.S.C. G.S.M.	B. PETERS
D. AMOS	W. TOWNDROW
B. BELL	R. WALFORD
K. BLACK (D.C. KENSINGTON)	P. WHITE
M. PERCIVAL	W. WOODS)

The plaque was rededicated at the family service attended by the Mayor of Richmond-upon-Thames, Councillor Pat Parsons, who unveiled the memorial plaque on the south wall of the church. Brenda Moore, Christopher and James Weeden, the daughter and sons of John Weeden, family and friends of those lost, Scouts from Texel (Holland), Scouters, Guides, Cub Scouts and Brownies from Richmond attended along with former members of the 1st Mortlake Group. Mike Nadin and Roy Masini represented Sea Scouting.

1954

25-7 June 1954

Senior Sea Scout Cruise – Tower Bridge to Maldon, Essex

They Did Not Forget their Drill

At six o'clock on Friday evening, 25 June 1954, a party of 23 London Sea Scouts set out from London's Tower Bridge for a weekend sail-training cruise to the River Blackwater on the east coast.

The entire party was on board a 52-foot ex-naval Sea Scout motor boat called the *Quintinian*, which was towing three 27-foot admiralty sailing whalers. The Sea Scouts were seated on the deck of the *Quintinian* learning about the various features of the river and the use of ship's lights as darkness fell.

They sailed through the night and at dawn were off Brightlingsea, which is the entrance to the River Blackwater. At this point the Sea Scouts manned the three whalers and rigged them for sail under the instruction the Assistant Sea Scout Leader, Geoffrey Preshner. Through Saturday they proceeded under sail down the Blackwater heading for Maldon, leaving the *Quintinian* to rendezvous at the same area on Sunday morning.

All went well and on Sunday morning the boats met up at sea as arranged. Once again the whalers were put on tow behind the *Quintinian* heading back on the long journey to Tower Bridge. After about an hour, the *Quintinian* stopped because of engine failure. With the wind coming offshore at about Force 4 all of the boats were being driven out to sea towards France. The *Quintinian* now radioed for assistance and a collier, which was heading for London, responded and came alongside. Towlines were attached to the *Quintinian* and the captain of the collier ordered that a few people should go into the last whaler in order to steer the tail. Geoff Preshner and three of the boys, Alan Day, John Heseltine and Malcolm Ward, all aged 15-16, undertook this duty.

The collier then set off at about 8-10 knots, which was too fast for the smaller boats, causing the last in the line to fill rapidly with water which was coming in through the drop keel casing. Recognising the imminent danger, Geoff Preshner made sure that all of the boys had their life jackets securely fastened. He then tried to indicate to the *Quintinian* the problem facing them in the hope of slowing the vessel and relieving the flooding of the whaler. Someone on the *Quintinian* then mistakenly cut the towline. Immediately, the whaler nose-dived under sea and went a long way down, throwing everyone into the water. The occupants came to the surface and the sea was empty. After a few minutes the whaler resurfaced but remained awash. Geoff indicated to the boys to swim to the whaler and spread around it and hang on. Understandably the boys were very distressed and had to be constantly reassured that they would be rescued. The sea was very cold

110 *Paddy Lawrence, Training Department, Scout Headquarters, addresses Deep Sea Scouts 'Get Together' at Baden-Powell House, South Kensington, London, in 1965.*

and after about 40 minutes a ferry was just about to dock at Clacton, but received the SOS and immediately set out for the distress area.

Having arrived there, the captain instructed two of the boys to swim towards his vessel. All the while the 400 passengers of the ferry lined the rail to observe the rescue and take photographs. At the same time another merchant vessel had arrived and lowered a rowing boat to assist in the rescue. Geoff and the third boy were picked up in this way. As result two boys were taken to Clacton on the ferry, and Geoff and the other boy were taken to London. They were given hot soup followed by a hot shower before bunking down for five hours' fast asleep.

On landing at Tilbury, they were met by reporters from the London newspapers who all wanted the story. This incident happened on what was regarded as a 'no news day' and appeared on the front page of the dailies on Monday. A week later Geoff received a telegram from the BBC inviting him to appear on the television show *Guess My Story* on 4 July. The programme had a panel of celebrities, including Jack Train, Helen Cherry and Jon Pertwee, who had to decide why the contestants had been in the news. This did not present them with too much of a problem because it had been in all the national newspapers.

Geoff continued to serve with distinction in Sea Scouting and the Sea Cadets for over 50 years and was awarded the Silver Acorn by the Scouts Association and the Sea Cadet Medal. Even after all these years this incident is still fresh in the mind of Geoff Preshner, now Lieutenant Commander (SCC), MBE, RNR.

1955

Sea Scout Jerseying

Miss C. Ashton from Leicester wrote to the author about how the letters were put on the front Sea Scouts jerseys just before and after the War.

In those days it was done by hand – I expect the work is done by machine now – and my mother and aunts did it, so I more or less grew up among 'the jerseys.'

In those days it was work that women could do at home especially if they had small children and if, like my two aunts, they lived near one of the Leicester factories (I believe it was Stretton's) and then went to a workroom nearby where the letters were cut out of thick paper and attached to the jersey with strong glue. (I remember going with my mother when I was about four; the work was done in the back room of a large terraced house and I saw the big pot of strong-smelling glue sitting by the hearth and open fire). A piece of thick canvas was then glued onto the inside of the jersey to back the letters.

The jersey then went out to the home workers, together with a supply of 'Mrs Smith's card', which was like wool but stronger; in the case of the Scouts it was white. The home worker then stitched over the letters, very hard work as she also had to go through the canvas backing.

Some of the jerseys then had the lettering backed with a piece of thin flannel. The Sea Scout jerseys were not the most popular, as the pay for them was not very good, but there always seemed more of them than anything else.

My mother gave up the 'jerseying' in the late 1940s, but my aunts kept it on for years afterwards. Sometimes mother would be persuaded to do a dozen or two if there was a big order. I have a piece of paper which records that in 1955 she was paid 18 shillings [90p] for 2 dozen Sea Scout jerseys.

1957 Whitsun

Longridge Scout Boating Centre opened on the Thames at Marlow to replace RRS *Discovery*.

112 *(Below) 1st Mortlake Sea Scouts Group Photograph – Jubilee Celebration, May 1959.*

Uniform Details

of the Sea Scout and Sea Scouter.

111 *(Above) Sea Scouting booklet re-published 1957. The diagram shows uniform details of a Sea Scout and a Sea Scouter.*

113 *A scene from the National Boating Centre, Longridge, Buckinghamshire – a Cub Scout just fishing while ITV looks on, c.1970.*

The London Sea Scout Meets 1949-84

For many Sea Scout Groups these Meets were a high point, and were normally organised every other year. The following are some accounts of these.

Geoff Preshner wrote about the history of the Meets:

> Once again nearly 1,000 Sea Scouts went to Camp at Chatham in Kent over the Whitsun weekend. These Sea Scout Camps at Whitsun, we call Whitsun Meets, have been held by the London Sea Scout Committee since 1949, first at a site at Erith, and subsequently in the grounds of Ingress Abbey, the shore establishment of HMS *Worcester* at Greenhithe. They culminated in the Meet of 1957 attended by 360 Scouts from 19 London Groups, also Surrey and Kent, together with the joint London Sea Scout Troop that later represented London Sea Scouting at the World Jamboree at Sutton Park.

The First Sea Lord, Admiral of the Fleet Earl Mountbatten of Burma, spent Whit Sunday afternoon in the Camp and presented an engraved glass dish to the retiring Captain-Superintendent of HMS *Worcester*, Captain G.C. Steele, VC, RNR, who had been host for so many years at Greenhithe. In making the presentation on behalf of London Sea Scouting, Earl Mountbatten was acting in his capacity as Commodore of Sea Scouts.

114 *The National Scout Boating Centre, Longridge, Buckinghamshire – memories of oil-drum rafting, c.1970.*

115 *The National Boating Centre, Longridge, Buckinghamshire – sheer enjoyment, c.1970.*

116   *The Chatham Sea Scout Meet, 5 June 1960. Lord Mountbatten addresses Sea Scouts and Sea Rangers.*

In 1959 by permission of Commander-in-Chief Nore, the Whitsun Sea Scout Meets were moved to Chatham Dockyard. Last year the Meet was again visited by the Commodore of Sea Scouts with 1,500 Sea Scouts in attendance.

A message received after the 1960 Meet, from the Commodore for Sea Scouts, Admiral the Earl Mountbatten of Burma

'My Dear Scouts,

In sending you this message I would like first, as your Commodore, to express on your behalf the thanks of us all to the Nore Command of the Royal Navy whose most generously-given assistance has made this whole weekend possible. Without their aid there could have been no Meet at Chatham, and I would have been denied the pleasure of seeing you. I would also like to voice your thanks and add my congratulations to all the Scouters who gave up so much of their time to organise the Meet. I am sure that their efforts are amply repaid, not only by the pleasure that they have given to so many of you, but also in the important effect of the Meet on the youth of the Country.

And I would like to thank every one of you for the grand welcome that you gave me. I am sure that similar events will be organised in future years and that they will strengthen the links that draw Sea Scouts together. It may be that, if circumstances permit, I shall be able to visit you again and I very much hope that you and your group will be there to meet me.

Yours very sincerely
Mountbatten of Burma
Commodore for Sea Scouts

Because the camp is always very near to water, camping and boating take up the major part of the camp.'

1970

Invited to return to Chatham by the Superintendent of the Naval Dockyard, just over 1,000 Sea Scouts and Sea Rangers attended the Meet. The weather was fine and there was keen competition during the regattas held for sailing and pulling boats, indoor rifle shooting, films and a disco in the evening, and the NAAFI shop was well supported.

In 1956 Chatham had become home to the standby or reserve fleet and also a number of operational ships were based at the Dockyard. For many of the young Sea Scouts attending this was

117   *The 99th Bristol (Cabot) Sea Scouts – boatwork.*

118, 119 & 120   *The Chatham Sea Scout Meet, 1961. 'The Great Tow' from London Bridge, arriving at HM Dockyard, Chatham on the River Medway, Kent.*

a mecca of Naval affairs. Many interesting ships were mothballed, and it was possible to see around these if the Shipkeeper or reserve crew allowed you to do so. Security was very tight, as this was still a fully-operational base, and there were many areas which were very much out of bounds, the Ministry of Defence (MoD) Police, both uniformed and CID, being very much in evidence. What was not known at the time was that the fleet of nuclear submarines were all being refitted and refuelled at Chatham between 1970 and 1983, the work being centred on the Nuclear Refitting and Refuelling complex based between nos 6-7 docks which had opened in 1968.

1984

The decision to close HM Dockyard Chatham, where the Sea Scouts Meets had been held since 1960, was announced in November 1981 but it was not until March 1984 that the yard finally closed, and the last London Sea Scout Meet was held there. In the intervening three years a final round of refits and repairs was undertaken, particularly during the short but unexpected 1982 Falklands War. The Chatham-based South Atlantic Patrol Ship HMS *Endurance* was adopted by various Sea Scout and Sea Cadet units, as is its successor which bears the same name.

One of my abiding memories of the 1984 Meet was being invited by the Chief Petty Officers to play bowls against them in the spacious hall of the now-empty Admiral Superintendent's official residence.

For some time the Sea Scout Committee searched for a new venue for the Meets, but very sadly, either on grounds of cost, distance or facilities, none could be found.

121 *The 4th Seven Kings Sea Scouts. Project 'Seven Kings', 1963-9. Launch of the 16-ton ketch by Mrs Gardiner, 1970.*

122 & 123   *The 4th Seven Kings Sea Scouts. Project 'Seven Kings', 1963-9. Laying the keel of the 16-ton ketch at Hargreaves Scout Campsite, Chadwell Heath (now Greater London).*

1974/5

Wake Up, Captain Mainwaring

From 1940 the Home Guard were on the 'front line' in the eventuality of an invasion across the English Channel. *Dad's Army*, a comedy television series, was located in the fictional seaside town of Walmington-on-Sea, Kent although most of the external scenes were filmed around Thetford, Norfolk. The series was broadcast on BBC Television between 1968 and 1977, gained an audience of 18 million viewers and is still repeated worldwide. Various episodes featured a local 'Sea Scout' Troop.

Tim Bell, who wrote the following article in the *Dad's Army Appreciation Magazine* issue of December 1999, contacted me. The episode in which he appeared was broadcast in October 1975. The storyline was that the Home Guard, at weekend camp, were disturbed by the Vicar, Verger and

124   *The 1st Reading Sea Scouts – Dragon Boat racing at Caversham, Berkshire, on the River Thames.*

Sea Scouts who also intended to camp there. The next morning finds three enemy airmen stranded in a rubber dinghy on a local lake nearby. Tim Bell recalled:

It all started with the bi-annual Thetford Scout and Guide Gangshow in November 1974. In the audience was a BBC researcher, talent spotting. Three months later the Leader of the 2nd Thetford, Ray Parish, was contacted by the BBC, as they wanted to tell us some 'exciting news!' I can remember the evening well – it was Troop night, and we were told we had been selected to be extras in a forthcoming episode of *Dad's Army – Come In, Your Time is Up!*

We were to film in June and would spend a Friday and all day Saturday filming. We were briefed about what we would be doing. They wanted somebody who could play a bugle to join in for filming on the Wednesday as well. I was honoured to be asked, and it seemed June would never come!

When it did we, as a Troop, met all the stars at the *Bell Hotel* for an evening meal on the Monday. We had our 'short back and sides' [haircut] complete with Brylcreem in the make-up caravan outside.

Wednesday was a scorcher. Ray and I sat chatting with Arthur Lowe [Captain Mainwaring] and Ian Lavender [Frank Pike], joined them for breakfast then boarded the coach for the Battle area at West Tofts. We were greeted by the producers, shown where everything was and told the rules about quiet, etc.

First watched the 'keep fit' scene and then the eating of the rabbit stew. Then came my bit; we pretended to have tent full of Scouts when 'Come on boys into the trees' was said by Frank Williams [the Vicar]. In fact it was only me in there. That only took about an hour to film. After lunch, Mary Husband took me and made me up, and explained what was going to happen (it turned out she would be 'Mum' to us throughout our time on set). I knew it was soon to be my turn as Bill Pertwee [Air Raid Warden] joked with me that if I got it right first time he would let me keep the sixpence [part of the plot]!

Now came the first shock; when the Beeb guy had come to our Scout hut he said he wanted the bugler to play Reveille. I can assure you I practised that until all the neighbours had moved out! But now here I was, and they wanted me to play it a bit different – they wanted it to sound a bit more 'painful'. They seemed pleased with the result so we were set.

We practised for about one hour then it was for real. It was planned for all the small tents to be full but it was so hot only Arthur was in his. I was very nervous but when the time came the butterflies went and there I was. It took two takes – as I recall in the first one my lips were too dry and the bugle just squeaked, then after the hilarity ceased we did it again and this time all went well. Everybody clapped and we broke for tea. The remainder of the day we rehearsed for the next day's filming. My exams were through so what the heck!

The next two days were spent filming the crashed German airmen with Clive Dunn/stunt man snorkel swimming and Bill Pertwee falling in the lake. Again on the Saturday we all met at the Bell, had breakfast and hopped on the coach. Today was Pirate day, the whole day devoted to the 2nd Thetford Scouts. Firstly was the arrival in the van, then the raft scene. It took many takes as some of us got the giggles, along with the crew! I was amazed how long it took to film, considering how short each section was in the finished scenes. We finished filming at 5 p.m. and went home buzzing with the day's events.

I did very well with £50 wages in my pocket plus sixpence of course. Mary explained that it is all they could give me due to Equity Union rules, but I was more than pleased. At the time I was 14, I am now 38 [2001] but I remember it as if it were yesterday. I stood in front of my school telling them of my escapades – they couldn't wait to see it go out. The only sad part is Ray (our Scout Leader) passed away in 1983. He was instrumental in it all and took most of the pictures which I still have (he, by the way, was the tallest pirate).

Tim Bell wrote to say:

I need to put the record straight and tell you that the 2nd Thetford were Land Scouts, cleverly transformed into Sea Scouts. This was done because they had no Sea Scouts close by. All of the uniform badges are painted. Jack Wheeler did just that and saw that 'Walmington' was spelt 'Warmington' on one of the uniforms! Naturally as the Home Guard were based by the sea it was only natural to have Sea Scouts in the episode and we at 2nd Thetford, enjoyed the transformation.

Postscript

During my research Jimmy Perry, who co-wrote the series with David Croft, contacted me to explain why he had written Sea Scouts into the series. He said he had found the Sea Scouts to be very smart and they illustrated the patriotic feelings of the time, particularly when he was in the Home Guard at the age of 16.

1974

Annual Report, The Scout Association 1974/1975, Time & Tide Magazine, *1975, the London Gang Show Fellowship*

The Farewell London Gang Show – *November*

'The greatest shop window for Scouting', as Baden-Powell described the London Gang Show, drew its final curtain on 2 November closing its two weeks at the Gaumont State Theatre, Kilburn. The house was full every night as this unique entertainment moved towards the achievement of 423 performances over 42 years. Visitors to the Farewell Show included the Prime Minister, the Rt Hon. Harold Wilson, Lord Rowallan, Lord Maclean and Chief Scout, Sir William Gladstone. The thunderous applause which greeted Ralph Reader at the end of the last show gave fitting expression to The Association's gratitude for his long and valuable service.

Sea Scouts were always well represented as members of the cast of the London Gang Show, as programme sellers and providing guards of honour required for VIPs, and particularly royalty and for the Commodore of Sea Scouts.

When I interviewed Ralph Reader for *Time & Tide Magazine* in May 1975 when reviewing his book *Ralph Remembers* (1975), he told me he had always considered himself to be a Sea Scouter. He recalled that, in 1937:

Five of us – all Sea Scouts – had an old Navy motor patrol boat moored on the river near Kingston. In the morning we would go out in our pulling boat, have breakfast on the motor boat and then go off to

Kingston Church. Back for lunch on the boat during the afternoon and after we had tired of yarning we would go our various ways. Myself, I usually work on my latest show or have a shot at writing a song or two before I turn in.

He was Skipper of the Gang.

He wrote the words and music to the song which will always be associated with the *Gang Shows*, *I'm Riding Along on the Crest of a Wave* (1934). Ralph Reader, CBE, died in 1982.

1975
Police Constable Stephen Tibble
The national press reported:

Stephen Andrew Tibble, aged 21, was a keen Sea Scout and Leader. He joined the Metropolitan Police on 12 August 1974, attended Hendon Police College, and had been a police officer for three months, posted to Fulham Police Station as PC179F in December 1974. He died on Wednesday 26 February 1975 when he was shot while assisting two plain-clothes officers in the execution of their duty.

PC Tibble died in Charing Cross Hospital at 4.50 p.m. leaving a 20-year-old widow.

125 *Sea Scout of the 99th Bristol (Cabot) operating a radio-controlled model ship, Longridge, Buckinghamshire, 1973.*

Dr John Barton, sitting at Hammersmith's Coroner's Court on Tuesday 4 March said, 'Quite clearly he knew what he was doing and knew it was his duty. He knowingly gave his life trying to stop an armed gunman'.

On Monday 10 March, 40 members of the 3rd Osterley Sea Scouts formed a guard of honour at the officer's funeral at Mortlake Crematorium. 1,000 mourners attended with officers from the Metropolitan Police, the Surrey, Hertfordshire, Sussex and Thames Valley Constabularies also present. Sir Robert Mark, Commissioner of the Metropolitan Police, gave the oration: 'The selfless devotion of this young man was to the cause which all police officers in Britain are dedicated – the protection of people'.

On Friday, 18 June 1976, PC Tibble was posthumously awarded the Queen's Police Medal for Gallantry and the Bronze Cross of The Scout Association for courage in the line of duty. Sir Robert Mark said 'We and the Public he served so selflessly are forever in his debt'.

'The Steve Tibble Award' provided to the 3rd Osterley Sea Scout Group by Wilkinson Sword is presented annually in his memory for service. The sword is a replica of the one used by Captain Cook.

1984

Mr Maurice Gardener and Scouting *magazine, August 1984*

MTB 102 – Full ahead – Both Engines

The Dunkirk Veteran which became a Sea Scout Training Ship in Norfolk

MTB (Motor Torpedo Boat) *102* was designed in 1936, launched in May 1937 and the Admiralty paid around £16,000 for her. She was 68 feet in overall length and one of the fastest vessels in the

126   *MTB 102, Norwich Sea Scouts.*

Royal Navy, with a speed of 43 knots or more. She was a heroine in the Second World War, a film star, and home to Sea Scouts.

In 1940, MTB *102* took part in the evacuation of Dunkirk. Used by Rear Admiral Wake-Walker as Flagship for the last two nights at Dunkirk, though heavily attacked, she was one of the last three ships to leave, after which MTBs were continually engaged in the waters of the Channel and North Sea. In 1944, MTB *102* embarked Winston Churchill and General Eisenhower to review the Fleet assembled for the 'D' Day landings.

In October 1945, '*102*' was sold into private ownership and converted into a motor cruiser. After 20 years she went on the market again and eventually fetched up in Norfolk where the 1st Blofield and Brundall Sea Scouts came into the story, and in particular Maurice Gardener, the Group Scout Leader. They were looking for a floating headquarters, and heard that an MTB was for sale, with land for moorings. At a cost of £5,000 a deal was brokered. When the illustrious history of MTB was discovered the idea of restoring her to her original condition was born.

In 1976 Kelso Films came on the scene seeking an MTB for use in their production *The Eagle has Landed* starring Michael Caine. They agreed to refurbish MTB *102* in her wartime appearance and then to return her to the Sea Scouts after filming as a fully-operational sea-going vessel.

The ship had to change nationalities into a German ship for the film. She also appeared in a 1977 documentary, *Soldiers of Orange*, during which time she was given replica torpedo tubes, guns and ammunition lockers and looked as she had done during her War service. During The Queen's Silver Jubilee celebrations *102* had the honour of leading the Royal Yacht *Britannia* upstream during the great River Thames Pageant. She also attended the 1979 Navy Days representing

127   *64th Birkenhead Sea Scouts.*

'Yesterday's Navy'. There were some raised eyebrows when she appeared at various events when it seemed that Sea Scouts were manning an apparently armed Naval vessel (all imitation).

She was taken over by the Norwich Area Scout Council and made regular trips to sea where she was used to train youngsters particularly in coastal navigation. On passage past Dungeness and up through Dover, messages came over the VHF radio from foreign trawlers, 'Polizei', being the only identifiable word – as they were fishing or otherwise in the wrong place at the wrong time.

The vessel is now owned by the MTB Trust dedicated to keeping her afloat, she travels around the coasts and is a VIP at various events.

1971-2009

Discovery Sailing Project

The project was founded in 1971 by the Discovery Committee who ran courses for Scouts and Guides on the RRS *Discovery*. The aims of the Discovery Sailing Project are the same as those of the Scout Movement and it exists to take Scouts and other young people to sea, aboard offshore yachts, in order to promote their development in achieving their full physical, intellectual, social and spiritual potential, as individuals, as responsible citizens and as members of their local, national and international communities. The Discovery Sailing Project operate:

Thermopylae Clipper, a 60-ton round-the-world yacht, which has accommodation for 124 trainees and three after guard.

Discovery DSP, a purpose-built 45 Sea stream 445 Cutter taking nine trainees and three after guard.

Alexander Fairey, a 34ft sloop used mainly for training of after guard.

The Sailing Project operates from its base on the River Hamble; its main cruising area is the south coast. It also takes part in the annual Tall Ships Race.

The Dockland Scout Project

The remarkable story of the Dockland Scout Project (DSP) spans over three decades, a registered charity in its own right with the Discovery Dockland Trust retaining a supportive role. Their aim is to run training courses for Scouts, Guides and others based on the training programme of the Scout and Guide Movements. The bias of their work is towards disciplined water activities for young people providing a unique base for Scouts in this country and from overseas. It is the only permanently-moored campsite in the UK situated in the heart of London – with scope to explore as the Docklands Light Railway is close by.

Conservation in Action – the Ship that came back from the Dead

In 1982 the Project acquired the ex-pilot cutter *Algol* now called *Lord Amory*. The Dutch-built 600-ton trawler spent part of the Second World War lying on the seabed. The *Algol*, a 150 foot/47

128   *Dockland Scout Project (DSP) Training Ship* Lord Amory, *formerly the ex-Dutch Pilot Ship* Algol, *600 tonnes, 150ft – the centrepiece of the project.*

metre, ex-Dutch Pilot Cutter, was built in Arnhem in the late 1930s and was launched in 1939. The Dutch Navy scuttled her to stop the enemy using the vessel. After hostilities ceased the ship was re-floated and used as a pilot cutter.

During 1976-7 she was given a major refit to equip her for work as a stationary pilot vessel and customs chaser. In this role the *Algol* was moored out to sea with 40-or-so pilots on board, who would be transferred when needed to ships needing guidance into and out of Rotterdam, and

occasionally used as a survey ship. The vessel was due to end her ocean-going days supplying North Sea oil rigs, but instead she was sold to the Dockland Scout Project.

Purchased for £30,000 by the Discovery Dockland Trust, a £39,000 refit was carried out. *Algol's* main engine and auxiliaries, all pumps, seacocks, rudder and propeller were removed and a great deal of the interior reorganised. A team of about 80 volunteers and helpers with specialist marine skills gutted the main engine room and built a new floor so that the space could serve as a conference

129   *Dockland Scout Project (DSP) workshop, store rooms, shower block and mess deck area,* c.2000.

130   *Dockland Scout Project – HQ Training Ship,* Lord Amory, *formerly Pilot Ship* Algol.

131   *The annual Devizes-to-Westminster Race – Sea Scouts from Longridge Canoe Club canoeing by Westminster Bridge, London.*

hall and lecture room. Two deck cranes fitted amidships were removed, along with the main anchor capstan, anchors and tons of anchor chains to provide forward storage space. The fo'c'sle became a wardroom, and central heating installed in *Algol*'s cabins. The entire task was an enormous one.

The Project was provided with a berth for *Algol*, new storage racks for canoes, equipment, with Portakabin facilities for office and administration use. A permanent shore-based building to the Project's own design was provided by the London Dockland Development Corporation at Dollar Bay. Grants and facilities were a great help in progressing the work.

The ship accommodates more than 50 people in two- to six-berth cabins. The residential project runs for about 30 weeks of the year. One-day and weekend courses are supplemented by evening activities including first aid, radio telephony, seamanship theory, boat maintenance, outboard engine servicing, repairs, and navigation. A fleet of over 100 craft is available from canoes to large offshore craft which can operate within the dock complex. DSP also operate on the River Thames and around the south and east coasts of England. The Project is considered one of the best voluntary-run water activities centres in the country.

2001

Sail Training Yacht Discovery

Extract – Scouting *magazine, August 2001*

Her name inspires a sense of adventure, a sleek, white ocean-going yacht, cutting a fine edge through the water. *Discovery* is the latest, specially-commissioned, addition to the Discovery Sailing Project, the offshore arm of the Dockland Scout Project, which is based at the West India Docks on the River Thames. After an absence of 15 years a vessel bearing the name *Discovery* has returned to the River Thames.

The £300,000 yacht was built in Falmouth to DSP specifications by Sea Stream International, with the assistance of Lottery funding and brought to London. Clive Fisher, the organiser, said it was a dream come true, a boat of a very high calibre, very much a 21st-century vessel.

Mike Nadin, Chairman of the Discovery Project, paid tribute to the ship with a famous name. 'It's a continuity of the spirit. Many of us on the old project were in awe of Captain Scott – he was one of our heroes. To have a state-of-the-art ship like this is magnificent.'

On Friday, 1 June, she was escorted under Tower Bridge by police and fire tenders on her way to the Project's Headquarters. She was moored overnight in Dollar Bay in West India Docks, lying alongside the *HQ Training Ship, Lord Amory*. At her naming ceremony the following afternoon, she was named *Discovery* by the guest of honour, Lady Philippa Scott, widow of Captain Scott's son, Sir Peter Scott. A blessing by the Rev. Steve Burgess completed the occasion. The yacht's arrival was cause for great celebration, and the excitement and joy could be felt all around.

The next three weeks were spent taking youngsters on short sailing trips on the Thames. Entered for the prestigious Cutty Sark Tall Ships Race she departed with a full complement at the end of June to sail from Antwerp to Alesund in Norway returning via Esbjerg, Bergen and Amsterdam to her operating base on the River Hamble in early September. The aim of the Tall Ships Race Series is to bring together youngsters aged 16 to 25 of many nationalities to promote international understanding.

2004-9

In 2004 DSP provided one of the facilities to promote the announcement of a new Chief Scout, Peter Duncan. In 2005 it assisted in the Nelson flotilla celebrating the 200th Anniversary on the River Thames, and in 2007 it hosted the European Sea Scout Armada to celebrate 100 years of Scouting.

132 *Peter Duncan on his appointment as Chief Scout in May 2004 visits Dockland Scout Project, West India Dock, London, to sample canoeing and other activities.*

European Scout Armada, 2007

DSP accommodated the London part of the Armada in late July and early August. Boats sailed from Norway and Poland to join up in Ostend with other boats from France, Portugal, Holland and Belgium before crossing the English Channel to Ramsgate and come up the River Thames to Docklands. Over 16 boats made the journey to London and 16 boats remained in Ostend due to the weather. The largest boat was the *Zawisza Czarny*, a 40-metre Polish yacht which moored alongside the *Lord Amory*. The Thames River pilots who piloted the *Zawisza* up-river donated the fee to help with the costs of the Armada.

In 2008 DSP were used to launch the 'Kids Outdoors' initiative, a campaign to inspire new outdoor activities for children.

133 *The 4th Streatham Sea Scouts boating at Putney, 2001. In the background is MV Ellen Elizabeths.*

2009

16 July 2009

The Prince of Wales launched 'YOU London'. In May 2009 the Dockland Scout Project was approached by The Scout Association to take part in the press launch of Project YOU (Youth Organisations in Uniform) and host the first part of the launch. This was a water activity morning with ten youth representatives from each of the nine partner Groups. It involved 90 YPs (Young Persons) plus DSP staff being on the water. It required the removal of all their boats on the lock side in front of the *Lord Amory* to allow a drop-slide climbing tower and zorbing (rolling downhill in an orb, generally made of transparent plastic) to take place at the same time. By 0800 DSP was a hive of activity with people erecting inflatable slides and an artificial climbing wall on the quayside. Police patrolled with dogs; including the pontoons where one the dogs clambered over a sailing boat and fell in.

The day was made very special by the attendance of Prince of Wales and the Duchess of Cornwall. Richard Hart and Lily Bourke of DSP escorted them around the various activities taking place on the water and on the quayside, talking to the different groups of young people and answering any questions. The Prince and the Duchess met representatives of the nine Groups before going down onto the pontoon to talk to the canoeists and watch one boatful of paddlers capsize into the water.

16-year-old Explorer Scout and young Leader Alec also helped show the Prince around the Project telling him about his Scouting experiences. 'I talked to the Prince about being a young Leader in Scouting, about how it involved me helping young people do all kinds of different activities. He was really interested in what I'd been up to recently through Scouting. He asked a lot about what activities I'd been doing at a recent activity camp called Gilwell 24.'

Finally everyone went onboard the Lord *Amory* for a cup of tea and cake.

2009

1-8 August 2009

National Sea Scout Jamboree – Sea Scout 100

This was held at Holme Pierrepont, Nottingham, celebrating the centenary of Sea Scouting in the United Kingdom. Over 2,000 Scouts attended a full water activities programme. Initially the weather was very wet; one of the most popular events was the water slide, where Scouts and ducks slid down together. Having witnessed the spectacle I am not sure who were the more entertained, the Scouts or the ducks – both returned repeatedly.

The Centenary of Sea Scouting

100 years ago, 7-21 August 1909, a camp was held at Beaulieu, Hampshire for Scouts to take part in activities on the water. It was from that date it is considered that Sea Scouting started.

Warington Baden-Powell, the founder of Sea Scouting in 1913, married Hilda Farmer from New Zealand. He died in 1921 and his ashes were interred at the Farmer family plot at St Andrews Cemetery, Fife.

134 *National Sea Scout Camp, August 2009. (Left to right) Frank Brittain (visitor), David Sturdee (Camp Chief), Geoffrey Preshner (Lieutenant Commander, Sea Cadet Corps, visitor).*

To mark the World Centenary of Sea Scouting in the United Kingdom on Sunday, 16 August, Sea Scout representatives from New Zealand, the USA, Ireland and other parts of the United Kingdom had arrived at the Headquarters of the 8th Fife Scouts.

On the Sunday morning more than 100 Scouts, the international contingents and distinguished guests assembled at the Parish Church of the Holy Trinity to join the congregation for the service marking the Centenary. An international flag party laid their flags at the altar. The Rev. Cameron Harrison used a nautical theme for the address and Scouts from New Zealand, Dublin and Fife gave the three readings, after which Roy Masini, Sea Scouter and historian, gave a talk to the congregation about the start of Sea Scouting.

As the participants left the church and made their way to the 8th Fife Scout HQ a four-masted Dutch sailing ship taking part in the St Andrews Harbour Gala Day came into view in the Bay, making an appropriate backdrop for the Centenary. At lunch, presentations were made by the Lord Lieutenant of Fife, Margaret Dean; Lieutenant Commander David Griffiths RN, Staff Officer Scouts representing Flag Officer Scotland; Derek Colley, Regional Commissioner for East Scotland; Jean Martin, District Commissioner for North East Fife and organiser of the event, and Ron Bird (New Zealand) who helped bring the event to fruition. The Hon. Michael Baden-Powell, grandson of the Founder, now a resident of Australia, recorded a DVD especially for the occasion, emphasising the international aspects of Scouting and its aim to bring about harmony between nations.

In the afternoon wreaths were laid at the graveside of Warington Baden-Powell followed by singing by members of the New Zealand contingent of a traditional Maori song about meeting together and understanding. A minute's silence was held, marked by two Sea Scouts from Limekilns, Fife, sounding 'the still' followed by the 'carry on' on the bosun's call.

Also attending the graveside ceremony were Eleanor Lyall, Chief Scout's Commissioner for Scotland; Andy Matthew, former Chief Scout's Commissioner for Scotland; Frances Melville, Provost for Fife, and Sir Menzies Campbell MP for North East Fife.

Funding was also made possible for the event through the generous assistance of Stephen Peck, Director of Programme and Development at Scout Headquarters, Gilwell Park, Chingford.

THE WORLD SCOUT EMBLEM - ITS MEANING

DUTY TO GOD

THE TWO FIVE POINT STARS

stand for truth and knowledge. The ten points represent the ten points of the original Scout Law

THE ENCIRCLING ROPE

symbolises the unity and family of the World Scout Movement

OBEDIENCE TO THE SCOUT LAW

SERVICE TO OTHERS

THE BOND, showing the family of Scouting

THE REEF KNOT which can't be undone no matter how hard it is pulled, is symbollic of the strength of world scouting's unity and family

THE WORLD EMBLEM IS WHITE, ON A ROYAL PURPLE BACKGROUND, IN HERALDRY, WHITE (OR SILVER) REPRESENTS PURITY, AND ROYAL PURPLE DENOTES LEADERSHIP AND SERVICE.

THE ARROWHEAD:

Lord Baden Powell, Our Founder said:

" Our Badge we took from the 'Northpoint' used on maps..........."

Lady Olave said later:

"It shows the true way to go"

135   *The World Scout Emblem – Its Meaning.*

NINE

SCOUTING INTERNATIONAL

TO SET THE SCENE

Sea Scouting was first formed in Britain, a seafaring nation, and soon became part of the international scene. However, where Scouting was suppressed and sanctions imposed, Sea Scouting was equally afflicted.

PART 1: 1908-20 – EARLY DAYS

No sooner was *Scouting for Boys* published in book form in May 1908 than the Movement rapidly spread to many other countries. British Scouts went abroad in small groups and, on a larger scale, international camps and jamborees followed.

1911

B-P wrote to his mother on 10 September: 'I strongly believe that Scouting will become soon a real international movement.' In the October 1911 issue of the *Headquarters Gazette* B-P recommended that a Foreign Department at Imperial Headquarters [IHQ] be created to maintain contact with Scouts abroad.

1913

3-11 July 1913

The Boy Scouts International Exhibition and Rally, Birmingham, England

This early milestone in the history of Scouting drew more than 30,000 Scouts from many parts of the world and became the precursor of the Jamboree. The majority of Scouts came from Britain and the Dominions, but also from much of Europe with a sizeable contingent from the USA.

This exhibition, opened by Princess Alexandra of Tec, and visited by Prince Arthur of Connaught, Sir Robert Baden-Powell (Chief Scout) and Lord Charles Beresford (Chief Sea Scout), fitted happily into its age. Favoured by good weather – not characteristic for large international Scout events – the exhibition encompassed all the activities covered by Scout Proficiency Badges.

The Sea Scout display took place before B-P and Lord Charles Beresford at the 60-acre reservoir at Edgbaston. There were all sorts of manoeuvres including a 'Whale Hunt' and a rocket apparatus rescue. After the shipwrecked crew were brought ashore, two scoutmasters were inadvertently left behind on the wreck! They nobly elected to come ashore by breeches buoy, but the hawser sagged and two very good yachting suits were 'ducked'.

1914-18

By January numbers were growing steadily with plans under consideration for further expansion. On the eve of War in 1914 there were 152,333 Scouts in the UK; by 1918 there were 193,731. The magnitude of the tragic conflict of the 1914-18 War did not see the demise of the Scout Movement, but gave it a new lease of life and a new dimension.

Still wartime, it was decided that provided the War was over by 1917 an Imperial and International event should be held in 1918. At IHQ in London committees were formed, responsibilities divided and where possible every contingency foreseen and provided for. The planning of this first Jamboree was an enormous feat of organisation in which B-P played the key role as General Commissioner. Invitations were despatched – every Scout Association was invited with 30 countries accepting.

An essential requirement was to obtain a picture of how Scouting had evolved in other countries during hostilities, so B-P nominated Hubert Martin, International Commissioner; other countries did likewise. Hubert Martin was named Director of the International Bureau created in 1922 and remained until his death in 1938.

136   *The Governor inspecting Hong Kong Scouts, c.1920.*

The First World War ended on 11 November 1918; it was decided the international rally postponed from 1918 would be held in 1920.

PART 2: 1920-9 – A LEAP FORWARD

In this chapter where no specific involvement of Sea Scouting is mentioned at a Jamboree, only the date and place are recorded.

From 1920 'Jamboree' took on a specific meaning associated with the largest gathering of youth that took place in the Scout Movement. Getting together young people from all nations was a new idea for which a name had to be found: B-P found it – 'Jamboree'. He was asked, 'Why do you call it a Jamboree?' (First used in US slang in 1872.) 'What else would you call it?'

This Rally had a far bigger significance than those previously held at Crystal Palace, Windsor and Birmingham. It marked the restoration of peace.

1920

20 July-8 August 1920

1st World Scout Jamboree, Olympia, London

Scouting had spread during the war years. The presence of the reigning monarch, King George V, the Queen and Princess Mary gave the Jamboree a Royal seal of approval.

Open to visitors from 11 a.m. to 9 p.m. with admission 1s. 3d. (£1.33 today) it afforded both Scouts and visitors the opportunity to mix with young people from a wide range of backgrounds and countries. 8,000 Scouts from 34 countries took part, a considerable achievement. Daily displays were given in the arena at Olympia where 3,000 Scouts also slept – a foot of earth and turf was laid to enable them to pitch their tents. A camp of 5,000 Scouts was set up in the Old Deer Park, Richmond where at one stage the Thames overflowed, flooding part of the camp.

115 Sea Scouts lived for the week on board the Training Ship *Northampton* moored in the Thames near Temple Pier. Their mornings were occupied in boat races, the Dublin Sea Scouts eventually proving the winners after a close race with Sea Scouts from the River Tyne.

Sea Scouts take part

The Jamboree Book 1920 recorded:

> The Sea Scouts were a 'well set up' lot and in the Grand Procession, in which they had the honour of representing the United Kingdom. They always looked extremely well [many had served as coastwatchers] and got a well-deserved cheer from the spectators.

> It was envisaged that the Sea Scouts were to show work aloft, derrick rigging and hoisting cargoes, but this did not prove possible [early Health and Safety]. The only seamanlike turn given was a display against a painted backdrop scene of a rocky coast with a ship at anchor. It was carried out remarkably well by the Sea Scouts from Dublin, using 'Captain Smith's' ship in the vast arena, 325ft x 85ft, for their life-saving rocket apparatus.

In the presence of many thousands of spectators, Robert Baden-Powell was acclaimed by the Scouts as Chief Scout of the World, a title which lapsed upon his death in 1941.

It was intended that Jamborees should be held every four years, but world circumstances have not always permitted this arrangement.

1924

1-10 August 1924 – Imperial Scout Jamboree, Wembley, London

The British Empire Exhibition was held at Wembley and it was suggested that as an accompaniment to it an 'Imperial Jamboree' should also be held. Scouts from 34 parts of the British Empire answered the call.

On Saturday, 2 August with 12,500 present the Prince of Wales, the guest of honour, witnessed the displays and attended the campfire. As ever it rained, and the main street of the Jamboree became a sea of mud, but the spirit remained excellent.

From The Imperial Jamboree Book *(1924);* Scouter *magazine, September 1924*

How the Sea Scouts manned the Stadium

> The Sea Scouts were chiefly in evidence being the fatigue party for changing scenery and bringing properties into the arena. They did the work quickly and well.
>
> In the Grand Procession [entry of Scouts of the Empire marching past with their flags] they made a lane for any Royals present. They formed a circle in the centre of the arena on which the Rally was held, and around the flagstaff during the rush in after the Grand Procession of Empire when the Prince of Wales was present. The rain was pouring down their necks but not a single one moved a muscle or scratched his nose – it did them great credit.
>
> On Sunday, the Sea Scouts in their white caps standing three deep made a picturesque framing to the aisle down which the Prince of Wales's and the Archbishop of York's procession passed for the Stadium Service.
>
> The Weymouth Sea Scouts [Dorset] gave an excellent display in erecting sheer-legs, getting up a 35ft mast, unrigging sheer-legs, and hoisting and breaking the Union Flag. The Sea Scout Troops did well in the tug-of-war competitions.
>
> Rear Admiral Thesiger felt glad that the Sea Scouts had an opportunity of showing themselves to be a healthy, united body. He did not wish to advertise, but it actually happened at Wembley that a Commissioner told him that he did not know Sea Scouts existed. He could only hope that now they had been seen there would be more Sea Scout Patrols in Land Scout Troops.

10-17 August 1924

2nd World Scout Jamboree – Ernmelunden, Denmark

From Wembley many of the Scouts set off for Denmark for the second World Jamboree, to be the pioneer of the now-accepted 'all camp' Jamborees in contrast to the indoor event at Olympia.

1926

1-9 August 1926

First International Sea Scout Conference and Regatta, Antwerp, Belgium

Extract from The Scouter, *October 1926*

This was attended by delegates from eleven nations, including Sea Scout contingents from northern Europe. 70 Sea Scouts also attended from the UK, the largest party of Sea Scouts from any one country.

Sunday, 1 August

The first few mornings were devoted to training for the regatta and sports competitions. The British Troop were second and third in the signalling (the Danish Team were first) and fourth in the rowing final.

Monday 2, Tuesday 3 and Wednesday 4 August

There was a reception by the Burgomaster at the *Hotel de Ville*, a trip around the docks in a tug, a concert at the Bourse, a visit to a Danish warship sent in honour of the Jamboree and commanded by a former Chief Sea Scout Captain Briand de Crévecoeur. They looked in vain for a British cruiser sent in honour of the occasion. There was a tour round the Zoological Gardens and Aquarium, a glance round the Cathedral; the Sea Scouts sang as they marched through the City streets, their silk Union Flag flying proudly in the breeze.

Thursday, 5 August

They rose at five o'clock, struck camp and packed their kit, then went by river steamer to Brussels where, after a short ceremony at the tomb of the Unknown Soldier, they were shown around the city by the District Commissioner for Brussels. They returned by steamer to Ruysbroeck, where the entire camp had been re-pitched by the Belgian Sea Scouts and Antwerp Rovers. The fleet of Sea Scout yachts and the guard-ship were now moored alongside the new camp – a wonderful feat of transporting, entirely carried out on the water where the regatta took place.

Sunday, 8 August

All the Sea Scouts went in the Dutch Scouts' auxiliary cutter, and other craft which she towed, to Rupelmonde, where the Burgomaster received them at the statue of Mercator. The next day they returned to Antwerp for Brussels (and Zeebrugge) to re-embark for England, reaching home ports on Tuesday morning.

They all had a wonderful time, even the Sea Scout who cut his scalp and was escorted to hospital by four policemen armed with swords and automatic pistols. (They had previously taken down his dispositions, in Flemish, in case there was an inquest, but he returned the next day with a smile and a clean bandage.)

Sea Scout Congress

The Congress, over three mornings, considered reports on Sea Scouting in their several countries. It soon became evident some countries such as Great Britain and Holland used Sea Scouting as part of Scouting in general. Others used Sea Scouting for the specific purpose of training boys for sea careers. They wore the same rig as British Sea Scouts and preserved most of the Sea Scout methods. The Swedish and Brussels Sea Scouts dressed exactly like their navy.

1929

30 July–14 August 1929

3rd World Jamboree (Coming-of-Age) – Arrowe Park, Birkenhead, Cheshire

The year 1929 marked 21 years since the publication of *Scouting for Boys* in 1908 calling for a special Coming-of-Age celebration, so it was decided to have the Third Jamboree that year in England.

The 3rd World Jamboree was held at 450-acre Arrowe Park, Birkenhead which welcomed in a most hospitable manner the invasion of over 50,000 Scouts from 71 countries with an estimated 320,000 visitors.

Arrowe Park gave B-P the idea for the Jamboree symbol: the Golden Arrowe. The official opening was performed on Wednesday, 31 July by the President of The Boy Scouts Association, the Duke of Connaught. The Prince of Wales, Chief Scout of the Principality, also attended.

The weather was appalling, with days of heavy rain. The clay soil could not absorb the water and became waterlogged – the 'Jamboree of Mud'.

Sea Scout Regatta and Pageant – The Incredible Adventures of Captain Curdle

From The 2nd Wallasey Sea Scouts History

The Sea Scout Regatta was staged at West Kirby, some miles away on 3 August. The 2nd Wallasey played a very active role in the Sea Scout display on West Kirby Open-Air Marine Lake.

This was a pageant and play, *The Incredible Adventures of Captain Curdle*, specially written and produced by Scoutmaster F.W. Wilkinson, Headmaster of Wallasey Grammar School, and was performed by Merseyside Sea Scouts. Rehearsals had started during the previous winter.

Came the dress rehearsal on the Friday, a gale the previous night had led to an island in the middle of the lake breaking adrift from its moorings and finishing up hard aground against the promenade wall; the pirate ship (mounted on a barge complete with masts and rigging) also blew away. The day was spent working at this disaster.

Saturday was Wet Bobs Day – it certainly deserved the epithet. The young gale that was blowing was making quite sure about the movement side of the afternoon programme.

The Chief Scout was there, and the B-P family, en masse, as full of beans as ever. Vice-Admiral A.V. Campbell, HQ Commissioner for Sea Scouts, attended. The Sea Scouts' Commodore, Prince George of Kent, was not there owing to his indisposition. The Chief Scout, in opening proceedings, read a message from Prince George:

'HRH the Prince of Wales gave me a message from [his brother] HRH Prince George, saying it was a great disappointment that, owing to illness and doctor's orders, he had been obliged to remain at home and could not attend the Sea Scout show. He had been greatly looking forward to seeing it and getting to know more of the Sea Scouts. But he sends his best wishes for the success of the show and thanks for all the work they have put into preparing it. His Royal Highness hopes that many of the present Sea Scouts will later go on to become seamen and that all of those will then join the Brotherhood of Deep Sea Scouts of which he is very proud to be the Commodore.'

In his opening speech B-P said:

'We have been trying to show the Scouts at their worst. We have turned on all the bad weather we could because I have told the boys that any boy can be a Scout in fine weather, but it takes a true Scout to remain cheerful in all circumstances. It is specially the case with Sea Scouts, and so we have turned on the very worst weather here to put them to the test; during the past few days their preparations have been knocked to bits by gale and sea. The island you see before you was sunk to the bottom of the ocean, their ship on the left has been dis-masted, and the other ship – I don't know where it has gone to – it has blown away.'

'I will not say any more – you want to see what they can do under difficulties. I have every hope and confidence that they will show themselves full of the right spirit of the sea and will smile and whistle under difficulties.'

The *History* continues:

The cast of the pageant were King Neptune, The Princess Happycacuana, mermaids, cannibals, a sea serpent and pirates. The adventure pageant did get underway. The actors were soon soaked and the cannibals all appeared strange with black faces streaked with white. Bonnie Prince Charlie coxed the whaler with the Highlanders rowing. His dress was a white jacket and trousers with various tucks and trimmings, looking just the thing for a lot of ragging afterwards.

After the first half hour or so, the wind got up to gale force again. The pirate ship, with its high freeboard and being mounted on a flat-bottomed barge, soon became unmanageable with its small outboard motor and drifted away towards the prom; then the island also started to drift off the scene. The rain became a deluge and most of the spectators departed, and eventually the decision was taken to call it off.

The Prince of Wales and B-P came down to the changing rooms to walk amidst the crowd of wet Scouts. The Chief Scout called for silence for the Prince of Wales to say how disappointed Prince George was not to be able to attend, and how they too must be disappointed to have to abandon the show after all the work that had been put into it. In the Chief Scout's words, 'Don't be disappointed boys; it is when times get really tight such as this that you really get to know whom your best friends are.'

At the close of the Jamboree a golden arrow and a hatchet were buried, with gilded wooden arrows presented to national contingents. B-P said, 'Now I send you forth to your homeland bearing the sign of peace, goodwill and fellowship to all your fellow men'.

The Fifth International Conference was held during the Jamboree which had a unique distinction – one of the bureau staff was challenged to a duel. The challenger was hastily removed from Arrowe Park by the leader of his delegation.

PART 3: 1930-9 – THE PRE-WAR YEARS

One Party – One State

Russia banned Scouting in 1922 and established the 'Pioneers'. When the Communists and Fascists seized power they forced Scout Associations to close or merge with state youth organisations of which membership was compulsory. Italy banned Scouting in 1927 and developed its own uniformed state youth organisations, the 'Balilla' [little boy] and 'Avanguardisti' [avant-guarde]. In 1933 the new government in Germany absorbed 'Scouting' into the Hitler Youth Movement. Sea Scouting was banned in all of these countries, likewise Sea Scouting.

Hitler Youth [Hitler-Jugend]

The Grossdeutsche Bund, a federation of many youth movements including a dozen Scout Movements, was prohibited. Baldur von Schirach was appointed Reichsjugendführer (Reich Youth Leader) of the Nazi Party by Hitler in 1933. Hitler Youth proclaimed it alone represented the youth of Germany. The organisation was in no sense voluntary, but was to a certain extent selective, since those boys who seemed unlikely to make good party members were rejected.

1933

March 1933 – Italy

B-P's visits to foreign countries were seldom of long duration, his European journeys usually being for specific purposes in connection with Scouting. In the spring of 1933 the Chief Scout and the Chief Guide, Lord and Lady Baden-Powell, visited Gibraltar and then travelled to the Palazzo Venezia in Rome to have an audience with Pope Pius XII, a warm supporter of the Boy Scouts.

B-P sought an interview with the Italian Prime Minister Benito Mussolini ('Il Duce') to hear more from him about the Balilla and Avanguardisti movements. Knowing of *Scouting for Boys* he had incorporated its ideas, now using them as a basis, through military training, for boys.

B-P's daughter Heather in *Baden-Powell – a Family Album* (1986) refers to a 'neatly-pencilled account by B-P' contained in her scrapbook of the 1933 meeting with Mussolini.

On 2 March [1933] the British Ambassador, Sir Ronald Graham, took me to see Signor Mussolini. He lives in the Great Palace in Rome, formerly the Austrian Embassy. We waited half an hour in the ante-room with 14th-century pictures. Mussolini's room was a great marble hall – with no furniture. Walls painted to represent pillars etc. In the four corners a writing table and reading lamp and three chairs.

The Duce awaited us there and came out, speaking fair English. Small, rather stout, in morning dress but genial and human with a low, soft voice, not a bit the bombastic or commanding figure one had expected. After a word or two of his admiration for the Boy Scouts, I said I had come to pick up hints from the Balilla – it had been arranged I should see them tomorrow. Also I was interested to hear how he made the working man take healthy exercise and play outdoor games.

He put his hand over his nose and stared hard with the whites of his eyes showing (a favourite way with him), and said as he lowered his hand flat on the table, 'We do it by MORAL force! Free passes on the railways, cheap tickets to entertainments and various privileges of that kind to those who go in for sports – until it has become the "Thing". This, coupled with drills, exercises and uniform – discipline of the Balilla will make the next generation a fine, manly race.'

We had about ten minutes' talk and in saying good-bye he accompanied us across the hall to the door.

B-P considered the Balilla to be an experiment in applying Scout training to Italian education and was impressed by the material resources committed to it, particularly to the 'Marinetti', the Italian equivalent of the Sea Scouts. He was disappointed in his hopes of softening attitudes towards Scouting in Italy and put in his confidential report to Scout HQ: 'The Balilla movement is as yet in its infancy. The important point to us is that it is an experiment in applying Scout training to education.'

Their Provincial Headquarters had modern health clinics, workshops, wireless equipment, cinema and dormitories together with enthusiastic instructors. B-P noted two essential differences from the Scout Movement: the Balilla sought to develop a strong nationalist system coupled with efficiency for military service; it was an official organisation not a private one.

In *The Scouter* magazine for April 1933 B-P wrote in his Outlook column about his visit to Mussolini and the Marinetti:

The Balilla is the equivalent in Italy of the Boy Scout Movement [using some scout-like training]. Signor Giovanni, the equivalent of a County Commissioner, took me to see a Troop Headquarters of the Marinetti, the equivalent of our Sea Scouts. This was a house on the banks of the Tiber containing offices, gymnasium, bathrooms, stores etc, with rowing boats on the river available for instruction, and a couple of full-sized square-rigged masts on the parade ground for sail and drill training. The boys, dressed in full naval rig, showed themselves very smart and keen at their work. Indeed the earnest and cheery keenness of all, officers and boys, was the striking part of whole show.

TS Mercury, *and the Hitler Youth*

C.B. Fry was offered the crown of Albania, but was principally remembered as the man who captained England at cricket of whom the cricketer John Arlott wrote, 'a most incredible man'. It is written, however, that he saw his life's work being the naval training ship *Mercury*, where he was Superintendent, on which the first Sea Scout training was carried out for B-P in 1909.

C.B. Fry's fascination with Nazism started in the spring of 1934. An invitation was extended to him to visit Germany, because of TS *Mercury*, his knowledge of youth training and connections with Baden-Powell and the Scout Movement, albeit over 20 years previously. Much of his time was spent with Baldur von Schirach, commander of Hitler Youth since 1933, and Joachim von Ribbentrop, then Hitler's Foreign Affairs Adviser, later German Ambassador to Britain and then Germany's Foreign Minister. C.B. Fry had a brief meeting with Hitler, with whom he was very impressed, and with Bernard Rust, the Minister of Education and Culture.

C.B. Fry's biography showed an uncritical acceptance of Hitler's views and the Nazi attitude towards the German people. Later Fry claimed that he had tried to persuade them to develop cricket in Germany to cement Anglo-German relations. His suggestion was not taken up.

In June 1934, as a result of C.B. Fry's German tour, a party of brown-shirted youngsters, members of Hitler Youth, arrived from Berlin to visit TS *Mercury*. They joined in some activities but otherwise did not socialise during their visit.

A young boy seaman on TS *Mercury* recalled that:

> We were forbidden to speak to the German party, although they joined in the drills forming their own platoon. The closest we came to socialising was whilst swimming from the ship. This was the only time when we met on an equal footing, and not even the Duty Officer in the safety boat could prevent such exchanges as usually pass between swimmers of any nationalities when they happened to meet in the water. At all other times they were kept severely apart; on board they slept in the fo'c'sle, well away from the midships sleeping deck, and took their meals in the Frys' home.

The German party were impressed with all they saw, and left with the impression that all Sea Scout training was on the lines of that carried out on TS *Mercury*.

During the next three years, the Hitler Youth made a great show of trying to make friends with the youth of other countries through camping, cycling clubs and school journeys. In 1935 the International Committee of the Boy Scouts World Bureau clearly articulated their position that Scouts 'have nothing in common with undesirable Hitler-Jugend'. By 1936 the membership of Hitler Youth stood at four million.

Contact with Hitler Youth Abroad

On journeys through Europe English Scout contingents and others were attentively welcomed by parties of Hitler Youth, who did their best to impress with their bearing and discipline.

Jack Beet, a Sea Scouter from Harrow, also to be a member of Ralph Reader's Gang Show, recalled driving all the way to Hungary for the Jamboree in July 1933 and had an uneventful journey apart from a two-mile stretch of road in Germany: 'Here we were stopped five times by different parties of Nazi Storm Troopers and each time thoroughly searched; it took us about two hours to do two miles.'

The 1933 Hungarian Jamboree was visited by members of the German Hitler Youth invited, with the Italian Balilla, as a gesture of goodwill. At the International Bureau in London in 1934, the Chief of Staff of Hitler Youth Karl Nabersberg continued to attempt to negotiate contacts, and also sought to meet the Scouts of France.

2-13 August 1933

4th World Scout Jamboree – Godollo, Hungary

With financial control imposed as a result of worldwide economic problems and growing unrest in central Europe, it was considered not to be the best time for a large international event. In Britain the permission of the Prime Minister, Ramsay MacDonald, was required, who agreed despite the need for financial stringency. The country had to be represented, and 9,000 Scouts from the Commonwealth and Empire attended.

The Jamboree was held in the Royal Forest of Godollo, near Budapest, and attended by 25,792 Scouts from 34 nations. The uncharacteristically excellent weather for a Jamboree was enjoyed by the assembled Scouts.

On 6 August 1933 the following advertisement appeared in the Jamboree newspaper *Magyar Cserkesz*:

COME TO THE SEA SCOUTS DISPLAY

The Sea Scouts will give a special free display for Scouts only on the island of Csepel, near Budapest, on 9 August. The Regent of Hungary will be present. Scouts from Austria, Finland, Great Britain, Hungary and Poland will take part. This explains the disappearances of parties of Sea Scouts that have been occurring in the last days – they have been going off to the river to rehearse.

Sea Scouts at the Jamboree

From Jamboree Magyar Cserkesz Budapest, *15 August 1933*

An article by a British Sea Scout well describes Jamborees from a Sea Scout perspective – which could well have been written today.

Many of you 'Land' Scouts at the Jamboree must have wondered what we Sea Scouts find to do, far away from boating facilities.

Whilst you are in your natural element, so to speak, in magnificent camping country, here we are 17 miles from the nearest river and almost as many hundred miles from the sea, with apparently nothing to do.

Well, it must not be forgotten that a Sea Scout, even if he does spend quite a large proportion of his time on the water, is essentially a Scout in the first place, and can camp, cook and chop with the best of you, being as much at home in camp as on the water. Then again we have several opportunities for indulging in swimming, and almost every afternoon will find us off to the nearest pool.

We have also many more foreign representatives than it would seem at first hand, and if you went down the Danube to Csepel Island on Monday afternoon with us, you would not have thought there was a scarcity of Sea Scouts. The whole of the Danube for almost as far as one could see was straddled with their kayaks, canoes, skiffs and various other type of craft, manned mostly by Hungarian and Polish Sea Scouts, but with a fair sprinkling of English and Dutch Bobs.

The only disadvantage of being a Sea Scout at the Jamboree is, being so few of us, we are looked on as a novelty by visitors to the camp, having to spend much more time than other Scouts signing autographs. Still, we do not mind this in moderation, and I am sure that we 'Wet Bobs' get just as much enjoyment out of the Jamboree as our 'Land' Scout brothers.

1937

31 July-9 August 1937

5th World Scout Jamboree – Vogelenzang-Bloemendaal, Netherlands

Although 10,500 had applied, the British contingent numbered 8,000, including contingents from the British Empire. The British headquarters party left London for Holland on the night of 26 July. Eight ships each took 1,000 British Scouts from England to Holland, the largest

137   *Danish, Greek, Dutch and British Sea Scouts at Vogelenzang station, 1937.*

138   *American Sea Scouts on Rotterdam Dock, 1937.*

flotilla of youth the modern world had at the time seen.

Queen Wilhelmina opened the Jamboree to 28,750 from 51 countries. Girl Guides welcomed the World Chief Guide, Lady Baden-Powell, to the arena, where there were daily displays. The programme of events followed the usual lines of previous Jamborees. The campfires were open to the public and were attended by 30,000 visitors.

There was a water camp for Sea Scouts and a 'Sea Scout Day' was held on Lake Kaas on 9 August, where Polish Sea Scouts gave a kayak display.

Hitler Youth target Scouting

In the years prior to the outbreak of the Second World War, parties of uniformed German boy cyclists criss-crossed the UK travelling on its highways in groups of around 20 receiving warm welcomes almost everywhere.

Nationally the Headquarters of the Boy Scout Association remained aloof about the visits, although Hubert Martin, the International Commissioner, argued against contact and that rebuff would be more likely to bring a genuine Scout movement back to Germany.

Until now this part of history has been very under-researched and reported. More recently there has been a degree of speculation amongst historians and social researchers about Robert Baden-Powell, and perceived discussion with Germany in the 1930s.

On 8 March 2010 The National Archives at Kew released the formerly-closed Security files on this subject. I have scrutinised the papers, and because the fresh information disclosed is part of the history of Scouting not previously published, a summary appears in this chapter.

Extracts from Security Service Operational File, 1937 – Visits of Hitler Youth

Summer 1937

The papers reveal MI5's anxiety about visits to Britain of members of Hitler Youth during 1937. These coincided with the appearance of Hartmann Lauterbacher, Deputy Leader of Hitler Youth, who had arrived in England ostensibly to study English. Letters intercepted by MI5 showed that Nazi Germany was seeking to expand the influence their youth movement by fostering closer relations with the British Boy Scouts Association.

MI5 also took a close interest in the visit of Jochen Benemann, a senior figure in Hitler Youth who arrived in London in January 1937, his third visit. In 1934 and 1935 he had tried unsuccessfully to set up joint Anglo-German Youth Camps – including one at Bryanston School, Blandford, Dorset – to develop closer links between Hitler Youth and the Boy Scouts Association.

In 1937 articles appeared in the *Daily Herald* warning that tourist parties of Hitler Youth were 'Spyclists' gathering information on Britain and attempting to establish closer links with the Boy Scout Movement.

These visits promoted debate in the *Birmingham Post* to the extent that Sir Vernon Kell, Director of MI5, asked to see the letters sent to the newspaper as he felt obliged to investigate public concerns about the sudden appearance of Hitler Youth. MI5's investigation of the articles led them to the view that the initial story had come from an anti-fascist freelance writer in Prague, and they were sceptical about the authenticity of the details referred to in the British press.

(French literature in 2000 on Hitler Youth visits to France record that the German cyclists mapped out the countryside and this information was used by the German army for the invasion of France in 1940.)

The Director wrote to the Home Office saying he had gathered from 'a most secret and delicate source' that five members of Hitler Youth and seven Boy Scouts were to do an eight-day tour together in the south of England and that Tamworth Boy Scouts might take part in a Hitler Youth Camp near Hamburg. (This visit did take place and the British Scouts were greatly impressed with all they saw.)

Sir Vernon Kell alerted police forces across the nation to the presence of Hitler Youth in the country. In all, seven Groups were identified who visited Essex, Worcester, Oxford, Cambridge, London, Scotland and Wales.

Thirty-seven German schoolboys from Berlin visited King Henry School, Sheffield and stayed in the homes of the families, also visiting Thomas Frith & Son and John Brown (Sheffield Steelmakers). The papers showed the Admiralty had approved the visit and the report implies the Hitler Youth only saw what they were intended to see.

19 November 1937

*Robert Baden-Powell's Meeting with the German Ambassador at the
German Embassy, London*

The MI5 file also details the efforts of Hartmann Lauterbacher, Chief of Staff of Hitler Youth, to foster relations with the Boy Scouts Association. Lauterbacher's efforts were paralleled by the German Ambassador, Joachim von Ribbentrop, who invited B-P and an unnamed Guide Commissioner to the German Embassy on the afternoon of 19 November to speak about the future of German-British relations and the role of youth organisations. Also present was Jochen Benemann, Hitler Youth Co-ordinator. The conversation revolved around how much Hitler-Jugend owed to Baden-Powell's pioneer work in the youth field. As with the Italian Balilla, they had taken parts of Scouting and adapted the programme to fit their conditions.

After the meeting B-P sought official advice on what attitude to take towards the German advances. The Security Service was noncommittal, waiting to see what developed.

B-P wrote a letter on 20 November to the German Ambassador. Not on The National Archives file, it is known to have expressed his grateful thanks for meeting Jochen Benemann and Hartmann Lauterbacher. He added,

> More especially I am grateful for the kind of conversation you accorded me which opened my eyes to the feelings of your country towards Britain which I may say reciprocates exactly the feelings I have for Germany ... I sincerely hope that we shall be able, in the near future, to give expression to it through the youth on both sides, and I will at once consult my Headquarters officers to see what suggestions they can put forward.

In a two-page internal memorandum B-P wrote to Hubert Martin, International Commissioner, recording his visit:

> Both [Lauterbacher and Benemann] are eager to see the Scouts get into closer touch with the German Youth Movement. I had a long talk with the Ambassador [von Ribbentrop] who was very insistent that true peace between two nations will depend on the youth being brought up on friendly terms together in forgetfulness of past differences ... He sees in the Scout Movement a very powerful agency for helping to bring this about if we can get into closer with the Jugend Movement in Germany. I told him I was fully in favour of anything that would bring about a better understanding between our nations.

24 and 29 November 1937

Hubert Martin's visits to MI5

Hubert Martin visited MI5 on 24 and 29 November when he handed over the memorandum Baden-Powell had written to him. The meetings are summarised as follows:

Mr Martin of the Passport Office is closely interested in the Boy Scouts Movement and said that Benemann had an interview with Lord Baden-Powell. He did not know the name of Lauterbacher.

Martin wondered what was behind Benemann's activities and thought there was some doubt about the sincerity of these German advances. He suspected there might be the intention of obtaining some advantage for Germany by providing Anglo-German friendship instead of resorting to more forceful methods

Martin was told that the activities of Benemann, in connection with the 'Anglo Circle', were a small part of large-scale German propaganda which aimed at promoting Anglo-German friendship.

Martin said that it had been recently decided that the British Boy Scouts should be allowed to wear uniforms (in Germany) and this was mentioned by Lord Baden-Powell to Benemann. According to MI5 information the decision seemed to have pleased the Germans.

MI5 were not in a position to advise Martin as to the policy which might be desirable for the Boy Scout Movement to adopt towards those German approaches. It was a matter of importance the leading people in the Boy Scout Movement might like to discuss with someone in Government.

MI5 concerns in the matter were simply to obtain information on activities such as Benemann's in view of the connections with foreign policy of the German Government, and their connections with the foreign organisation activities of the National Socialist Workers Party. They were interested in who was developing the Hitler-Jugend Movement among young German residents here. The file shows a list of 51 people (unfortunately illegible) who Lauterbacher visited while in London.

Martin said that in Lord Baden-Powell's absence, he had left the management of the international aspects of the Boy Scouts Movement in the hands of himself and Lord Somers, and he thought the latter should discuss the matter in the proper quarters.

The MI5 papers note:

Mr Martin, Passport Office, telephoned on 8 December to say Lord Somers had a conversation with Lord Camborne, Under Secretary of State for Foreign Affairs, who strongly deprecated close relations with the Hitler Youth. Martin said that Baden-Powell had talked of his difficulties with the Socialist Press when the [British] Scouts had appeared at a Fascist demonstration in Germany. This had necessitated forbidding the boys to go in uniform, but the embargo had now been withdrawn.

139 *Sea Scouts entering St Helena Bay. Watercolour by Robert Baden-Powell.*

To help this, von Ribbentrop had suggested that if possible they should send one or two leaders to meet the leaders in Germany and talk matters over, and especially he would like Baden-Powell to go and see Hitler after he came back from Africa. Baden-Powell had added that he had lifted a ban on Scouts wearing uniform whilst visiting Germany in the hope that British youngsters would head up visits to the Third Reich.

A statement issued by the World Organisation of Scout Movements in Geneva on 10 March 2010 about the release of National Archives papers on the meeting between Baden-Powell and the German Ambassador interpreted the tone of the reply by B-P as 'polite and diplomatic' but nothing more. B-P made no comment on von Ribbentrop's proposals (of close relations).

A week after his meeting with the German Ambassador, B-P left for Kenya on 26 November where he spent the winter of 1937. He returned to the UK for a short period in 1938 before permanently returning to Kenya on 27 October 1938. There is no evidence that any meeting with Hitler ever took place. Lord Baden-Powell was a man of proven honour and integrity. Many were deceived by Hitler, including the Prime Minister.

1938

In October Hubert Martin CVO, CBE, became seriously ill and died the next month aged 59.

PART 4: 1940-5 – THE WAR YEARS

Scouting was suppressed or dissolved in the Channel Islands and most European countries, Iran and Japan.

Scouting continued in secrecy by a Patrol of Scouts of the 11th Jersey Troop. One day the Gestapo raided the house in which they met, where they found a wireless, ammunition and photographs, all of which were forbidden. The Scouts were out at the time and escaped interrogation. On VE Day (Victory in Europe, 8 May 1945), the Scouts put on their hidden uniforms, and together went into town, greeting the liberating British soldiers and sailors – a truly jubilant band.

1940

SS Handbook – Blueprint for Nazi Britain

Had the invasion taken place in 1940, Scouting would have been banned, and sanctions imposed, applying equally to Scouts and Sea Scouts, particularly with regard to the use of boats.

From Invasion 1940, The Nazi Invasion Plan for Britain by SS General Walter Schellenberg – *Introduction by Prof John Erickson (2000)*

In August 1940, the German Gestapo (secret police) prepared a secret handbook for distribution to their occupation forces on the anticipated invasion of Britain. SS Chief Reinhard Heydrich believed that the swift and total dismantling and destruction of the infrastructure of British society was the way to victory.

The document covered the main aspects of British life which included the Scout Movement. It also included 'The Special Wanted List Information GB' of 2,820 British subjects who, it was planned, would be seized within days, among them being Winston Churchill, Lord Baden-Powell, Richard Lunt (Secretary of the International Boy Scout Bureau then based in London) and Hubert Martin.

Documents prepared by SS General Walter Schellenberg described Lord Baden-Powell, Chief Scout, and officials of international Scouting in Britain as 'tools of British Intelligence', and the Scout Movement as a 'disguised instrument of power for British cultural propaganda' and 'an excellent information source for the British Intelligence Service'. Furthermore, 'Lord Baden-Powell was run as an agent against Germany during the last war'.

Some 2,000 copies were printed but almost all were destroyed during an air raid on Berlin in 1943. Three copies were captured by the Allied authorities, but it was more than 50 years later in 2000 that a translation from French first appeared.

Baden-Powell – My Adventures as a Spy

The 'Special Wanted List Information GB' remains an unnerving document. While it seems a fallacy to have suspected the 'International Boy Scout Movement' as an SIS (Secret Intelligence Service) appendage, Robert Baden-Powell wrote several books on the subject, principally *My Adventures as a Spy* (1915). The type of intelligence-gathering of which B-P wrote appears to be of the pre-1909 variety, before MI5 and MI6 were formed.

The only foreign visit made by B-P thought to be connected to intelligence-gathering was that he was asked by the Government to make some enquiries about the reported use of German submarines using Spanish ports at the time when he went to France and Spain as Chief Scout in April 1918 to inspect Scouts there.

The rumours that B-P was in Germany on Secret Service work have persisted for many years even until today, despite his emphatic statements to the contrary. Writing in *Lessons from the Varsity of Life* (1933), B-P said on spying in Germany, 'I think the foundation of these rumours may probably have lain in our War Office, where sometimes it was found useful to start a hare to see whether and how far confidential information leaked out.' The Scout Association make the point that he was too busy in other ways to go off to Germany working on such a mission.

If Baden-Powell had been engaged in spying from the formation of the Scout Movement in 1908, the histories on B-P would need to be rewritten. The diaries available give little detail other than an 'appointment for B-P Adjutant-General – for the "New Army" in 1914', attendance at a number of unspecified Government meetings in central London in the autumn of 1914, and B-P's drawings of a recruitment posters 'Are YOU in this?' for the First World War effort.

1941

Lord Robert Baden-Powell died on 8 January 1941, was given a military funeral, and was buried at Nyeri in view of Mount Kenya. It was fitting that senior military officers and Scouts bore him to his last resting place.

Second World War, 1939-45

With the Second World War came the test – could Scouting survive prohibition, propaganda and persecution? In Occupied Europe and the Far East, boys and girls and their leaders maintained a belief in Scouting and Guiding. Jamborees which should have been held in 1941 and 1945 could not take place, but in 1945, plans were immediately made for a Jamboree to be held in 1947.

1944

Lord Somers, Chief Scout, died on 14 July 1944. The appointment of Lord Rowallan as Chief Scout was announced on 22 February 1945 to coincide with the birth of the founder. 'Operation Overlord' on D-Day, 6 June 1944, had been successful but Germany was not totally defeated, and the new Chief Scout had been denounced by the leaders of Hitler Youth.

Lord Rowallan wrote in his autobiography *Rowallan* (1976):

> Even after the unconditional surrender was ratified in early May [1945], there was no question of my being allowed into Germany to light the torch in the rubble. With tyranny crushed, the defeated nation might have seemed ripe for conversion to the Scout cause. I had been denounced, and though the allies were in Berlin, vestiges of the Hitler Youth Movement, the inhuman opposite of Scouting, remained. The time was not ripe, and it was wiser to stay away.

As country after country was liberated, clearly the spirit of Scouting had not suffered, but rather had been tested.

1945

15 August 1945

Colonel J.S. Wilson, Director of the Boys Scouts' International Bureau, was called to a meeting with Lord Rowallan and Field Marshal Lord Montgomery at Scout Headquarters, London, as the Field Marshal wished to speak about the difficulties of bringing good order into the British Zone in Germany, and the trouble caused by bands of German youths wandering about without discipline. 'Monty' went on to propose an Army Order be issued that these boys should be collected and formed into Scout Troops with British Officers and NCOs as their leaders.

Colonel Wilson wrote of the meeting:

> Lord Rowallan rightly said that the development of Scouting in foreign countries was Wilson's responsibility on behalf of the International Committee. 'I take it, Sir, that yours is a short-term plan to tide the British Zone through the winter. We have a long-term plan that in time – three years, five years, seven years, we don't know how long – we will be able to get a natural Scout Movement established not only in Germany; but perhaps the world as a whole; if you start Scouting as part of the Occupying Army, then there is little – if any – hope of our plan succeeding.'

> Then, feeling very bold and knowing that I could be demobilised whenever I had completed my wartime task – SOE [Special Operations Executive] closed down formally on 15 January 1945 and some of the agent work was taken over by MI6 – I added: 'If you will forgive me for saying so, this file is mine not yours.' There was a heavy and seemingly long silence. Then, to give the Field Marshal full credit, he said, 'Well, I suppose if that is the case I must give up my idea'.

> It was many months before we felt that it was advisable to launch the long-term plan about which we had spoken.

Scouting in Germany had started in 1909 and was suppressed in 1934. It was re-established after 1945 but with a proviso that 'Marine Scouts' would not be permitted.

Report by MI5

This is new research is drawn from a report issued in 1944 from their operational file by the Security Services released by The National Archives in March 2010.

MI5 wrote,

> The Hitler Youth is not a Boy Scout or Girl Guide organisation. It is in no respect comparable to any organisation for young people known in the Western World. It is a compulsory Nazi formation, which has consciously sought to breed hate, treachery and cruelty into the mind and soul of every German child – in the true sense of the word, 'education for death'.

The MI5 report led me to uncover a Supreme Headquarters Allied Expeditionary Force (SHAFE) document which had been drawn up from intelligence sources and issued in 1944. The 322-page SHAFE Evaluation and Dissemination Section G-2 (Counter Intelligence) document was unclassified on 23 April 1973:

> The Naval Hitler-Jugend was generally composed of boys living in coastal regions and furnished replacements for the German and Merchant Navy, under the supervision of naval personnel and included all phases of naval activities. After a three-to-four-year course the boy had learned to row, man row-boats, barges and sailing boats, basic communications and the employment of the various types of naval craft. The most exhaustive training was offered in the Reich Naval Sports Schools and the sailing training vessel *Horst Wessel*. Badges were awarded at the end of each stage of training. The uniform differed entirely from the ordinary Hitler-Jugend uniform, and was almost identical with the blue uniform worn by the German Navy. Members carried out both inland and coastal duties.

> The Marine Hitler-Jugend had been very popular in northern Germany and reached a membership of 62,000 boys. It made demands upon the individual boy both in terms of time, physical and mental accomplishment. Before the War training exercises were carried out in the Baltic Sea on the two German Navy sail training ships.

> Boys from coastal areas and waterways around Germany, were encouraged to join Marine Hitler Youth Units. In the north, the Marine Units were particularly sought after, since many youths in Hamburg, Bremen and Kiel were already familiar with sailing craft and kayaks.

Today in Germany there are a small number of Sea Scout Groups, which still draw their members from similar areas to those mentioned above.

PART 5: 1946-59 – POST-WAR YEARS
1945/46

A recently-liberated France, despite many difficulties during two years of preparation, invited Scouts and Guides of all nations to their 6th World Scout Jamboree – of Peace.

1947

9-18 August 1947
6th World Scout Jamboree (Peace) – Moisson, France

Extracts from Sea Scouts and the Jamboree *by Horace Taylor, Travelling Commissioner for Sea Scouts, and* The Scouter, *November 1947*

The Jamboree took place at Moisson, on a curve of the River Seine about forty miles from Paris, with a small island providing the Sea Scout base camp. The official opening by General Lafont, the Camp Chief, took place at dusk on Saturday, 9 August. 24,152 Scouts from 70 Countries attended; the British contingent numbered 5,330.

Sea Scouts

In addition to the 400 Sea Scouts of Great Britain in county contingents, there was a party of 24 representing Britain at the Sea Scout camp.

Twelve of the party were chosen from various parts of the United Kingdom and sailed with Denham Christie and Horace Taylor from Newhaven to Moisson on a 70ft motor cruiser named *Loyang*, the first ship to arrive there, in six days. In honour of her arrival with the British Sea Scouts a gun was fired and the Union Flag hoisted on the main flagstaff of the Camp Marin.

Ten 1st Mortlake Sea Scouts sailed to the Jamboree in their own pinnace *Minotaur* of Dunkirk fame, skippered by their Group Scoutmaster, Tom Towndrow, taking seven days on the trip. Becalmed in the English Channel was the four-ton cutter *Larrie Larmouth* sailed from Chichester by Sub-Lieutenant Alan Watts, RNVR, and Mr Hillier, of the Southbourne Sea Scouts.

140 *Sea Scout 'Camp Marin' – World Jamboree at Moisson, France, 1947.*

Horace Taylor recalled:

We scarcely dropped anchor than we were being smartly semaphored from the Camp signal station – in French. That took us aback and in order to give ourselves time to collect our wits our Yeoman of Signals parried with a rapid flow of Morse, in English. In the meantime, a boat had put out from the island and the message of welcome from the Camp Chief of the island was continued verbally. We went ashore and, after having 'made our number' with the French Scouters who were in charge of the Camp Marin, we were shown to our campsite, a clearing amongst the trees bordering onto the river like the other Sea Scout delegations.

At Camp Marin, for ten days the Sea Scouts of nine nations lived together and used the common language of the sea. Despite different routines and languages, the Sea Scouts found they had much in common with each other. No matter in what language orders are given, boats are managed in much the same way and all craft of a class respond similarly to the same treatment, irrespective of nationality.

There is also a point in the day's programme when the custom of the sea decrees that all the varying routines shall coincide. Thus at eight bells of the morning watch [8 a.m.] 1,000 Sea Scouts were stunned into silence by the roar of a gun. In the rush which followed there could be heard 'Ting-ting, ting-ting' from various parts of the island as one ship's bell after another rang out the time of eight o'clock in the morning.

Meanwhile, everyone at attention, the colour parties solemnly hauled up their national flags. A shrill pipe from the bosun's call – Carry on! – and the medley of sound of a rousing camp broke out once more into full volume.

141   *A replica of the Viking ship* Hugin *near Ramsgate, Kent, which sailed from Denmark in 1949 crewed by Danish Scout Guild. 2009.*

Closing

> The final march-past was in the human formation of a carrick bend, the symbol of the Jamboree. The bridges were so arranged that the Scouts marched along the pattern of the carrick bend, 24,000 people en masse passing over one bridge and under another.

Scouting survived the war years, but few realised that within a few months Scouting in Czechoslovakia and Hungary would again be suppressed.

3-12 August 1951

7th World Scout Jamboree (Simplicity) – Bad Ischl, Austria

18-25 August 1955

8th World Scout Jamboree (New Horizons) – Niagara-on-the-Lake, Canada

1957

1-12 August 1957

9th World Scout Jamboree (Jubilee) – Sutton Coldfield, Warwickshire

From Jubilee Journal, *1-12 August 1957, The Boy Scouts Association*

Planning started in the spring of 1955. Three purposes of this event were to celebrate the Centenary of the birth of the Founder, to celebrate the Golden Jubilee of the Brownsea Island Camp, and to proclaim the 50th Anniversary of Scouting (1907-57). 35,000 Scouts from 90 countries camped in the 2,400 acre Sutton Park; 9,772 attended from the United Kingdom alone.

It was opened on 1 August by the Duke of Gloucester, KG, President of the Boy Scouts Association, who arrived by helicopter.

On Saturday, 3 August the site was visited by Her Majesty the Queen, Patron of the Boy Scouts Association and HRH Prince Philip, the Duke of Edinburgh. The roads of the camp were lined with campers and visitors several deep. As the party arrived at the Jamboree, the Royal Standard was broken from the main staff. The Queen spent six hours with the Scouts, of which half was a three-hour tour of the seven sub-camps.

The Scouts camped for 12 days in weather which ranged from a heat wave to the now-traditional night of a great storm – 'Jamboreerain' – which flooded parts of the campsite.

The *Jubilee Journal*, the 24-page camp newspaper, had a staff of 50 writers, photographers, journalists, artists and others. 500 reporters, photographers and radio commentators from many nations attended. 'The largest sound radio and television operation outside London in our history' was how the BBC described the Jamboree. The Jamboree story was seen and heard by millions throughout the world. I visited the Jamboree and was completely overawed by it.

Sea Scouts on Powell's Pool – 'Having Fun On, In and Under the Water'

Sea Scouts camped at the southern end of Sutton Park in preparation for the Sea Scout Display on Saturday, 10 August. It was held on Powell's Pool in front of a packed audience in the presence of the Prime Minister, The Rt Hon. Harold Macmillan MP, with current, past and future ministers seeing how Scouts from many lands lived side by side.

The Sea Scout display included sailing and paddling in a wide variety of craft ranging from barrels to Viking ships. There were demonstrations of under-water swimming and rescuing with rocket apparatus. The display opened with 27 Red Ensigns broken from 27 buoys by an equal number of swimmers.

The Return of the Loch Ness Monster

One of the earliest games played by Sea Scouts (including B-P who used it in the very early days of Sea Scouting) was the 'Whale Hunt'.

The 'Loch Ness Monster' soon appeared, made of canvas on a frame and powered by several outboard motors – a remarkable feat of construction. The 64th Birkenhead Sea Scouts attacked it, but it swallowed one whole boat and its crew, before it was eventually cut in two by a gallant St George, a single Sea Scout.

More serious practical demonstrations followed showing rocket rescues from wrecks by the Sea Scouts from Gainsborough, Lincolnshire and Eccles, Lancashire.

Sea Scouts from London showed an activity which had seldom previously been seen in England but which the French Sea Scouts had taken up some years previously – underwater swimming and exploration. The London Sea Scouts combined their demonstration with a saga about Neptune and his court, and a 'Crossing–the-Line' ceremony.

The finale to the Sea Scout display occurred when full fleet of boats came into the arena, unfurled brightly-coloured pennants, and ended singing the Jamboree Song and, appropriately, the Scout Gang Show song *Crest of a Wave*.

The Jamboree was closed by the World Chief Guide, Olave, Lady Baden-Powell, who said, 'The end is only the beginning'.

17-26 July 1959

10th World Jamboree (Building Tomorrow Today) – Laguna Islands, Philippines

PART 6: 1963-2009 – TOWARDS THE 21ST CENTURY

1-11 August 1963

11th World Scout Jamboree (Higher and Wider) – Marathon, Greece

The World Jamboree was held on the Plain of Marathon, scene of the battle in 490 B.C. between the Ancient Greeks and the Persians. A 20,000-seat amphitheatre was the focus of the camp around a Greek village. The Jamboree was attended by 10,394 Scouts from 89 countries. The largest contingent was 1,498 Scouts from the UK at a cost of £85 each [about £2,000 today]. More than 300 journalists attended.

At the time of the Greek Jamboree I was a Sea Scouter working in the International Department of The Scout Association, amongst the duties of which was responsibility for British Scouts visiting abroad. For the Greek Jamboree, it was decided to charter 20 aircraft from the four major airlines to carry the UK contingent. I handed over the Association's cheque for £126,565 [£1,677,625

142   *The yacht* Ocean Scout, *operated by Rickmansworth Sea Scouts at Boulogne, April 1970.*

today] for the charter – the largest cheque I have ever handled. In 2010 it was still recorded as the largest UK Scout airlift ever.

31 July-9 August 1967
12th World Scout Jamboree (For Friendship) – Farragut State Park, USA

2-10 August 1971
13th World Scout Jamboree (For Understanding) – Asagiri Heights, Mount Fuji, Japan

3-12 August 1975
14th World Scout Jamboree (Norjamb '75) – Lillehammer, Norway

1979

The 15th World Scout Jamboree was scheduled to have been held in Neyshabur, Iran, in 1979 but was postponed towards the end of 1978 due to the Iranian political situation.

The World Scout Organisation announced 'World Scout Jamboree Year', in order to multiply by thousands the spirit of a Jamboree by holding at short notice several World Scout Jamborees in a series of camps in Canada, Sweden, Switzerland and the USA.

4-16 July 1983

15th World Scout Jamboree (The Spirit Lives On) – Kananaskis County, Alberta, Canada

31 December 1987-7 January 1988

16th World Scout Jamboree (Bring the World Together) – Cataract Park, Sydney, Australia

8-16 August 1991

17th World Scout Jamboree (Many Lands, One World) – Soraksan National Park, South Korea

1994

June 1994

From 102 News, Winter 1994 – Maurice Gardener, Blofield & Brundall Sea Scouts

Account of the Visit to HMS Norfolk in Bermuda by Richard Chambers, 1st Blofield Sea Scouts and Nicholas Willment, 11th Norwich Sea Scouts

We flew to Bermuda on 18 June from Gatwick. Experiencing problems with immigration at both ends because of our one-way tickets, so we had to prove we were Scouts. We were met by the liaison officer Surgeon Lieutenant Newton who took us to a beach party given by some of the crew. We spent our time on Bermuda touring the island including its capital Hamilton, and watched part of the Queen's Birthday Parade. This tour was kindly arranged and paid for by the Royal Navy.

HMS *Norfolk*'s departure from Bermuda was delayed by 24 hours which allowed us to do some snorkelling and more sightseeing including a look around the Old Royal Naval Docks on the island.

We sailed on 22 June with an early start. We were entertained by some spectacular scenery of Bermuda's coastline including the coral reefs lying offshore. With Bermuda fading into the distance the reality of life on board a modern warship began as we were put to work in the various departments of the ship.

During eight days at sea we worked in every department of the ship including standing three morning watches (4 a.m.-8 a.m.). Some of our activities included Astro navigation, a meteorology lesson, a tour of the engineering department and the operations room, stripping down a 30mm gun, and watching an anti-submarine exercise. I even assisted in the medical centre with an operation and with documenting the emergency medical stations.

Despite it looking like hard work we managed to take time out from our busy schedule with a barbecue on the flight deck on Saturday night, and a charity run on the Sunday morning (a mile each round the ship's deck). The trip was rounded off by a mess dinner on the Wednesday. We arrived at Devonport late Thursday night but due to the tides had to wait until the following morning before we could dock. We saw some amazing things, such as dolphins at 6 o'clock in the morning and whales in the afternoon. We both learned a lot and wish we could go again.

1-11 August 1995
18th World Scout Jamboree (The Future is Now) – Dronten, Netherlands

27 December 1998-6 January 1999
19th World Scout Jamboree (Building Peace Together) – Picarquin, Chile

28 December 2003-7 January 2004
20th World Scout Jamboree (Share our World, Share our Cultures) – Sattahip, Thailand

2007
28 July-8 August 2007
21st World Scout Jamboree (One World, One Promise) – Hylands Park, Chelmsford, Essex

From One World, *Official Newspaper of the 21st World Jamboree,* Scouting *magazine, October/November 2007*

In 2007 Scouting celebrated its Centenary. Almost 100,000 people of all nationalities participated in, worked in, or visited the 686-acre site at Hylands Park in Essex, which had been turned into a global Scouting City.

The Duke of Kent welcomed the Scouts to the United Kingdom and read a special message from the Queen. Prince William and the Duke of Kent were taken on a tour of the site to see how Scouting had evolved.

40,000 Scouts from 160 countries attended the Jamboree, incorporating the celebrations held on 1 August, the date agreed to celebrate the founding of Scouting. The UK contingent was 4,594 plus 1,510 staff. 50,000 attended the day visitors' experience.

On Saturday, 28 July the Royal Regiment Parachute Display Team – The Tigers – delivered the World Scout Flag by air into the arena – the largest crowd in front of which they had ever jumped.

On his tour Prince William sampled vegetarian sausages with onion and tomato ketchup cooked on a camp stove and said the sausages were a luxury compared to what he ate in the Army. A nearby camper commented, 'He is going to be an awesome King'.

143 *The 21st World Jamboree 2007 – a displayed waxwork model of Robert Baden-Powell, Chief Scout of the World, shown wearing the Silver Wolf – the highest award made by The Scout Association – for services of the most exceptional character, first awarded 1920.*

On Tuesday, 1 August Carl XV Gustav the King of Sweden visited the Jamboree; he was well prepared, having been a Scout for 50 years, and wore his Scout uniform, blue jeans and wellington boots.

Making Splash

Jamboree Water Activities were provided for around 4,000 participants over the eight days, 2,000 overall each morning and afternoon. The Activities were held at Alton Waters Reservoir, where they could enjoy a water-themed day. For most participants it was their first time in a boat.

Three days before the start of the event, 120 kayak instructing teams arrived to begin training including an international group from Ireland, America and Canada. The main training was devoted to developing instructors' visual demonstration skills – which took a lot of practice. There were 400 kayaks and 100 sit-on kayaks, plus 200 kayaks loaned from Scout Groups around the UK.

There were about 600 participants on the water at the largest session, added to this 121 instructor kayaks making 694 kayaks, a record for the amount of kayaks on the water at any one time. Nearly 9,000 participants were introduced to kayaking during the event. Kayaking at Splash was a huge success.

144 *The 21st World Jamboree, 2007 – the UK Pavilion.*

145   *Eurosea 9 – Sea Scout Leaders' Seminar at Larch Hill, Co. Dublin, Ireland, May 2008. Delegates attended from Belgium, the Czech Republic, Denmark, Germany, Finland, France, Ireland, Italy, Lithuania, the Netherlands, New Zealand, Norway, Poland, Portugal, Slovakia, Spain, Sweden, the UK and the USA.*

Richard Hart said the Dockland Scout Project provided their boats for the Jamboree at the Water Activity Centre at Alton Waters. To get the boats from London Docks to the site and back was a logistical problem, taking eight return trips – a total of 3,000 miles. Gigs, sailing dinghies, canoes and safety boats were provided.

Ron Bird said that New Zealand Sea Scouts with the support of Hamburg Sud, Ports of Tauranga (NZ) and Tilbury (UK) and many others arranged to have sent two of their new fibreglass

146   *A replica of the Viking longship* Sea Stallion, *30 metres in length, displayed at the National Museum of Ireland, Dublin, 2008.*

147   *A visit to Twickeree, Richmond's Scout Camp, at Marble Hill Park, Twickenham, Middlesex, in 2009 by Texel Scouts (Holland) who care for the graves of the 1st Mortlake Sea Scouts who drowned in 1950.*

5.2 metre (17ft) sailing/pulling cutters to be used during the period of the Jamboree. The two cutters were transported 12,000 nautical miles by container to and from the Jamboree.

Rafting – Pirates Ahoy

48,000 participants for rafting were split into eight teams of 60 people. Each person was given basic water-safety training and buoyancy aids. They built their rafts and were excited to get on, out onto the water; 400 barrels, 2,400 poles and 12.5 km of rope were made available.

All Scouts spent a day away from the Jamboree site working within the community on projects including clearing footpaths to repairing and painting a playground.

FIREWORKS

At the spectacular finale thousands of voices echoed around the arena renewing their Scout Promise. The ceremony ended with the line, 'We have come together and made the dream of One World, One Promise a reality.' Magnificent fireworks lit the arena. Peter Duncan, Chief Scout said of the Jamboree 'The sheer buzz'.

148   *Wreaths laid at the grave of Warington Baden-Powell to mark the Centenery of Sea Scouting in St Andrews, Fife, by Susie Clements and Eleanor Linton, 8th Fife Scout Group; Brendon McRae and Hamish Thorpe, New Zealand; and Eleanor Lyall, Chief Commissioner for Scotland. Sea Scouting has spread worldwide.*

TEN

THE ADMIRALTY AND SEA SCOUTS, 1910-2009

PART ONE: EARLY DAYS 1910-19

1909-10 – Sea Scouts: A Section in its Own Right

Early on Robert Baden-Powell saw a requirement for a 'Sea Scout' Section; in 1909 he turned for guidance to his brother Warington, who had a naval background, and also consulted Admiral Lord Charles Beresford, who had commanded the Channel Fleet between 1907 and 1909. In October 1910 the *Headquarters Gazette* of the Boy Scouts Association laid down the first policy for Sea Scouts, giving authority for a uniform of normal Scout rig but with naval cap; the distinctive Sea Scout jersey followed soon afterwards.

1911

In March 1911 Robert Baden-Powell wrote to the Admiralty for permission to establish Sea Scouts as 'Seamen and Coastwatchers'. Approval was given, and a growing number of Scout Troops on the coast became Sea Scouts. Arrangements were made for them to use equipment of the Royal Naval Volunteer Reserve (RNVR) and receive tuition from naval instructors paid for by the Navy League. Formed in 1894, the League was the foremost naval interest group and was able to influence naval affairs. The Navy League were raising similar questions about recognition of the Boys' Naval Brigades to those by Robert Baden-Powell for Sea Scouts, prompting a Parliamentary Reply:

Boys' Naval Brigades
Hansard, 13 March 1911 – Written Answers (Commons)

Sir Henry Kimber asked the First Sea Lord of the Admiralty whether the same privileges that are granted to the Cadet Corps by the War Office [may be extended] to those companies of the Boys' Brigade who may wish to comply with similar conditions.

Mr McKenna: The question of the possibility of extending official recognition to Boys' Blue Jacket Brigades and somewhat similar rules to those prescribed in the War Office Regulations for Cadet Corps has been under consideration, but the requirements and conditions of the Navy and Army are not analogous in this respect, and it is not anticipated that any general scheme can be adopted.

June 1911

Admiral Lord Charles Beresford, a well-known, popular figure with a naval and parliamentary career, was appointed Chief Sea Scout.

1911-14 – Admiralty Discussions

The Admiralty acknowledged the Sea Scout Branch was growing, witnessed by the popularity of Warington Baden-Powell's book *Sea Scouting for Boys.* It had received an application from a Naval establishment to start a Sea Scout Troop for Junior Seamen, which raised questions about the use of Treasury money for their accommodation and equipment.

The case for recognition of Boys' Naval Brigades and Sea Scouts had been put to Rear Admiral Jellicoe, Second Sea Lord, responsible for manning and discipline in the Royal Navy. There was some confusion as to which of the various units referred to were 'Sea Scouts, Sea Cadets or Boys' Naval Brigades'. It had been noted that an adult had been seen in the naval uniform of a Post Captain, when clearly he was not. 'Table manners observed were clearly not those of an Officer.'

Under the new scheme the 2nd Wallasey, becoming Sea Scouts in May 1911, had no uniform beyond the sailor's round cap. The leaders invented their own uniforms of blue tunics, blue breeches and puttees. Baden-Powell had proposed Sea Scoutmasters wore 'ratings' round caps instead of peaked caps. He was quietly dissuaded by one of the several admirals on the Sea Scout committee at Scout Headquarters on the grounds that the rating's round cap would not travel well in a kit-bag and therefore the peaked cap should remain … admirals did not wear ratings' caps!

On 1 August 1914 Acting Admiral Jellicoe was recalled as Second-in-Command of the Grand Fleet. The decision about the recognition of the Boys' Naval Brigades and Sea Scouts was again discussed, but put aside in December 1914 as the Admiralty had more important issues upon which to concentrate concerning the defence of the realm.

1914-18 – THE FIRST WORLD WAR
1914

August 1914

30,000 Sea Scouts provided assistance to the Coastguard Service between August 1914 and March 1920, many 'Land' Scouts also putting on the Sea Scout jersey. Log book entries showed their active engagement: 'Warned destroyer off rocks'; 'Provided night guard over damaged sea plane'; 'Went with patrol boat to blow up mine'.

The War ended on 11 November 1918, and at the cessation of hostilities the Secretary of State for War issued letters of gratitude to Sea Scouts and Cadet Units, commending them for the important role they had fulfilled.

1918

November 1918

This certificate, provided by Coastwatching Scout J.J. Potter, was sent by the Chief Scout to Coastwatching Sea Scouts:

THE GREAT WAR 1914-18

THE CHIEF SCOUT'S MESSAGE

OF CONGRATULATIONS and THANKS to the COATSTWATCHING SCOUTS

The Germans having surrendered their fleet to the Silent Sea Power of Britain I take the opportunity of congratulating and thanking you, Coastwatching Scouts, for what you have done to back up our Naval Forces, throughout the War, by acting as their second line ashore. You have done valuable work and you have done it well. You may always feel proud of the bit you did in the Great War.

Yours fraternally
Robert Baden-Powell
Nov. 1918

1919

Expansion of the Sea Scout Branch

Archives show that Sir Robert Baden-Powell – with his vision of an expansion to 30,000 members – recognised the importance of the Sea Scout Branch providing training for both the Royal and Merchant Navies.

In March 1919 Admiral of the Fleet, Sir David Beatty, GCB, GCVO, DSO, First Sea Lord, accepted the appointment of Chief Sea Scout, replacing Admiral Lord Charles Beresford.

On 23 April Sir George Le Hute, Headquarters Commissioner for Sea Scouts, wrote on the request of the Chief Scout to Admiral Commanding Coastguard and Reserves about the possibility of the Coastguard Service being greatly curtailed, in which event Sea Scouts would be placed at the service of the Admiralty for any duties they may wish them to undertake.

10 September 1919

Admiral Lord Charles Beresford, CGB, GCVO, the first Chief Sea Scout, died aged 73.

25 September 1919

In 1913 and 1917 the Navy League unsuccessfully approached the Admiralty for recognition. In 1919 the League again applied to the Admiralty for recognition of its 34 Boys' Naval Brigades, which was granted subject to an annual efficiency inspection by an officer on the staff of the Admiral Commanding Reserves, and the title 'Navy League Sea Cadets' was adopted. This was followed by the Sea Lords at the Admiralty officially recognising the Sea Scouts as a 'Central Association in the Sea Cadet Corps'.

PART 2: THE ROYAL NAVAL RECOGNITION SCHEME

Sea Scouting and Admiralty Recognition

Presently there are about 350 Sea Scout Groups in the UK (and one in Gibraltar), of which 101 Sea Scout Groups are allowed to wear the dark blue rectangular badge depicting a crown and anchor, the sign of 'Royal Naval Recognised' Sea Scout Groups.

RN Recognised Sea Scouts are not financially supported by the Ministry of Defence (MoD) to the extent of the Sea Cadet Corps, apart from an annual capitation grant to The Scout Association. This grant is the basis of the Admiralty Fund to which Recognised Sea Scout Groups can apply for assistance towards the purchase of, and access to, naval equipment and training, facilitating activities afloat, while still remaining independent of naval control.

A Selection of Sea Scout Admiralty/RN Recognition Reports and Activities

The reports provide an interesting historical and social insight over a period of almost 90 years. Of the 100 reports researched, the following is but a small sample of those written over the years:

1920

1st Mortlake Sea Scouts Admiralty Inspection

The Troop's first Admiralty Inspection took place on Tuesday 20 April 1920, and the Inspecting Officer was Captain Thesiger, RN, accompanied by Rear Admiral Hickley, RN, and Sir George Le Hute.

Captain Thesiger expressed himself as favourably impressed by the Troop's cheery spirit, said that in dress and general smartness they were well turned out, that its foot drill was good, and he considered the keenness of the Troop to be of meritorious quality.

As the result of this visit, Captain Thesiger presented the Troop with a small silver oar, which was subsequently mounted, and used as a trophy for competitions in elementary Scouting and seamanship.

Source: *Fifty Years of Sea Scouting in Mortlake 1909-59.*

1922-3

ADMIRALTY RECOGNITION

April 1922 – Five Sea Scout Troops in the Scheme

The 1st Mortlake, 23rd Dover, Liverpool (West Toxteth), Gravesend and Southport Sea Scouts received RN Capitation for 1921.

In a debate in the House of Commons on 31 July 1922 about RN Capitation, HM Treasury questioned the use of naval and military pensions and grants.

Sir A Shirley Benn asked the Financial Secretary to the Treasury how many units of the Sea Scout Branch of the Boy Scouts Movement have been recognised, and if any obstacles are being placed to the recognition of further units?

Mr Young: Five such units have been recognised since the Boys Scouts Association was recognised by the Admiralty in September 1919. The Treasury has asked that additional units of Cadet Corps, etc, shall not be recognised pending further consideration of the extent to which provision can be made for grants to such bodies in present financial circumstances.

New requirements for the Admiralty Recognition Scheme were issued in February 1923 – there was to be no expenditure of public funds for new Groups.

1924

1st Mortlake Sea Scouts Admiralty Inspection

On 8 April 1924 the 1st Mortlake underwent its annual Admiralty Inspection, which on this occasion was made by Captain N. O'Neil, RN. Eleven officers and 85 boys were mustered on parade.

Classes in signalling, boxing, compass, knots, splicing and seamanship were examined, and standards of ability under all these headings found to be entirely satisfactory.
The official report read:

149   *1st Mortlake Sea Scouts, c.1921.*

'The standard of intelligence was high, and showed careful and good instruction. Boat work was regularly carried out. Physical drill was very well carried out. The Troop possesses the best band I have heard during one-year inspections of Sea Scouts and Sea Cadet Corps. The Scoutmaster deserves great credit for the cheerful tone and intelligence of this well-organised Troop.'

Source: *Fifty Years of Sea Scouting in Mortlake 1909-59.*

1926

At the Annual General Meeting of the Council of the Boy Scouts Association held on 1 February 1926 Admiral of the Fleet Earl Beatty, OM, GCB, GCVO, DSO resigned from the Council.

During the years 1925 to 1940 no records can be found at The Scout Association Archives or in Group histories and publications of any Admiralty Inspections being carried out of Sea Scout Troops.

1926-9

In February 1926 Admiral of the Fleet the Earl Jellicoe, GCB, OM, GCVO was elected to the Committee of the Council of The Boy Scouts Association.

In February 1929 HRH Prince George (later the Duke of Kent) was appointed President of the Sea Scout Branch; he was also referred to as Commodore, Sea Scout Branch.

1935-6

On 20 November 1935 Admiral of the Fleet the First Earl Jellicoe of Scapa, GCB, OM, GCVO died.

On 11 March 1936 Admiral of the Fleet the First Earl Beatty of the North Sea and Brooksby, GCB, GCVO, DSO died.

1939-45 – THE SECOND WORLD WAR

Papers at The National Archives, Kew, show the Treasury considered coastwatching during the First World War had been too expensive, therefore the Sea Scouts would not be financed in the same way during current hostilities. With War more in the skies, Sea Scouts found other ways of using their specialised knowledge. One notable activity was the Thames River Emergency Service operated by the Port of London Authority; most of their crews were taken over by the Royal Naval Patrol Service in late 1941. Large numbers of Sea Scouts joined the Royal Navy or boating sections of other services. Requests were again made by the Admiralty for Sea Scouts to volunteer for convoy signaller duties.

PART 3: THE ADMIRALTY'S 'Y' SCHEME OF ENTRY INTO THE ROYAL NAVY 1941-5

1941

The December 1941 issue of *The Scouter* announced:

Young men of 17 years of age and above may now volunteer to enter the Navy (including The Fleet Air Arm) or the Royal Marines under the 'Y' Scheme. Under the arrangements, a candidate who is accepted will become a member of the Navy but will be placed on an unpaid reserve until he is called up for Service, which will not be before he reaches the age of 18. Fuller details will be found in a leaflet entitled *Entry of Young Men in the Navy and Combined Recruiting Centre or to Imperial Headquarters.*

As the Coastwatching Service in the First World War is an important part of Sea Scout history, equally the 'Y' Scheme, little researched by historians, is a central part of their history during the Second World War. The 'Y' scheme recruited educationally-qualified (School Certificate holders or higher) young men whilst still at school and who were potential officer material. This Scheme also permitted Sea Scout Groups which attained certain levels of proficiency to apply for stores and grants to train young men in basic seamanship before entering military service.

1942

14th Richmond Sea Scouts/1st Mortlake Sea Scouts

During February 1942, instruction of 'Y'-entry candidates started at Alder Road, Mortlake, London SW14. The 14th Richmond Sea Scouts combined with the 1st Mortlake Sea Scouts for Tuesday evening parades, giving the advantage of a more diversified corps of instructors. Paignton Sea Scouts also gained Admiralty Recognition in that year.

The 'Y' Scheme Live

Philip Marshall, aged 16, a junior bank clerk living with his family in Stoke-on-Trent, cycled daily to work. One day a female clerk from another local bank failed to arrive for a routine meeting to exchange documents, the casualty of a stray bomb. As a consequence Philip Marshall volunteered for the 'Y' Scheme.

He signed an agreement to join the Sea Scouts until he reached the age of 18. At their meetings they marched up and down, each holding aloft a flag, and when the leading 'ship' dipped his flag, they all turned 90 degrees to port, or starboard, or did something even more complicated. He wondered whether the ability to manoeuvre a fleet at sea, usually the province of an Admiral, would be of much use to youngsters, but they did learn to distinguish port from starboard, bow from stern, how to tie a bowline-on-the-bight instead of a granny knot, and other mundane though possibly life-saving skills.

Four days after his 18th birthday, Philip was taken to HMS *Raleigh*, a shore base in Torpoint, Cornwall, for training as an Ordinary Seaman. The first shock was seeing the heavily-bombed Plymouth and Devonport, and their wrecked houses. The second shock was being ordered about in groups, sleeping in crowded dormitories, and eating mass-produced food. Even the classrooms and physical education lessons were not unlike school, though some subjects were new.

The days passed quickly. Sometimes they rowed the cutter up-river to the Tamar Bridge and back; sometimes they were trusted to cross the Torpoint ferry to Devonport. For his group, that just meant the WVS (Women's Voluntary Service) canteen. Sometimes the nearby anti-aircraft battery was firing, and once they sat on the ferry at night and watched a plane come down in flames, like a distant firework. No-one cheered; after all they could not be absolutely certain that it wasn't one of 'ours'.

In the mid-December passing-out parade, they were a lot older and wiser. After Christmas leave, joining instructions were received – three of them in the Scheme were to travel to Northern Ireland to join HMS *Londonderry*. Philip Marshall went on to serve in Belfast and in Freetown, Sierra Leone, West Africa. Some of the other 'Y' Schemers were sent to serve in cruisers, battleships, or aircraft carriers. An early 'Y' Scheme Inspection report:

Admiralty Inspection Report – 2nd Reading Sea Scouts

In 1942 the newly formed Sea Scout Troop trained hard to work up to apply for Admiralty Inspection under the 'Y' Scheme. The inspection took place at their riverside base on 22 April 1942.

The Inspecting officer was Commander Rossitter, RNR, who was accompanied by Mr A.E. Mackenzie, Sea Scout Commissioner for training and Master of RRS *Discovery*.

During a two-hour programme Commander Rossitter saw Patrols being instructed in many subjects from knotting and splicing to signalling and navigation and physical training class.

The Commander congratulated the leaders R.E. Huggins and S.E. Johnson on the efficiency and discipline of the Troop. They were awarded full Admiralty Recognition as a Unit authorised to give pre-entry training under the Royal Navy's 'Y' Scheme.

Source: 2nd Reading Sea Scouts Group History

On 25 August 1942 HRH the Duke of Kent, Commodore of Sea Scouts, was killed in a flying accident near Oban, Argyllshire.

Admiralty Inspection Report – Southbourne and Aldwick Sea Scouts

Name of Unit	Southbourne and Aldwick	Number 48
Date of Inspection	27 November 1942	

GENERAL REPORT UPON THE INSPECTION:

Southbourne and Aldwick paraded at full strength, and showed themselves to be a very efficient Unit – smart and well disciplined.

The syllabus of training is of a moderate standard, and is efficiently taught by well trained Youth Instructors. Their Headquarters, a converted farm warehouse lent by Mr Charles Brundrett, Group Scoutmaster, provides every facility for training. Instructional equipment appeared good and efficient. I recommend this unit for Admiralty recognition.

W.L. Rossitter
Commander RNR

Hansard, 17 February 1943 – Sea Cadet Corps and Boy Scouts Association

After the 'Y' Scheme had been running for a year or so the following written Parliamentary Answer was made:

> Mr Perkins asked the First Lord of the Admiralty whether he is satisfied that the arrangements for co-operation between the Sea Cadet Corps and the Boy Scouts Association are working satisfactorily and will he extend the scope for the further development of the Sea Scouts?
>
> Mr Alexander: I am satisfied with the co-operation existing between the Admiralty and the two organisations mentioned. The number of Sea Scout Units receiving Admiralty recognition is still increasing.

During 1943, 47 Sea Scout Groups were inspected by the Admiralty Representative and attained the required standard under the 'Y' Scheme.

1944

In March 1944 a Southsea newspaper published an article by Sub Lieutenant J.D. Pearce, RNVR, Sea Scout Adviser (South) to promote Sea Scouting and the 'Y' Scheme:

LITTLE-KNOWN WORLD OF THE SEA SCOUTS

It is amazing after 34 years how little is known by the general public of Sea Scout Activities, and only in recent years has their training and efficiency become fully recognised.

Sea Scout training is different from the accepted method of training ship or nautical school. Its effects are obtained through adventurous experiences on water, whether inland or at sea, and not through formal instructions between decks.

FOR TOUGH YOUTHS

The Sea Scouts is not an organisation for small boys, but is capable of giving excellent training for youths up to 18 and 19, and owing to the strenuous activities a certain standard of toughness is required.

That the value of this training is recognised by the Admiralty is shown by the fact that about 3,000 Sea Scouts have received Admiralty recognition as being capable of giving instruction under the 'Y' scheme on naval entry.

The 'Y' scheme gives special chances to suitable candidates for promotion to commissioned rank, and it is because the Sea Scouts believe they can produce the officers that the Navy needs in war time that they are so happy to co-operate in the scheme.

The number of these 'recognised' Sea Scouts troops is steadily increasing. There are eleven in Hampshire.

The Sea Scouts are also co-operating with the Ministry of Transport in connection with the entry into the Merchant Navy.

WORK IN THE BLITZ [Air Raids]

Since the beginning of the war a large number of Sea Scouts have attended pre-Naval training courses held in the famous Royal Research Ship *Discovery*, and some extremely good work was done by Scouts operating from the ship up and down the London river during heavy air raids.

Like all Scout groups, Sea Scouts are self-supporting financially, and naturally their headquarters vary considerably.

While the Sea Scouts are doing everything they can to carry their full share of training under the war effort, they have not forgotten that their object is to produce good citizens, and to give the British boy who has the sea in his blood the chance of learning something of the ancient craft of seamanship, and they are doing all they can to attain this object.

Admiralty Inspection Report – Southbourne and Aldwick Sea Scouts

Name of Unit   Southbourne & Aldwick   Number [48]

Date of Inspection   9 May 1944

GENERAL REPORT UPON THE INSPECTION:

The continuity of very good work is most pleasing. The only attention I have to call is to the Morse signals. I congratulate the Group Sea Scoutmaster, Mr C. Brundrett, and those who took part in the great effort to rescue an Airman, who unfortunately lost his life when a part of the Aeroplane in which he was flying crashed into the creek at Prinsted during dark hours, which meant wading through mud a great distance and eventually bringing him ashore under very great difficulties. Knowledge of the above subject clears any doubts upon such undertaking. A Unit most worthy of Admiralty Recognition.

W.L. Rossitter
Commander RNR
Inspecting Officer

The *Observer*, Saturday, 2 September 1944

THEY WERE PREPARED

SEA SCOUTS RESCUE TRAPPED AIRMAN

For their courageous endeavour to rescue an airman who had been involved in a flying accident earlier this year at Prinsted, Hants., the Deputy Chief Scout, Sir Percy Everett, sent a letter of commendation to the 1st Southbourne Sea Scout Group [Sussex]. This Group has, like other Scout Troops in the District, gained a distinguished record of war service, having lived up to the motto 'Be Prepared'.

In his letter dated 14 July 1944 to the Southbourne Group, Sir Percy Everett wrote:

'I have heard with the greatest possible pleasure of the smart and courageous action of the Southbourne Group in their endeavour to rescue an airman who had been involved in a flying accident at Prinsted.'
'You and your Scouts behaved with remarkable bravery and resource and did what you could, at some risk to yourselves, in your endeavour to release the airman.'
'I do want, on behalf of the Chief Scout and myself, to congratulate you all most warmly on this fine piece of work. You have well upheld the tradition of our Scout training to "Be Prepared," and I know that you will continue to maintain a very high standard in your Group, so that whatever comes along you will be ready to do your best to help.'

Percy Everett
(Sir Percy Everett)'

Composite account compiled from Official Records: The Observer, *Saturday, 2 September 1944; The Group History of 1st Southbourne Sea Scouts; Adrienne Voller – WWII People's War.*

TRAGIC MID-AIR COLLISION

The full details of this tragic air accident, not released until many years later, are taken from various accounts, as follows:

At 8 p.m. on the evening of 8 February 1944 two RAF planes, a Mosquito Night Fighter and a Wellington Bomber, collided in the air over Southbourne.

The Mosquito crashed about a mile away heading for a small open space attempting to avoid nearby houses, both airmen losing their lives. The Wellington was cut into two in front of the rear gunner's turret, the tailpiece slowly twisting round and round, falling into the muddy creek left by the ebb tide, 100 yards offshore. The front section, containing six of the crew, fell in flames into a field at Southbourne and all inside died instantly. The rear turret containing Sergeant Varley 'fluttered down into Prinsted Harbour like a sycamore leaf', according to the account of two Sea Scouts who were standing outside their Scout headquarters.

As the tide was out, several members of the Troop waded out to the wreckage, which was in some three feet of soft mud. The conditions were far from ideal for such a hazardous rescue, and the Scouts faced danger but this did not deter them. By the illumination of a searchlight playing across the desolate mudland, and with the sticky mud clinging to everything and everybody all the while, after considerable clearing of debris had been done the Sea Scouts, helped by adults who had by now arrived on the scene, broke into the turret using a hacksaw, removed the 303 Browning machine gun and endeavoured to extract the rear gunner who was slumped over his machine gun. This took some while as his feet were trapped, but at last he was released minus one boot. The Sea Scouts thought the air gunner was still alive because of the warmth of his hand. The large and heavy young man was half-carried, half-dragged to the shore where a small crowd of civilians and servicemen were waiting, but he was pronounced dead at the scene.

During 1944, 70 Sea Scout Groups inspected under the 'Y' Scheme.

1945

April 1945

Admiralty Recognised Groups in the Scheme numbered 100.

Pre-Naval entry courses were held on RRS *Discovery*, attended by 2,500 Sea Scouts, one in four gaining a commission during the period of hostilities.

8 May 1945

The War in Europe ended.

Some comments on Admiralty Inspections 1920-45

The Inspecting Officer [IO] said we were well-turned-out and foot drill was good, but we lacked elementary knowledge.

He criticised severely the lack of elementary knowledge in both Scouting and Seamanship.

IO: The Troop possessed the best band I had ever heard.

The IO said he had never seen sail drill on land before.

The IO was a fatherly soul.

The report was a little too good, and he gave us credit for astronomy, which we did not do.

A younger and stricter officer came for the next inspection. His eagle eye did not miss much.

We constructed a breeches buoy which we thought was not very well done, but the IO seemed pleased.

The day was one of the wettest I have every known.

On only one occasion did we receive stores, very useful equipment, together with six colossal great iron snatch blocks which would have held a battleship.

On marching; 'The Scouters made a valiant attempt, but a not-very-successful effort to keep all in one step and some show of dressing in the ranks'.

RRS *Discovery* survived the bombing with very few scars. The last pre-navy course was held on *Discovery* in May 1945 and after the War she reverted to use for Sea Scout training.

After the War the RN 'Y' Scheme was redeveloped into the new Admiralty Scheme whereby a limit of 100 Groups of Sea Scouts in the United Kingdom at any one time were granted recognition.

During 1945 the Admiralty Inspecting Officer, Lieutenant Commander Rossitter RNR, retired and was presented with a carved plaque in appreciation of his help and kindness during the previous four years. His duties were assumed by Lieutenant Commander Askins, RNR.

Part 4: The Admiralty/RN Recognition Scheme 1946-2009
1946

In a post-retirement letter written in 1946 to *The Scouter*, Commander Rossitter said that now hostilities had ceased and victory achieved, his time had come, as for many others, to pack his bags and return to his pre-war occupation. Since 1941 he had served as Liaison Officer, visiting many units. He expressed his sincere thanks for all the devoted labours of many in the training of Sea Scouts during the past years of war. His inspections had been made a pleasure by the high standards of training for Admiralty Recognition, and the fine spirit of voluntary loyalty and self-discipline. He fully realised that it was no small sacrifice to choose the harder path of service. The Sea Scouts would carry on, like all other Scouts, whatever adjustments may be needed by the coming Peace.

He said Scout training constituted the best preparation for qualities of character. The coolness of Scouts during blackouts, the bombing of London and other cities, has been most marked. Whilst aboard *Discovery*, with everyone feeling the stress, he was always was greeted with a smile and cheery word.

He was immensely proud of the Scouts, knowing the claims of world Scouting was the main foundation for world peace.

1947

Rear Admiral Viscount Mountbatten of Burma was appointed Commodore for Sea Scouts.

September 1947

The Admiralty approved the use of a badge to be worn by members of Admiralty Recognised Units, an anchor surmounted with a Naval Crown and the word 'Admiralty' in gold on a navy-blue background. A smaller version of this badge is still worn proudly today.

1948

London Sea Scouts attended the unveiling of the Earl Jellicoe and Earl Beatty memorials in Trafalgar Square, London.

1951

Synopsis of 1951 Inspecting Officer's Report:

There were 98 Admiralty Recognised Units. Numbers remained steady and were about 46% of all Sea Scouts in the country (4,579). The numbers of Recognised Units were about 28%. The general standard of seamanship and Sea Scouting was very satisfactory. The entry of Admiralty Recognised Sea Scouts into the Royal Navy was satisfactory. The interest taken in and the encouragement given by the Royal Navy were of considerable value. About 4,500 Sea Scouts were in Admiralty Recognised units.

COMMANDER F.D. BROWN
Inspecting Officer
For Admiral Commanding Reserves

Source: Scout Association Archives.

1952

On 15 April 1952 approval was given for RN Recognised Sea Scout Groups to use a Red Ensign defaced with the Arrowhead Badge surmounted by an Admiralty Crown in the fly.

1953

100 Sea Scouts from Admiralty Recognised Units invited aboard HM Ships to see the Spithead Review. They did normal ships' crew duties and were complimented on their bearing and turn out.

1954

Admiralty Inspection Report – 1st Mortlake Sea Scouts

ADMIRALTY INSPECTION UNIT NUMBER 92

1st MORTLAKE SEA SCOUTS

The Admiralty Inspection took place on 7 May 1954 and was carried out by Rear Admiral Commanding Reserves, Rear Admiral Alan Scott Moncrieff, CBE. The ceremonial parade on the river bank took very much the same form as in the previous year, in that the march past led by the band took place at Leydon House, with *HL(S) [Harbour Launch (Steam)] Minotaur II* lying off the foreshore moored off Ship Lane for inspection immediately after the review of the Group personnel. Admiralty recognition approved.

Source: 1st Mortlake Group History 1909-59

RRS *Discovery* became too expensive for the Boy Scouts Association to fund. She was handed over to the Admiralty for a nominal £1 for use as an RNVR Drill Ship and Flag Ship of the Admiral Commanding Reserves, who was also responsible for the Admiralty Recognition Scheme for Sea Scouts and Sea Cadets.

1955

Synopsis of 1955 Inspecting Officer's Report

Sea Scout numbers declined during the year but the Branch continued a vigorous existence. A total of 94 Sea Scout Troops were qualified during the year, including one at the Royal Naval School on Malta.

The enthusiasm and initiative of all concerned have enabled the high standard of the previous years to be maintained in the face of ever-rising cost of boats and maintenance. Many Sea Scouts had visited HM Ships and Establishments.

Source: The Boy Scouts Association

1956

In 1956, 99 Admiralty Qualified Sea Scout Groups were registered.

Extracts from Inspecting Officers' comments published in Annual Reports of the Boy Scouts Association 1956-60

1956: The number of Admiralty Qualified Sea Scout Units increased to a total of 97. Good reports were received of the inspections made by Lieutenant Commander P.C.S. Black, the Admiralty Inspecting Officer who has now taken up other duties. We would like to express our appreciation of the way in which Lieutenant Commander Black has carried out these inspections during the last two-and-a-half years. He has won the admiration and respect of all the Scouters and Scouts who have met him.

1957: The Admiralty Inspecting Officer reported a small increase in the number of Sea Scouts. There were 96 Qualified Sea Scout Units recognised by the Admiralty. Rear Admiral Geoffrey Thistleton-Smith, CB, GM, personally inspected eight units and expressed himself as well pleased with what he saw. For the first time Sea Scouts were on duty at the Boat Show at Olympia.

1958: After three years' service as Admiralty Inspecting Officer Lieutenant Commander R.C.E. Watkins retired at the end of 1958. A "Thanks Badge" was presented to Lieutenant Commander Watkins as an expression of gratitude for his great service to Sea Scouting in connection with the Admiralty Scheme.

1959: The Admiralty Inspecting Officer reported there were 94 Admiralty Qualified Units. 40 Sea Scouts from Admiralty Qualified Units enlisted on regular engagements and 24 had joined the Royal Navy for National Service. 20 had entered the RNVR. 79 entered the Merchant Navy and three joined Royal Naval Cadet Ships.

1960: Lieutenant Commander Wareham RN reported that all of the 98 Admiralty Qualified Units had been inspected. There had been an improvement in the quality and quantity of boats used and in the standard of nautical instruction given. The number of Queen's Scouts had increased by 50%. During July 35 Sea Scouts had spent a day at sea in HM Ships taking part in Exercise Shop Window – a demonstration of the modern Navy in action. The Golden Jubilee of Sea Scouting celebrated this year included participation in the International Sail Training Race in July.

Overall, the reports were good with some increases in numbers, some fluctuations, but an improvement in quality.

1961-2

Admiralty Qualified Sea Scout Groups reach 100 – the maximum number.

1963-4

The yearly report of the Royal Naval Inspecting Officer, Lieutenant Commander Peter Cane, recorded 'Sea Scout Groups continued to maintain a high standard'.

The Royal Navy Flying Scheme was opened up to Admiralty Qualified Sea Scout Groups in 1964.

The 99th Bristol (Cabot) Sea Scout Journal recorded that access to these scholarships was one of the benefits of RN Recognition. Four Venture Scouts from the Group obtained their Private Pilot's licence.

Extract from 99th Bristol (Cabot) Sea Scouts Journal
Royal Naval Flying Scholarship – Paul Naish

Shortly before Christmas, the Scouts were having their festive party, when Tony [Bartlett] presented me with a pamphlet advertising a three-week at a civil flying club where I could obtain 30 flying hours, ten of which were to be solo. It seemed no time before I was at Biggin Hill in Kent going through severe scrutiny by a board of naval officers. After two days they decided they had seen enough of me, and I found I had passed.

On 11 July, I left Bristol in the early hours bound for Carlisle. At the station a van took us to the airfield to join the 17 others on the course. After a preliminary talk we settled down for the night and prepared for the day ahead.

It was a hectic routine. For the first eight days we were given six one-hour lectures daily from meteorology, air law, mechanics and aerodynamics for the Cessna 150, a small two-seater with fantastic manoeuvrability and handling. There was little time remaining each day to do much flying, but I did get a few hours in during the first week.

150   *An Admiralty Inspection of the 99th Bristol (Cabot) Sea Scouts, 1962. Boats are being towed by an RNR cutter during the Admiralty Inspection. RN Inspecting Officer: Lieutenant Commander P. Wareham, RN.*

The next two weeks consisted of waiting for bad weather to clear, revising for exams, learning 150 checks off by heart, and squeezing in 30 hours flying time. When told we were to fly solo, I was under the impression that I would handle the plane whilst an instructor accompanied me and got me down safely. How wrong can one get? He made sure he was OK by not being in the plane at all! After seven hours above ground, of which I had control of the plane for only a few, the instructor landed, jumped out, told me to do a short circuit and walked away. The aircraft was known as Foxtrot Oscar but when reporting to the control tower that I was ready for take-off, I referred to the plane as 'Foscar Oxtrot'. As time went on, so did my progress – I carried out spins and stalls, cross country flights, short landings and take-offs, practice engine failure, fires and emergency landings – all eventually mastered.

The day came to return home. I can only presume the chief instructor was satisfied, as he hardly said a word to me during the sixty-minute flight.

I find it difficult to believe I was alone, 4,000 feet above ground, flying over the Scottish Highlands with the wind blowing past you at 100mph. It's a lonely sensation but you feel free, far away from the civilisation below.

In November 1964 Admiral of the Fleet Earl Mountbatten of Burma, Commodore of Sea Scouts, presented the 1st Sandown (1st Isle of Wight) Sea Scouts with their Royal Naval Recognition Pennant (first inspection) during his tour as Governor of the Island.

1965

Synopsis of 1965 Inspecting Officer's Report

The majority of Units are well up to standard, but the total of Units continues to decrease, although the situation is beginning to stabilise. The building of new headquarters and modernising continues apace. The number of canoes being built is increasing, and the number of RN Cadet Ships continues to be encouraging. There is a very keen spirit amongst the Sea Scouts, and tremendous efforts are continually being made.

I have thoroughly enjoyed this, my first year, of inspections and coming to close quarters with the Scout Movement. There is a very keen spirit amongst the Sea Scouts and tremendous efforts are continually being made by Scouters and parents alike to meet the requirements of the younger generation without breaking with the basically sound principles of Scouting.

Wherever I have travelled I have been treated with great courtesy and generosity and I take this opportunity to thank all concerned for helping me so much in my work and I look forward, with optimism, to 1966.

C.J. Whiffen
Lieutenant Commander RN

Source: Reports supplied by the late Eric Musgrave.

151   *4th Seven Kings Sea Scouts building their 30ft-ketch at Hargreaves Camp Site, 1963.*

1967

The total number of RN Recognised Sea Scout Groups was recorded as 93.
'Admiralty Recognition' was renamed 'RN Recognition'.

1972

Royal Naval Inspection Report – 4th Streatham Sea Scouts

1.   I carried out the Inspection at the Headquarters in Streatham and at the Boat House Putney
      on Tuesday 19 September 1972.

      My first duty was to inspect *Venture Spirit* (steel ship's lifeboat) which they are converting to
      a General Purpose Work Boat; it has been fitted with an ex-MoD (N) engine and has been

decked in. I examined this boat with a critical eye and must congratulate them on the effort made; it has taken three years' work and they hope to launch it at the end of the year.

On arrival at the boat house, I was greeted by the SL, and was then piped into the Muster area, where I met the County Commissioner and witnessed colours. My next duty was to inspect the Group; the turnout was of a high standard, both in numbers and in the general appearance. I finally inspected the Cub Pack which was also a keen team. (My questions caused some worried looks, as indeed did my bends and problems, though a lot can be put down to 'Inspectionitis'.)

It was pleasing to see a Scout [Dirk van Beek] with his Pilot's badge, as such an award is rare in Scouting Groups, the exam being more difficult than most and covering such topics as practical Navigation (coastal) by day and night and a thorough knowledge of the 'Rules of the Road'.

2.   (The activities were too limited, even allowing for the time of year, but they were well carried out.) Two gigs and the dinghies were put afloat and I was invited to join them in the Venture Scout gig, which I stroked up the river (with the tide) and coxswained down the river in a race. The boats were well handled with the oarsmanship being of a high standard. I then visited the class being instructed in Pilotage and was well satisfied with the standard. The Inspection concluded with prayers said by the Group minister, my comments and the Lowering of Colours.

3.   The Inspection was witnessed by the Assistant County Commissioner for Sea Activities Mr Perkins, District Commissioner Mr Sutton and Assistant District Commissioner Mr Evans.

4.   Since the last inspection the following awards have been granted:

Scout Standard	9	Advanced Scout Standards	4
Chief Scout Award	4	Coxswain Badge	1
Pilot Badge	1		

5.   One Scout from this Group has joined BRNC.

6.   This was a good Inspection; the Group has tremendous enthusiasm and very good leadership. It was a pleasure to see so many Venture Scouts, whose example and keenness impressed me greatly.

There is a feeling of strength within this Group, which points well for the future and I recommend continuation of Royal Navy Recognition.

Signed G.R.P. WEAVER
Lieutenant Commander, RN
Inspecting Officer for
Admiral Commanding Reserves

Source: The Author

152   *Royal Naval Inspection of 99th Bristol (Cabot) Sea Scouts by Staff Officer, 1972.*

1975

Tip Top Sea Scouts

David Harwood wrote in the January and February *Scouting* on RN Groups that there were 300 registered Sea Scout Groups, of which 100 were Royal Naval Recognised Sea Scout Troops. Scout headquarters received an annual grant (in 1975 22½p) for each Sea Scout in a Recognised Group between the ages of 12 and 15, and also grants were paid for each Chief Scout's Award, Advanced Scout Standard, Scout Standard, Coxswain, Pilot, Fireman and Ambulances Badge.

The Inspecting Officer was Lieutenant Commander Gerry Ginn. Although shore-based, the posting was not deskbound or static and he travelled widely. He invariably went by train, often writing inspection reports, and frequently called at Scout HQ to collect further details of his programme.

Critics of the Royal Naval Recognition Scheme claimed that it formed 'elite' Sea Scout Groups. David Harwood thought that this was unfounded – the Royal Navy was prepared to recognise 100 Groups which he felt reflected credit on the Scout Movement in general. Groups recognised had to work hard to maintain the standard, initial recognition for which was high. In his opinion, the Scheme was of great benefit to The Scout Association.

Statistics and Achievements – Royal Navy Recognition

Scouting *magazine, March 1975:*

There were 99 Recognised Sea Scout Groups, in which were 3,700 Sea Scouts and over 700 Venture Sea Scouts. The number of Sea Scouts dropped very slightly over the previous year, but the number of Venture Scouts rose by just over 20%. About 45% of Sea Scouts achieved their Scout Standard, and 17% had the advanced Scout Standard. Coxswain's Badges were gained by 27 Sea Scouts (fewer than 1%) and the Pilot Badge was gained by 6 Sea Scouts (0.2%). 91 members of Recognised Groups gained places in the Royal or Merchant Navies during the previous year – a very significant number.

Synopsis of 1975 Inspecting Officer's Report

Qualified Admiralty Sea Scout Units

The total number of Sea Scouts in RN Recognised units is just under 4,000 (3,974), together with 898 Venture Scouts – 22½% of the number of Troops – on average one Venture Scout for five in the Troop.

These 4,000 Troops achieved 54 Queen's Scouts Awards, 287 Chief Scout Awards, 34 Duke of Edinburgh Gold Awards, 66 Silver and 84 Bronze. There were also 662 Advanced Scout Standard Awards.

Proficiency Badges: 18 Pilots, 27 Coxswains, 179 Venture Awards, 196 RYA [Royal Yachting Association] and 78 BCU [British Canoe Union] qualified.

Of the 105 Groups inspected, five lost their RN Recognition, three had their recognition withheld and 28 were under warning.

General Comments: Lieutenant Commander Cressey RN:

'It has been a great privilege to have been associated with Sea Scouting for the past fifteen months. Many groups are still short of boats or make do with unsuitable ones, most are tackling the problem of both RYA and BCU qualifications, some are short of Scouters and the problem of finance is ever present; yet all strive with untiring energy and devotion to produce good citizens, good Scouts and good seamen. One has learnt that Scouting must never be allowed to stand still, and on the Water Activities side it most certainly does not, as on each visit I have made to a Group there has always been something new to see or new ideas being brought into practice. Points of comment, so far as I am aware, have always been received in the spirit in which they were delivered and I hope have been of some help.'

Source: *Cabot Bulletin – 99th Bristol Sea Scouts*

1977

The 2nd Cowes (St Mary) celebrated their Golden Jubilee in February with the opening of their new Group Headquarters by Admiral Lord Mountbatten, Governor of the Isle of Wight and Commodore of Sea Scouts. The £20,000 Headquarters was filled to capacity for his arrival. The Group sent a telegram to the Queen in her Jubilee year, and she replied with congratulations on the Group's Golden Jubilee.

153 *His Excellency The Admiral of the Fleet, The Earl Mountbatten of Burma, Governor of the Isle of Wight (1969-74), inspects the 2nd Cowes (St Mary's) Sea Scouts, who were there to open the new Scout Headquarters, as Commodore of Sea Scouts.*

In June 1977 Sea Scouts from the 17th Colchester Sea Scouts had a grandstand view from HMS *Sultan*, a shore base at Lee-on-Solent, of the Review of the Fleet by the Queen at Spithead. They later boarded HMS *Brighton*, one of the frigates in the Review, and were joined by Sea Scouts from the 29th Glasgow, steaming out of Portsmouth as HMY *Britannia*, with the Royal Family on board, sailed into the Harbour. The Sea Scouts helped the ship's company in 'manning the ship' as they sailed along the English Channel to Dover.

Royal Naval Prize

This prize was instituted in 1973 by Rear Admiral I.G.W Robertson, formerly Admiral Commanding Reserves, to encourage Sea Scouts from Royal Naval Recognised Groups to obtain the Pilot's Badge, requiring a high standard of nautical knowledge. The presentation of the prize was discontinued in 1979. On 1 April 1979 the title of Admiral Reserves lapsed and his functions, including responsibility for the Sea Scouts and Sea Cadets, transferred to the Commander-in-Chief Naval Home Command (CINCNAVHOME) in Portsmouth. The office is now held by the Flag Officer Scotland, Northern England and Northern Ireland (FOSNNI) and Flag Officer Reserves.

List of Prizewinners 1973-9

1973: 16-year-old Cardiff Sea Scout, Martin Westwood.

1975: David Donaldson, 15-year-old Sea Scout, 6th Newtownards, Northern Ireland.

1976: Christopher Gorringe, 6th Barry Sea Scouts (South Wales).

1977: Stephen McCrory, 6th Newtownards Sea Scouts.

1978: Nicholas Matthews, 1st Blofield and Brundall Sea Scouts, Norwich.

1979: Timothy Calk, 1st Blofield and Brundall Sea Scouts.

Presentations of the prize usually took place on board HMS *Discovery*.

154　*The 70th Anniversary Camp of the 99th Bristol (Cabot) Sea Scouts, 1979. Lieutenant Commander D. Uden, RN, Staff Officer (Scouts) cuts the anniversary cake.*

RN Recognised Sea Scouts – The Swimming and Diving Championships

The first National Sea Scout Swimming Gala took place at HMS *Ganges* in the early 1970s. Since the 1970s competition has been held mostly at HMS *Raleigh*. The standard of competition improved each year, with individual records being broken. In 2008, 250 Scouts and Explorers took part in the gala, accommodated at HMS *Raleigh*. On arrival, Groups must guarantee a full team of swimmers. As usual, the enthusiasm shown by all involved is very impressive. Participating Groups compete for the Otter Trophy presented to Lord Baden-Powell in 1910 by the Royal Naval Life-Saving Association.

1979

The Seventieth Anniversary Sea Scout Meet

This special event in the history of the Sea Scouts was marked on August Bank Holiday 1979 when Rear Admiral Charles Williams opened the three-day Seventieth Anniversary Sea Scout Meet at Chatham Naval Dockyards. Activities included sailing, rowing, barbecues, discos, knock-out football and cricket.

Earl Mountbatten had been invited to attend the Sea Scout Meet but declined due to his forthcoming traditional family holiday at Classiebawn Castle near Mullaghmore, Sligo, in the north-west of the Republic of Ireland.

Remembering their Commodore

Lord Mountbatten, Commodore of Sea Scouts, 25 June 1900-27 August 1979

On Monday, 27 August Lord Mountbatten, aged 79, and six companions were in his boat, *Shadow V*, which had set off from the fishing village of Mullaghmore. At around 11.30 a.m. a explosive device planted on board detonated. Lord Mountbatten was killed, together with one of his twin grandsons and a young local boy from his estate.

The news of the death of Lord Mountbatten was at first received with disbelief by those at the Chatham Sea Scout Meet. As soon as the tragic news was confirmed, colours were lowered to half-mast and the Hon. Greville Howard, a former Assistant County Commissioner for Sea Scouts, spoke movingly about Lord Mountbatten and their naval service together during the Second World War. It was agreed that the Sea Scout Meet should continue as that would have been the wish of our late Commodore.

Scouts shared the nation's horror and shock when Earl Mountbatten and members of his family were killed. Lord Mountbatten was appointed Commodore of Sea Scouts in January 1947, and held the appointment until his death. Whilst Viceroy of India, he was also Chief Scout of that country. He was extremely knowledgeable of Scouting, and demonstrated his understanding of the 'Post Advance Party Scouting' which recommended major changes to the Scout Movement. As President of the Romsey District Scout Council and Governor of the Isle of Wight, his interest and involvement in the Movement never diminished.

On Sunday, 18 November 1979 a Service of Thanksgiving for the life of Lord Louis Mountbatten, Commodore of Sea Scouts, took place at All Hallows by The Tower, London. The service was held for all London Sea Scouts and Sea Rangers, and was extremely impressive. Over 450 people attended, filling the church to capacity. Over 40 colours were paraded, including the national colours of the Scout Association. The service was conducted by the Rev. Peter Kefford with the Rev. Philip Blewett.

The service was based on the funeral service held in Westminster Abbey, for which Lord Mountbatten himself had chosen the hymns. The lesson was read by a Sea Scout from the 4th Streatham, and the address given by Lieutenant Commander the Hon. Greville Howard.

Rear Admiral C.B. Williams, Flag Officer, Medway, was represented by Staff-Commander D. Fowler, and other guests included Commander Phillip Cressey, Royal Navy Inspecting Officer, the District Commissioner, and six Scouts from Lord Mountbatten's home district of Romsey.

Nobody fortunate enough to be present will forget an occasion on which a sense of loss was succeeded by a great feeling of pride and gratitude. (The singing of the hymn *For Those in Peril on the Sea* added even greater poignancy to the moment, binding the congregation together as one.)

'A telegram of sympathy and loyalty was sent to Her Majesty the Queen.'

There has been no Commodore of Sea Scouts since that date.

Some other Comments on and about Admiralty Recognised Groups at their Admiralty Inspections 1946-83

Capability and/or ambition is missing.

Ignorance of procedure gave rise to self-consciousness and indecision.

UNIFORM (Scouts)

Shoes to be of a plain, black type, well polished and with plain laces. Socks to be dark blue in colour.

Trousers must be of the official dark blue pattern, well creased, with no lumpy objects worn on belt or carried in pockets.

Jerseys should be of adequate size and correct pattern, with badges sewn on as shown in the sketch. Great care should be taken to see that there is no chance of underclothing showing at the neck, as this ruins the appearance of an otherwise smart scout. Washing should be done with luke-warm, soapy water, the badges, etc. being scrubbed gently.

Neckerchiefs to be washed and pressed frequently and folded neatly in such a way that the creases are symmetrical and there is room for a 50p piece in the triangle at the back. Lanyards to be scrubbed frequently - it is best to have a spare one. Never pull the knot through. When the correct adjustment has been made to allow the lanyard to go over the head and lie on top of the "Discovery" knot of the neckerchief, a stitch or two should be put in the lanyard knot to stop it slipping and causing an accident in rough play, etc.

Caps should be well-cared for and in good condition. They should be scrubbed but not blancoed. Tally bands to be tied in a neat bow as sketch and then ironed and secured with a stitch if necessary. Never untie the bow once it has been cut to size.

The "S" of the word "SCOUTS" to be above the nose

Watch Flash

Group
District
Patrol
County
¼" between each badge
R.N.
SEA SCOUTS
"Standard" (top ¼" below the "S"
World Badge (top ¼" below the "S")
Pursuit   Service
Boatman, Cox Mate or Cox.
Interest

Room for a 50p piece or old fashioned penny

A sea scout's appearance is ruined if he allows his hair to grow too long. It is a condition of membership that hair should be kept reasonably short.

Members are expected to arrive and depart in correct Number One Uniform. Coats to be carried and not worn unless it is raining or cold. We are in the eye of the public when arriving and leaving our headquarters.

Always bring: Clasp knife with spike, pencil, dark blue shorts, plimsolls (white if possible), white T-shirt in summer.

155 *Tying a Sea Scout tally band (cap ribbon). Blue caps in winter were abolished in 1956 for white caps to be worn all year round. The 99th Bristol (Cabot) circulated their own instructions about Sea Scout uniforms. The tying of the 'tiddly bow' included putting a farthing or a sixpence inside the knot of the tally band to bring good luck (not part of the instructions). The purple ink of the instructions shows it was produced by a spirit duplicator – a low-volume printing method mainly used by schools, churches and youth organisations, alcohol being the main component.*

156   *99th Bristol (Cabot) Sea Scouts Admiralty Inspection, 1985.*

On navigation: I think it would be as well for the boys to be thoroughly conversant with all the symbols on a chart before proceeding to actually navigate. Such things as the meaning of the tides, the heights of lighthouses given, how charts are made, etc.

The tendency of Sea Scouts wearing their caps on the back of their heads is spreading. This must not be allowed. The Inspecting Officer (IO) sets a lot of store by such things as clean boots and properly-worn caps.

The standard of training is probably unsurpassed by any other Sea Scout Troop.

A few Troops own yachts!

The IO said I was very short for a Sea Scout. I said, 'Yes Sir, I am only eleven.'

IO: 'That's a tiddly bow; is that a small coin under the centre of the overhead knot?' Young Sea Scout: 'Yes, Sir.' IO: 'Was your father in the Navy?' Young Scout: 'No Sir. My Patrol Leader makes and sells the bows for half-a-crown [2s. 6d.]'.

157   A Royal Naval Inspection, 1985, of the 99th Bristol (Cabot) Sea Scouts. Inspecting Officer: Lieutenant Commander Scott.

After a watery exercise, the IO was taken back to the HQ where he received the traditional Navy tot.

I hated the knotting relay.

The Inspection, even an Admiralty one, was preferable to a Latin test or a Geometry lesson.

The breeches buoy was the longest we have ever made.

The juniors were trying their best to commit suicide by racing home-made willow and canvas coracles.

The IO seemed to enjoy the good tea provided by the Committee, and this may have influenced him when writing the report.

The Rear Admiral said, "Well, tell me what you want me to do and I will do it.'
The wind forgot to turn up.

Apart from a few errors of judgement, the handling was good.

Very smart, but surprised at the number of misplaced badges.

IO in gig: 'Your manoeuvre of man overboard was well carried out'. Venture Scout (also a police cadet):

'Yes Sir. It was almost at this spot last week we pulled an attempted suicide out of the river. The man was not pleased'.

A lot of sweat and anguish goes into the preparation for the Inspection.

The magic words – 'the Group should retain its Recognition'.

We had a lot of laughs and some tears.

The first visit of an unknown IO is a bit of a trial.

Before the Inspection, our intrepid ladies were busy with polish, needles, thread and face flannels.

More training is needed in coming alongside and where to put your hands.

1984
Whitsun 1984

The last London Sea Scout Meet was held at HM Dockyard Chatham due to closure of the establishment.

1985
June 1985

Royal Naval Inspection Report – 13th Guernsey Sea Scouts

The 13th Guernsey Sea Scouts have been based for many years in an old German Communications bunker next to the Beau Sejour Leisure Centre. Being below ground level, the temperature inside the all concrete bunker remained constant but a musty smell pervaded most of the rooms which are on two levels. Beavers, Cubs, Sea Scouts and Venture Sea Scouts represented the Group at their Royal Naval Inspection carried out by Lieutenant Commander John Scott at Castle Cornet.

Source: *Scouting* magazine

1992

The first edition of the *Sea Scout Journal* was published in January 1992 by Sea Scouters for Sea Scouters. It continued publication until 1998, and is much missed.

1993

Lieutenant Commander Devine reported in 1993 that the Royal Navy paid about £13,000 in grants to The Scout Association. He said that the Scheme encouraged a high standard of progress and seamanship expertise in its members, and he was always reassured to see how well they did in the various regattas, particularly at national level and around the country.

158 *Royal Naval Inspection, 1992, of the 3rd Frodsham Sea Scouts by Lieutenant Commander Scott, RN.*

1994

Census Returns

Sea Scout Journal, *Edition 11 (Summer) – study published on the 1994 census figures for Sea Scouts*

The census identified 8,749 male and 516 female Sea Scouts in 403 Troops, an average of 23 members per Sea Scout Troop, compared with a national average of 17 members per Scout Troop. Sea Scout Groups were spread over 81 counties, distributed as follows:

Channel Isles – 5, Isle of Man – 1, Northern Island – 6, Wales – 15, Scotland – 18, Shetland – 1, leaving the bulk of more than 360 Groups in England. Hampshire had the greatest number of Groups – 28 Troops with 823 members.

Venture Sea Scouts totalled 2,099, of which 464 were female Sea Scouts.

Totals in Sections by age:

Age	Sea Scouts						Venture Sea Scouts				
	10	11	12	13	14	15	15	16	17	18	19
%	10.57	24.10	23.21	19.90	15.48	6.91	15.04	31.73	27.98	19.24	10.39

Generally it seems that Sea Scout Groups accounted for between 25,000 and 30,000 members. On this information the highest proportion of Sea Scouts was in the 11- to 12-year age group, and for Venture Scouts in the 16- to 19-year age group.

APRIL 1994 TO MARCH 1995

RN Recognition Scheme – 'Proposed Defence Cuts'

The *Sea Scout Journal* carried a major feature about the Royal Naval Defence review, meaning the loss of the Staff Officer Scouts at Naval Home Command as the Navy planned to devolve the duty to seven area Sea Cadet Officers who would organise inspections. News quickly spread within the Sea Scout fraternity.

'Staff Officer to go in the latest Defence Cuts'

After decades of having a dedicated man at the Admiralty, The Scout Association was told that the status quo (the existing circumstances) was not an option.

Post of Staff Officer Scouts Reprieved

The Autumn 1994 issue of the *Sea Scout Journal* reported that the post of the Royal Navy's Staff Officer Scouts had been reprieved, and it was announced that it was to remain until at least April 1996. Further discussions were scheduled to take place between The Scout Association and the RN with a view to maintaining the Scheme but substantially reducing running costs.

1995

Royal Navy Recognition Scheme Changes Abandoned

The *Sea Scout Journal* of July 1995 reported: 'The New Commander in Chief has ordered the scrapping of the threatened changes to the Royal Navy Recognition Scheme.'

'This came as a great relief to those Recognised Groups and made a more certain future.'

1996

More recently RN Recognised Sea Scout Groups became eligible to attend four large events facilitated by the Royal Navy, which are: Summer Camp (Sea Scouts) and Explorer Camp at HMS *Bristol*, Portsmouth; Soccer Sixes at HMS *Bristol*, Portsmouth; and Swimming Galas at HMS *Raleigh*, Plymouth.

RN Recognised Sea Scouts Summer Camp

The Summer Camp centrepiece is HMS *Bristol* berthed at Portsmouth. The 200 Sea Scouts and 80 Leaders experienced ship-borne life for the week. Organised in Divisions of 24, Scouts took part in either an activity camp consisting of powerboating, sailing, kayaking, trekking on the South Downs, a day visit to Action Stations and the Historic Dockyard and a day sailing expedition which will earn them the Basic Nautical Skills Badge or they take courses in powerboating, sailing or canoeing which lead to RYA (Royal Yachting Association) and BCU (British Canoe Union) recognised awards.

RN Recognised Sea Explorer Camp

Held on board HMS *Bristol* each autumn up to 120 Explorer Scouts, supported by 60 Leaders, experience activities including kayaking, dinghy sailing, power boating, mountain biking and a 'naval activity day'. Each activity stretches those involved. Additionally, there is opportunity for some to gain nationally-recognised qualifications, such as competent crew and in power boating.

RN Recognised Sea Scouts Soccer Sixes Competition

The Soccer Sixes is based in HMS *Bristol* and uses HMS *Excellent*'s sporting facilities. 24 Groups send two squads of eight with accompanying Leaders to Portsmouth for a goal-packed weekend of close competition for Cups and Plates. The penalty shoot-out competition especially tests their mettle under pressure.

159 *Sea Scouts sailing offshore.*

RN Swimming Galas

These commenced in the 1970s. The Royal Navy Recognised Sea Scouts Swimming and Diving Championships are now based at HMS *Raleigh*, the Royal Navy's New Entry Training Establishment, at Torpoint, Cornwall, around 250 taking part.

RN Recognition Scheme – New System of Assessment

As ever moving with the times, an improved system was introduced for each inspection whereby the entire Group, its members, the administration, buildings and all its equipment, and its standards of Scouting attainments were assessed and marked, to establish where each Group rated on the RN Recognition Scheme.

2004

Form RN4 – RN Inspection and Recognition

The self-assessment system of marking on the form RN4 was introduced in 2004 to provide an evaluation of a group's standards and attainments.

Area 1: Training – nautical skills, activity badges and other awards
Area 2: Equipment – boats & equipment, building and facilities
Area 3: Membership – age ranges, appearance, role of young people
Area 4: Adult Leadership and Support – group organisation and structure, and
Area 5: Naval Knowledge and Participation – participation in the RN Scheme.

A Unit is given the form for completion before its Royal Naval Inspection. The Group Leader assesses the Unit against the criteria statement shown, and indicates how closely it meets it by entering a number between 1 and 20 in the Group Assessment boxes. The Inspecting Officer scores the form similarly, which in turn generates whether Recognition is granted, renewed, temporarily suspended or withheld.

2009

Royal Naval Inspection Report – 2nd Beeston Sea Scouts June 2009

Members of 2nd Beeston Sea Scouts were present and correct for the Royal Naval Inspection of their base at Barton Island on the River Trent last week.

Lieutenant Commander David Griffiths has the task of inspecting just 100 Sea Scouts units across the UK that have Royal Naval Recognition, and he arrived from his base to inspect the river base of the Scouts on Barton Island.

Navy Recognition brings with it a range of extraordinary benefits, such as access to the facilities of HMS *Bristol*, the training ship at Portsmouth. Once lost, RN Recognition is hard to regain and the members of 2nd Beeston, ages ranging from six-year-old Beavers to the oldest Explorer Scouts, as well as their leaders, were determined to show Commander Griffiths what they were made of.

He was piped aboard the Island after being brought across the river by a team of accomplished oarsmen on board the skiff *Styx*. The Scouts had been practising their pulling technique in preparation for the event, and were highly proficient. Other dignitaries invited to Barton Island for the inspection included the Mayor and Mayoress of Broxtowe as well as South West Notts District Commissioner Stuart Stanton and Deputy District Commissioner Colin Kemp.

Commander Griffiths inspected the Scouts – the ship's company – smartly lined up for flag break, speaking to each of them about the badges they'd gained. He then observed their prowess on the water once they had changed out of uniform ready to take part in activities that included kayaking, rowing (pulling) and sailing.

Commander Griffiths said he would be looking for a good scouting programme, the equipment available, qualifications gained and safety on the water as part of a marks-based inspection.

160   *A unique group photograph taken on board HMS* Bristol *of the four most recent Royal Naval Staff Officer Scouts, 1997-2007.*

'One of the things I do look out for is smartness and discipline,' he added. 'I noted the Scouts and the young Beavers here were all very disciplined during flag break. Not everyone achieves that high a standard.'

Before taking leave of the Island and heading back to the land-based HQ at Lilac Grove, Beeston, for a buffet, Commander Griffiths told the young people they had passed their Inspection.

'I would like to compliment all of you on what you have here,' he said. 'You have a wonderful setting, some excellent and well-maintained equipment, a wide range of activities to choose from and a good set of strong leaders. What's most impressive, though, is the way you all work together as one team'.

Source: *Beeston Express*, Friday, 26 June 2009.

Further comments on and about Admiralty Recognised Groups at their Admiralty Inspections 1984-2009

The danger is they may lose Scouts to the Sea Service faster than recruitment.

The Venture gig crew are as good as any the RN can produce.

The sign over the 'Galley' doorway read 'Canteen'. The Inspecting Officer took a poor view of this: 'Not on any ship I have visited'.

IO: 'Who on earth sewed on that Badge?' Reply: 'Auntie'. 'Well, give Auntie my compliments, but she must really try to do better'.

Comment as colours were hoisted: "It's not a race, you know; there are eight seconds allowed for that".

Some cap tally bows could have been trimmed more neatly and cut to a shorter length.

Having no Cubs or Beavers we are able to provide more grown-up Scouting.

More attention to polishing of shoes would have enhanced the overall impression.

On presentation of Twenty-Year Service Certificates, 'I remember them joining as First Formers – which is probably where 40 years of my life went to'.

The canoe squad were finding new ways to commit suicide.

IO to Scout District Commissioner: 'Who meets in the adjoining boathouse?' Answer: 'The local Sea Cadets'. IO: 'I think I will do a spot check'. Much ringing of the door bells; after about ten minutes the boathouse door is opened by a Sea Cadet Chief Petty Officer, who turned pale on the spot.'

In the *3rd Shoreham Sea Scouts Group History* Les Goodbody wrote on Inspecting Officers: 'And so they have come and gone, all kindly friends, polite, interested in our problems, appreciative of small services we have rendered to them when the occasion arose, an example to us all.'

Royal Navy Inspecting Officers 1920-2009

Date	Inspecting Officer
1920	Captain B.S. Thesiger RN
1923-4	Captain N. O'Neil RN
1943-5	Lieutenant Commander W.L. Rossitter RNR
1946-7	Lieutenant Commander W.J. Askins RN
1949-50	Lieutenant Commander Morrison RN
1951-3	Lieutenant Commander F.D. Brown RN
1954-5	Lieutenant Commander P.S.C. Black RN
1956-8	Lieutenant Commander R.C.E. Watkins RN
1959-62	Lieutenant Commander P. Wareham RN
1962-3	Lieutenant Commander C.J. Hallam RN
1963-4	Lieutenant Commander P. Crane RN
1965-7	Lieutenant Commander C.J. Whiffen RN
1968-72	Lieutenant Commander A.F. Ginn RN
1973-4	Lieutenant Commander G.R.P. Weaver RN
1976-7	Lieutenant Commander P. Cressey RN
1978-9	Lieutenant Commander D. Uden RN
1984-90	Lieutenant Commander J. Scott RN
1991-3	Lieutenant Commander J. Scott RN
1993-5	Lieutenant Commander J. Devine RN
1996-8	Lieutenant Commander Haynes RN
1999	Lieutenant Commander Millington RN
1999-2001	Lieutenant Commander M. Ellis RN
2002-4	Lieutenant Commander R. Williams RN
2004-6	Lieutenant Commander J. Haynes RN
2006-	Lieutenant Commander D. Griffiths RN

Sources: This information has been collated from Admiralty and RN Inspection reports. The dates may vary in some instances due to variations in postings.

ROYAL NAVY RECOGNISED SEA SCOUT GROUPS, 2009

1	4th Gillingham	35	3rd Frodsham
2	3rd Portchester	36	1st King Norton, Birmingham
3	1st Oulton Broad	37	1st Blackfords, Cannock
4	13th Ipswich	38	11th Torbay (Barton)
5	4th Epping Forest South (Bancroft)	39	4th Streatham, S. London
6	Newbold-on-Stour	40	3rd Bingley
7	1st Guernsey	41	1st Avoch
8	3rd Walsall	42	10th Christchurch
9	2nd Cowes	43	Vacant (1st Corsham provisional)
10	1st Batchworth, Rickmansworth	44	4th Heswall (St Peter's)
11	1st Lytham-St-Annes	45	1st Lilliput, Poole
12	15th Macclesfield	46	2nd Beeston (Parish Ch Gp), Notts
13	Vacant	47	35th Bournemouth
14	2nd Warwick	48	1st Southbourne, Emsworth
15	2nd Whitstable	49	4th Allerton, Liverpool
16	36th Epping Forest South	50	Holy Trinity, Margate
17	18th Inverness	51	1st Felpham
18	4th Dovercourt, Harwich	52	17th Colchester
19	1st West Bay, Bridport	53	6th Itchen, Hamble
20	4th/6th Leigh-on-Sea, Southend	54	12th Halifax
21	8th Faversham	55	1st St Peter's-in-Thanet
22	4th New Forest East, Hythe	56	1st Petersham & Ham, SW London
23	3rd/5th Lancing	57	1st Clifton, York
24	1st Hertford	58	1st Sutton Coldfield
25	25th Southampton (Northam)	59	8th Worthing
26	8th Norwich (Norwich School)	60	4th Thames Ditton, SW London
27	64th Birkenhead	61	2nd Durrington
28	2nd Abingdon	62	9th New Forest South (Lymington)
29	6th Torbay	63	1st Watchet
30	Leander Kingston, SW London	64	19th Exeter
31	14th Tonbridge	65	1st Bungay, Lowestoft
32	3rd South Shields	66	21st Sunderland (St Andrews)
33	3rd/6th Shoreham	67	6th Ramsgate
34	9th Stafford	68	1st Blofield & Brundall, Norwich

69	1st Luton	86	33rd Lancaster
70	11th Norwich	87	1st Barry
71	1st Thorpe St Andrew	88	1st Warsash
72	19th Tynemouth	89	9th Itchen (Woolston)
73	3rd Chalkwell Bay, Southend	90	29th Glasgow
74	1st Molesey, SW London	91	6th Newark
75	4th Knowle, Solihull	92	2nd Fareham
76	2nd Deal	93	5th Woodbridge, Suffolk
77	1st Cleethorpes	94	15th Long Eaton, Nottingham
78	30th Norwich	95	1st Cuddington, SW London
79	1st Cogenhoe, Northampton	96	4th Canvey Island
80	1st Park Gate, Fareham	97	6th Barry
81	Dartford Cambria	98	1st Standlake
82	5th Gosport	99	4th New Forest North (Eling)
83	1st Reading	100	6th Falmouth
84	3rd Poole	101	Gibraltar
85	17th Sutton Coldfield		

Source: Lieutenant Commander David Griffiths RN

1920-2009 – Sea Rangers

The Sea Scouting fraternity regard the Sea Rangers as being a sister organisation which merits a whole chronicle of its own, though space only permits a brief history.

At the beginning of the 20th century there were few opportunities for activities for young people, but in 1908 and 1910 Scouting for boys and the Girl Guides were started by Robert Baden-Powell. A Scout rally was held at Crystal Palace in 1910 where a number of girls attended wearing their version of the Scout uniform. B-P asked his sister, Agnes, to assist him, and in the same year the Girl Guides were formed; by 1916 a Ranger Section was introduced for the older girls.

1920: Sea Guides were started for girls who were interested in boating activities with Veronica Erksine as their head.

1922: Dame Katharine Furse, who had been Director of the Women's Royal Naval Service (WRENS) during the First World War, was appointed head of Sea Rangers, giving inspired leadership. In its formative years, the Sea Guides section was run by ex-WRENS.

1926: 61 Sea Guide ships were commissioned. Sea Ranger crews are named after ships of the Royal and Merchant Navies.

1927: Sea Guides became Sea Rangers.

1937: A new era in seamanship began in the Sea Section when 270 Sea Rangers took part in nautical training aboard the Training Ship *Implacable*, moored in the upper reaches of Portsmouth Harbour. This training was to prepare them for service in the WRENS, if re-established when war was declared, thus reviving the original intentions of those who started the Sea Guides in 1920.

1939-45: During the Second World War, in 1940 Sea Rangers trained under a scheme called the Home Emergency Service, and in London they joined the River Emergency Service, which demanded high standards of discipline and fitness. Many Sea Rangers joined the WRENS when old enough. Sea Rangers also gave assistance to the Red Cross and Air Raid Precautions/Civil Defence.

1943: In 1943 Princess Elizabeth joined the Sea Ranger Ship (SRS) *President*, and Princess Margaret joined the crew of *SRS President III*, later renamed SRS *Duke of York* by King George VI.

1945: In 1945 the Admiralty granted Recognition to Sea Ranger crews that fulfilled the necessary conditions of efficiency, etc, and in the same year 6,000 Sea Rangers celebrated their Silver Jubilee.

The Guide International Service was formed to carry out relief work in Europe in the aftermath of the Second World War; Sea Ranger leaders were the first to volunteer.

1947: Princess Elizabeth became Commodore of Sea Rangers; the position was taken over by Princess Margaret in the same year.

1965: On relinquishing the appointment of Commodore of Sea Rangers, in 1965 Princess Margaret became a very hard-working President of the Girl Guides, and would ask to see their new publications in advance to comment upon them. After a meeting, which 'HRH' attended with Guide Commissioners, came a meal. A note was passed by one of the Commissioners to another: 'Whatever can I say if I am sat opposite "Maggie"?' By one of those quirks, the note finished up with 'HRH', who read it aloud, and said dryly with a smile, 'Who's "Maggie"?'

1966: *Tomorrow's Guide* was published, which detailed the future reorganisation of the Guides. Sea Rangers were to be absorbed under the umbrella of 'Ranger Guides', losing their separate identity, but the Sea Rangers were allowed to continue for the time being. The debate continued from

1968 to 1971. Princess Margaret, Commodore of Sea Rangers, wrote at length that some sort of compromise could continue, with the Sea Rangers wearing their distinctive uniform but adopting the new Guide programme.

1973: The Girl Guides decided they were no longer to have a nautical section, and the Sea Rangers ceased in March 1973. An independent association was formed to take on the activities of Sea Rangering.

1982: Sea Rangers had close links with Chatham Naval Base which continued for many years with Sea Rangers taking part in the Chatham Meets, ending when Chatham Naval Base closed in 1982.

Today, members of the Sea Rangers Association, whose ages now range from ten to 21, still canoe, sail, go offshore, and participate in the Tall Ships' Race and the Duke of Edinburgh's Award Scheme. Close links still exist today between the Sea Rangers Association and Sea Scouting.

1856-2009 — SEA CADETS

The inclusion of a short narrative about Sea Cadets in this history of the Sea Scouts is because their early origins are broadly similar, and in the early days up until 1914 there was absorption between the two organisations. Also, in 1919 both were RN Recognised at the same time. There has often been confusion between the Sea Scouts and the Sea Cadets as they are both uniformed youth organisations with a similar maritime ethos, but with different funding procedures and training traditions.

The Sea Cadet Corps dates back to the Crimean War (1854-6) when sailors returning home formed Naval Lads' Brigades to help orphans in the sea ports, but there was then no national organisation. The Sea Cadets in the UK can be traced back to the Kent port of Whitstable where the first of the Naval Lads' Brigades was established. The Navy League adopted the Brigades in 1910. The early Naval Lads' Brigades were independent and their histories are scant.

December 1908: Another organisation, the British Boys' Naval Brigade with its Headquarters in South London was launched, and by April 1909 battalions were listed in Wandsworth, Battersea, Greenwich, Lambeth and Birmingham. In May 1909 their name changed to the National Naval Cadets, then changed again to Scouts of the Sea, and later to Sea Scouts of the Empire. There was no further mention of these units but their members most probably joined the Navy League Boys' Naval Brigade or the Sea Scouts around 1914.

1910: The Naval Lads' Brigade was renamed Navy League Boys' Naval Lads' Brigade. By 1914 the Navy League Boys' Naval Lads' Brigade were well established resulting in a number of early Sea Scout Troops transferring to the Sea Cadet Corps. From those early days, a thriving youth movement grew, drawing on the ethos of the Senior Service to provide training and adventure with a nautical theme for young people.

The Navy League applied to the Admiralty for recognition of the Brigades. Robert Baden-Powell, in his discussions with the Admiralty about Sea Scout Recognition, is on record as saying that he did not wish the Boy Scouts Association to come under government control.

1919: Recognition was granted by the Admiralty for Sea Cadets and Sea Scouts.

1942: The title Sea Cadet Corps was adopted and the units were numbered. The Corps came under the control of the Admiral Commanding Reserves with administrative matters handled by the Navy League, now called the Sea Cadet Association.

1947: Sea Cadets received co-sponsorship from the Admiralty which agreed to supply uniform, boat training facilities and limited pay to adults who retained appointments in the RNVR.

1976: The Navy League was renamed the Sea Cadet Association. The title of Admiral Commanding Reserves lapsed, and responsibility for the Sea Cadet Corps and the Sea Scouts was passed to the Commander-in-Chief Naval Home Command in Portsmouth (CINCNAVHOME). The Sea Cadet Charter was revised and replaced with a Memorandum of Agreement.

2004: The Sea Cadet Association with the Marine Society formed the charity The Marine Society & Sea Cadets.

January 2005: The *Navy News* reported that the Sea Cadet Association received from the MoD £4,380,000 to provide a Headquarters structure and national training facilities.

2009: The Capitation Fee The Scout Association receives from the Royal Navy for 100 Admiralty Recognised Sea Scout Groups out of 350 or so Sea Scout Groups overall, was £60,000.

SELECT BIBLIOGRAPHY

In my research, the following books provided background information:

Adams, W.S., *Edwardian Portraits*, Martin Secker & Warburg Ltd (1957)

Andrew, Christopher, *The Defence of the Realm – The Authorised History of MI5*, Penguin Group, London (2009)

Anon., *Jack Cornwell: The Story of John Travers Cornwell, VC*, Hodder & Stoughton, London (1916)

Arthur, Sir George, *Life of Lord Kitchener, Vols 1, 2 and 3*, Macmillan & Co., London (1920)

Auten, Lieutenant-Commander Harold, *'Q' Boat Adventures*, Herbert Jenkins Ltd, London (MCMXIX) [1919]

Baden-Powell, Heather, *Baden-Powell: A Family Album*, Alan Sutton Publishing, Gloucester (1986)

Baden-Powell, Robert, *My Adventures as a Spy*, USA Reprint (1915)

Baden-Powell, Robert, *Boy Scouts Beyond the Seas*, USA Reprint (1913)

Baden-Powell, Lieutenant General Sir Robert, *Quick Training for War* (MXMXIV), Herbert Jenkins Ltd (1914)

Baden-Powell of Gilwell, Lord, *Girl Guiding*, C. Arthur Pearson Ltd, London, 19th edition (1951)

Baden-Powell of Gilwell, Lord, *Lessons from the Varsity of Life*, C. Arthur Pearson Ltd, London (1934)

Baden-Powell of Gilwell, Lord, *Rovering to Success*, Herbert Jenkins Ltd, London (1930)

Baden-Powell of Gilwell, OM, Lord, *Paddle Your Own Canoe*, Macmillan & Co. Ltd, London (1939)

Baden-Powell, Agnes (in collaboration with Sir Robert Baden-Powell, KCB), *How Girls can Help to build up the Empire*, The Girl Guides Association (1912), this edition reprinted 1993

Baden-Powell, Sir Robert, *Scouting and Youth Movements*, Ernest Benn Ltd (1929)

Baden-Powell KC, W., *Sea Scouting and Seamanship for Boys*, Brown, Son & Ferguson Ltd, Glasgow (1912)

Bakowski, June, *Rose Hill 1832-2008: The History of one of England's Oldest Prep Schools*, Rose Hill School (2008)

Bartimeus, *Naval Occasions*, William Blackwood & Sons, Edinburgh (1915)

Batten, Rex, *The Leysdown Tragedy*, Friends of Nunhead Cemetery (1992)

Beacon, Admiral Sir R.H., *The Life of John Rushworth, Earl Jellicoe*, Cassell & Co. Ltd, London (1936)

Beaumont, Marguerite de, *The Wolf that Never Sleeps*, The Girl Guides Association, London (1991)

Beesley, Patrick, *Room 40 British Naval Intelligence 1914-18*, Hamish Hamilton, London (1982)

Beesley, Patrick, *Very Special Intelligence: The Story of the Admiralty's Operational Intelligence Centre, 1939-1945*, Greenhill Books, London (2000)

Bell, William M., *Guernsey Green*, The Guernsey Press Co. Ltd, Guernsey (1992)

Bennett, Geoffrey, *Charlie B: The Life of Admiral Lord Charles Beresford*, Peter Downey Ltd, London (1968)

Bennett, Rodney M., *The Archer-Shees against the Admiralty*, Robert Hale & Co. (1973)

Bennett, Geoffrey, *Naval Battles of the First World War*, Pan Books (1974)

Bennett, Geoffrey, *The Battle of Jutland*, David & Charles, Newton Abbot (1972)

Bihet, Molly, *A Child's War: The German Occupation of Guernsey as seen through Young Eyes*, The Guernsey Press Co. Ltd, Guernsey (1994)

Bond, Geoffrey, *The Evans of the Broke Story*, Arco Publications, London (1961)

Bonnet, Geoffrey, *The Battle of Jutland*, Wordsworth Editions Ltd, Hertfordshire (1999)

Bonney, George, *The Battle of Jutland 1916*, Sutton Publishing Ltd, *Gloucestershire (2002)*

The Boy Scouts Association, *The Royal Research Ship Discovery, The History of Captain Scott's Famous Vessel*, London (1951)

Brigland, Tony, *Q Ships: Sea Killers in Disguise*, Redwood Books Ltd, Wilts (1998)

Brittain, Frank, *Milestones of 100 Years of Hertfordshire Scouting*, Hertfordshire County Scout Council (2008)

Brooks, John, *Dreadnought Gunnery and the Battle of Jutland – The Question of Fire Control*, Routledge Taylor & Francis Group (2005)

Browne MA, Tom, *Sea Scouting*, Morrison & Gibb Ltd, London (1951)

Brownrigg Bt, Rear Admiral Sir Douglas, *Indiscretions of a Naval Censor*, Cassell & Co., London (1920)

Burston, Ivor, *I Joined the Navy and Saw the World*, Wellington Printers, Somerset (1985)

Campbell, Rear-Admiral Gordon, *My Mystery Ships*, Hodder & Stoughton Ltd, London (1930)

Campbell, John, *Jutland: an Analysis of the Fighting*, Conway Maritime Press, London (1998)

Carew, Anthony, *The Lower Deck of The Royal Navy 1900-1939*, Manchester University Press, Manchester (1981)

Carlton, L.A., *Gallipoli*, Transworld Publishers, London (2002)

Cassar, George H., *Kitchener: Architect of Victory*, William Kimber, London (1977)

Caulfeild CBE, RN, Captain James M., *Sea Scouts Coast Watching Areas, Letter to Boys and Inspection Routines*, 17th Edition (1933)

Chatterton, E. Keble, *Gallant Gentlemen*, Hurst & Blackett Ltd, London (1933)

Chatterton, E. Keble, *Q Ships and Their Story*, Sidgwick & Jackson Ltd, London (1922)

Chatterton, E. Keble, *The Epic of Dunkirk*, Hurst & Blackett Ltd, London (1940)

The City of Portsmouth Council, *W.L. Wyllie, RA, The Portsmouth Years*, Portsmouth (1996)

Coates, Tim, *Defeat at Gallipoli*, The Stationery Office, London (2000)

Coles, Alan, *Three Before Breakfast: The Sinking of* HMS *Aboukir, Hogue and Cressy*, Kenneth Mason, Hampshire (1979)

Collins, L.J., *Cadets: The Impact of War on the Cadet Movement*, Jade Publishing Ltd, Lancashire (2001)

Collis, Henry, Hurll, Fred, Hazlewood, Rex, *B-P's Scouts*, Collins, London (1962)

Cookridge, E.H., *Inside SOE*, Arthur Barker Ltd (1966)

Costello, John and Hughes, Terry, *Jutland 1916*, Futura Publications Ltd and George Weidenfeld & Nicolson Ltd (1976)

Coysh, Victor, *Swastika Over Guernsey*, Guernsey Press Co. Ltd, Guernsey (1983)

Cross, Arthur and Tibbs, Fred, *The London Blitz*, Dirk Nishen Publishing, London (1989)

Cruickshank, Charles, *The German Occupation of the Channel Islands*, The Guernsey Press Co. Ltd (1975)

Crum, Major Frederick, *Scouts and Sniping in Trench Warfare* (c.1917)

Dark, Sidney, *The Life of Sir Arthur Pearson Bt, CBE*, Hodder & Stoughton Ltd, London (1922)

David, Lieutenant John, *Lower Deck*, RNVR, Macmillan & Co. Ltd, London (1945)

Dickens, Captain Peter, *Night Actions: MTB Flotilla at War*, Peter Davies, London (1974)

Dimmock, F. Haydn, *Bare Knee Days*, C. Arthur Pearson Ltd, London (1939)

Dimmock, F. Haydn, *The Scouts' Book of Heroes*, Arthur Pearson, London (1919)

Drewery, Mary, *Baden-Powell: The Man Who Lived Twice*, Hodder & Stoughton, London (1975)

Drewery, Mary, *Window on my Heart: Olave Lady Baden-Powell GBE*, Hodder & Stoughton, London (1977)

Eadon, Stuart, *Kamikaze, The Story of the British Pacific Fleet*, Crécy Books Ltd, Bristol (1995)

Eadon, Stuart, *Sakishima and Back*, Crécy Books Ltd, Bristol (1995)

Edwards RN, Commander Kenneth, *Seven Sailors*, Collins, London (1945)

Everett, Sir Percy, *The First Ten Years*, The East Anglian Daily Times (1948)

Ewing, A.W., *The Man of Room 40: The Life of Sir Alfred Ewing*, Hutchinson Ltd, London (1939)

Fawcett, H.W. and Hooper, G.W.W. (eds), *The Fighting at Jutland*, Chatham Publishing, London (2001)

Fevyer, W.H., Wilson, J.W. and Crabb, J.E., *The Order Of Industrial Heroism*, The Orders & Medals Research Society (2000)

Fiennes, Ranulph, *Captain Scott*, Hodder & Stoughton, London (2003)

Filmer, Keturah, Diary & Memories [unpublished extract], Walworth, August 1912

Finer, Herman, *Mussolini's Italy*, Victor Gollancz Ltd, London (1935)

Fleming MA, CF, Rev. John A., *The Last Voyage of His Majesty's Ship Britannic*, Wordsmith Publications, Buckinghamshire (1998)

Foot, M.R.D., *SOE: The Special Operations Executive, 1940-1946*, The Mandarin Press, London (1990)

Frame, T.R. and Swindon, G.J., *First In, Last Out: The Navy at Gallipoli*, Kangaroo Press Ltd, New South Wales (1990)

Furse GBE, RRC, Dame Katharine (Director of the Women's Royal Naval Service (1918) and Sea Rangers (1922)), *Hearts and Pomegranates*, Peter Davies Ltd, Glasgow (1940)

Gardner, W.J.R., *The Evacuation from Dunkirk, 'Operation Dynamo' 26 May – 4 June 1940*, Naval Staff Histories (2000)

Garnett, Lieutenant-Commander H.W. Stuart, *Seamanship for Scouts*, Wells Gardiner & Co. Ltd (1914). Completely revised with new chapter by Tom Browne, MA, Wells Gardner, Darton & Co. Ltd, Surrey (1952)

Gilcraft, *Sea Pie*, George Philip & Son Ltd, London (1934)

Girl Guides Association, *Sea Rangers*, Girl Guides Association, London (1934)

Girl Guides Association, *Sea Sense: A Handbook on Sea Rangering*, Brown Son & Ferguson, Glasgow (1963)

Gliddon, Gerald, *VCs of the First World War*, Budding Books, Sutton Publishing, Gloucestershire (1997)

Godfrey, Arthur, 14th Richmond Sea Scouts, *Second to None, The Story of the 14th Richmond 1921-1990*

Goodey, Charles and Rose, Jack, HMS *Europe*, The Royal Naval Patrol Services Association, Lowestoft (1977)

Gordon, Andrew, *The Rules of the Game: Jutland and British Naval Command*, John Murray (2005)

Gove, Eric, *Big Fleet Actions*, Brockhampton Press, London (1998)

Grant, Robert M., *U-Boat Hunters*, Anthony Rowe Ltd, Eastbourne (2003)

Granville, Wilfred and Kelly, Robin A., *Inshore Heroes: the Story of the Little Ships in War & Peace*, London (1961)

Grieve, Hilda, *The Great Tide*, The County Council of Essex (1959)

Hammond, Sylvia A.M.V., *From Mercury to Mines: The Story of Lieutenant Commander Roy Berryman Edwards, DSO, RN*, Hammond Publishing, J.E.M. Digital Print Services in Kent Ltd (2006)

Hampton, Lord, *Scouting Sketches*, C. Arthur Pearson, London (1925)

Harman, Nicholas, *Dunkirk: The Necessary Myth*, Hodder & Stoughton, London (1980)

Harris, Steven, *Images of England, 100 Years of Scouting*, Tempus Publishing, Gloucester (2008)

Harris, Steven, *Legalised Mischief, Volumes 1-4*, Lewarne Publishing, London (2002, 2003, 2006, 2008)

Harris, Steven, *Scout Island!*, Lewarne Publishing, London (2007)

Harrison, Thom, *Living Through the Blitz*, Penguin Books (1978)

Harrold, Dr Jane and Porter, Dr Richard, *Britannia Royal Naval College 1905-2005*, Richard Webb Publishers, Dartmouth (2005)

Harwood, David, *Scouts in Action*, G. Bell & Sons Ltd, London (1963)

Hazlewood, Rex, *Scouting*, Frederic Muller, London (1969)

Hazlewood (ed.), *The Diamond Jubilee Book of Scouting 1907-1967*, C. Arthur Pearson Ltd, London (1966)

Heilbrun, Carolyn G., *The Garnett Family, The History of a Literary Family*, Allen & Unwin (1961)

Henderson GM, D.V., *Heroic Endeavour*, J.B. Hayward & Son, Suffolk (1988)

Heren, Louis, *Growing Up Poor in London*, Indigo Cassell Group, London (1973)

Higgs, Dorothy Pickard, *Life in Guernsey under the Nazis 1940-1945*, Toucan Press, Guernsey, Channel Islands (1979)

Hill, Richard, *Lewin of Greenwich, The Authorised Biography of Admiral of The Fleet Lord Lewin*, Cassell & Co., London (2000)

Hillcourt, William with Baden-Powell, Lady Olave, *Baden-Powell, The Two Lives of a Hero*, The Gilwellian Press, New York (1992)

Hoey, Brian, *MacLean of Duart: The Biography*, Country Life Books, Middlesex (1986)

Horne, Alistair, *The Lonely Leader, Monty 1944-1945*, Pan Macmillan Ltd, Basingstoke (1995)

Hough, Richard, *Mountbatten, Hero of our Time*, Book Club Associates, London (1981)

Humphries, Roy, *Dover Patrol 1914-1918*, Sutton Publishing, Gloucester (1998)

Humphrey, Stephen, *Southwark History 1901-1982*, Sutton Publishing, Gloucester (1999)

Hunter, Margaret, *The Story of Discovery*, Dundee Industrial Heritage Ltd, Dundee (1996)

Huntford, Roland, *Shackleton*, Abacus, London (1996)

Jarvis, John, *Tack of Life*, Woodfield Publishing, West Sussex (2000)

Jay, Peggy, *Loves & Labours*, Weidenfeld & Nicolson, London (1990)

Jeal, Tim, *Baden-Powell*, Pimlico, London (1995)

Jeffrey, Keith, *MI6 1909-1949*, Bloomsbury, London (2010)

Jeffries, Ron, *Just an Essex Lad*, SPS Communications (2009)

Jellicoe, John Rushworth, *Battle of Jutland, 30 May-1 June 1916*, Official Dispatches, Admiralty 1920, The Naval & Military Press Ltd, East Sussex

Jellicoe of Scapa, Admiral Viscount, *The Grand Fleet 1914-1916*, Ad Hoc Publications, Suffolk (2006)

Jones, Max, *Robert Falcon Scott Journals: Scott's Last Expedition*, Oxford University Press, Oxford (2005)

Jones, Max, *The Last Great Quest, Captain Scott's Antarctic Sacrifice*, Oxford University Press, Oxford (2003)

Joseph, Michael, *Victoria Cross at Sea*, John Winton, London (1978)

Kerbrech, Richard P. de, *The Last Liners of the White Star Line, MV Britannic and MV Georgic*, Shipping Books Press, Shropshire (2002)

Kerr, J. Lennox and James, David (eds), *Wavy Navy*, by Some Who Served, George G. Harrop & Co. Ltd, London (1950)

Kirby, Norman, *1100 Miles with Monty*, Sutton Publishing Ltd, Gloucestershire (2003)

Knightly, Phillip, *The First Casualty*, Prion Books, London (1975)

Knippel, Marilda Yuyama, *John Travers Cornwell, VC* [private publication prepared for HMS *Raleigh*]

Koch, H.W., *The Hitler Youth 1922-1945*, Dorset Press, New York (1988)

Labat, Pierre, *The Marvellous Kingdom*, Odhams Press Ltd, London (1956)

Lacquer, Walter, *Young Germany: A History of the German Youth Movements*, Translation Books, New Brunswick, USA (1984)

Lake, Deborah, *The Zeebrugge and Ostend Raids 1918*, Pen & Sword Ltd (2002)

Liddle, Peter H., *The Sailor's War 1914-1918*, Blandford Press (1985)

Lloyd George, David, *War Memoirs of David Lloyd George. Vol 1*, Odhams Press Ltd, London (1938)

London, Charles, *Jutland 1916*, Osprey Publishing Ltd, Oxford (2000)

Longmate, Norman, *The Real Dad's Army*, Arrow Books, London (1974)

Lord, Walter, *The Miracle of Dunkirk*, Wordsworth Editions Ltd (1998)

MacDonald, Robert H., *Sons of the Empire, The Frontier and the Boy Scout Movement 1890-1918*, University of Toronto Press, Toronto, Canada (1993)

Macintyre, Captain Donald, *Jutland*, Evans Brothers Ltd, London (1957)

Macintyre DSC, RN, Ret'd, Captain Donald, *Jutland*, Pan Books (1960)

Macksey, Kenneth, *Invasion – The Alternate History of the German Invasions of England, July 1940*, Greenhill Books, London (1990)

Mahy, Miriam M., *There is an Occupation*, The Guernsey Press Co. Ltd, Guernsey, Channel Islands (1992)

Maloney, Alison, *Something For The Girls: The Official Guide to the First 100 Years of Guiding*, Constable & Robinson, London (2009)

Marchant KBE, LLD, Sir James, *Youth and the Race*, Kegan Paul, Trench Trubner & Co. Ltd, New York (1923)

Marr, Scout (James William Slessor Marr), *Into The Frozen South*, Scout Marr of the Quest Expedition, Cassell & Co., London (1923)

Marshall, Howard (retold by), *With Scott to the Pole*, London Country Life Ltd (1947)

Massie, Robert, *Dreadnought Britain: Germany and the Coming of The Great War*, Pimlico Books, London (2004)

Matthews, W.R. (Dean Emeritus of St Paul's), *Memories and Meanings*, W.R. Matthews, Hodder & Stoughton, London (1969)

Mayne, Richard, *Channel Islands Occupied*, Jarrold & Sons Ltd, Norwich (1985)

Maxstone-Graham, John, *Titanic Survivor, The Memoirs of Violet Jessop*, Sutton Publishing, Gloucester (1998)

McCann, Graham, *Dad's Army – The Story of a Classic Television Show*, Fourth Estate, London (2001)

McL Ranft MA, D Phil, FRHistS, B.L., *The Beatty Papers*, Scolar Press for the Navy Records Society (1989)

McGregor, W.H., *Making Men: The History of Boys Clubs and Related Movements in Great Britain*, University of London (1953)

McKee, Christopher, *Sober Man and True*, Harvard University Press, London (2002)

Milford, Humphrey, *The Scouts Every-Day Book*, Oxford University Press, London (1941)

Mills, Simon, *HMHS Britannic: The Last Titan*, Shipping Books Press, Shropshire (1996)

Mizzi, J.A., *Scouting in Malta*, Progress Press Co. Ltd, Valletta, Malta (1989)

Montgomery of Alamein, Bernard, *The Memoirs of Field-Marshal the Viscount Montgomery of Alamein, KG,* Collins, London (1958)

Morris, Ronald, *The Captain's Lady*, Chatto & Windus (1985)

Morris, Ronald, *The Indomitable Beatie*, Sutton Publishing, Gloucestershire (2004)

1st Mortlake Sea Scouts Branch (compiled by), *Fifty Years of Sea Scouting in Mortlake, 1909-1959*, 1st Mortlake Sea Scouts Branch, B-P Scout Guild (1959)

Mulholland, John and Jordan, Alan, *Victoria Cross Bibliography*, Spink & Sons Ltd, London (1999)

Nagy, Laszlo, *250 Million Scouts*, Darntrell, Chicago (1985)

The Naval and Military Press Ltd, *Jack Cornwell: The Story of John Travers Cornwell VC, Boy 1st Class* (1916)

Nevill, P.B., *My Scouting Story*, Roland House Scout Settlement, London (1960)

Nevill, P.B., *Scouting in London 1908-1965*, The London Scout Council 1913-65 (1966)

Noyes, Alfred, *Trapping the U-Boats, Mystery Ships Trapping the U-Boats*, Hodder & Stoughton, London (MCMXVI) [1916]

Oddone, Patrick, *Dunkirk 1940*, Tempus Publishing Ltd (2000)

Odhams Press (eds), *Fifty Amazing Secret Service Dramas* [Including Lord Baden-Powell's *My Adventures as a Spy by J. Southworth*], Odhams Press, London (1937)

Padfield, Peter, *The Battleship Era*, Pan Books, London (1972)

Padfield, Peter, *Rule Britannia: The Victorian and Edwardian Navy*, Routledge & Kegan, London (1996)

Parkinson, Alan F., *St John's School, Walworth: Past and Present Celebrated* (2006)

Percival, John, *For Valour – The Victoria Cross: Courage in Action*, Methuen London Ltd in association with Thames Television International Ltd, London (1986)

Perry, Jimmy, *A Stupid Boy – Jimmy Perry: The Autobiography of the Creator of Dad's Army*, Century, London (2002)

Phillips, Lucas, *Cockleshell Heroes*, Heinemann Ltd, London (1956)

Piggott, Jan, *Dulwich College: A History 1616-2008*, Dulwich College, London (2008)

Picht, Dr Werner, *Toynbee Hall and the English Settlement Movement*, G. Bell & Sons Ltd, London (1914)

Plummer, Russell, *The Ships that Saved an Army*, Patrick Stephens Ltd, Northamptonshire (1990)

Pocock, Geoffrey A., *The Legion of Frontiersmen*, Phillimore & Co. Ltd, Chichester, West Sussex (2004)

Pocock, Geoffrey A., *Outrider of Empire: The Life and Adventures of Roger Pocock*, The University of Alberta Press (2007)

Poolman, Kenneth, *The British Sailor*, Arms and Armour, London (1989)

Quorm, Roger and Wyllie, John, *W.L. Wyllie*, Chris Beettes Ltd (1981)

Reader, Ralph, *It's Been Terrific*, Werner Laurie London (1953)

Reader, Ralph, CBE, *Ralph Reader Remembers*, Bailey Brothers & Swinfen Ltd, Folkestone (1974)

Reynolds, E.E., *Boy Scouts*, Collins, London (1946)

Reynolds, E.E., *Boy Scouts Jubilee*, Oxford University Press, London (1957)

Reynolds, E.E., *The Scout Movement*, Oxford University Press, London (1950)

Reynolds OBE DSC, Leonard C., *Dog Boats at War*, Sutton Publishing, Gloucestershire (1998)

Reynolds, L.C., *Gunboat 658*, William Kimber, London (1955)

Reynolds, L.C. and Cooper, H.F., *Mediterranean MTBs at War, Short MTB Flotilla Operations 1939-1945*, Sutton Publishing Ltd, Gloucestershire (1999)

Rich, P.J., *Chains of Empire*, Regency Press, London (1991)

Ritchie, Carson I.A., *Q-Ships*, Terence Dalton Ltd, Suffolk (1985)

Rolfe, Vic, *Three Flag Hoist*, The University of Reading (2004)

Rosenthal, Michael, *The Character Factory, Baden-Powell and the Origins of the Boy Scout Movement*, William Collins Sons & Co. Ltd, London (1986)

Roskill, Stephen, *Admiral of the Fleet Earl Beatty*, William Collins & Co. Ltd, London (1980)

Rowallan, Lord, *Rowallan: The Autography of Lord Rowallan*, Paul Harris Publishing, Edinburgh (1976)

Royal Geographical Society, *South With Endurance: Shackleton's Antarctic Expedition 1914-1917*, Tamiko Rex Book Creation, London (2001)

Royle, Trevor, *The Kitchener Enigma*, Michael Joseph, London (1988)

Saunders, Hilary St George, *The Left Handshake*, Collins, London (1949)

Savours, Ann, *The Voyage of the Discovery*, Virgin Books, London (1992)

Schellenberg, Walter Keegan John, Erickson, John, *Invasion 1940: The Nazi Invasion Plan for Britain*, SS General Walter Schellenberg, St Ermin's Press (2000)

Scholkamp, Dr Stephen and Raun, Helmut, *100 Jahre Pfadfinder in Deutschland 1909-2009* (2009)

Scott, Peter, *The Eye of the Wind – An Autobiography*, Hodder & Stoughton, London (1961)

Scott, Lieutenant Commander, *The Battle of The Narrow Seas*, Country Life Ltd, London (1945)

Scott, R.F., *Scotts' Last Expedition* (Extracts from personal journals), Modern English Series, John Murray, London (1940)

The Scout Association, *An Official History of Scouting*, Hamlyn, London (2006)

The Scout Association, *The Founder, Scouting* magazine series, London (1997)

Shackleton, Ernest, *Shackleton: The Polar Journeys*, Birlinn Ltd, Edinburgh (2002)

Sharma, Trara Chand, *Scouting as a Cocurricular Activity*, Sarup & Sons, New Delhi (2003)

Sica, Mario (ed.), *Playing the Game, a Baden-Powell Compendium*, Macmillan & Co. Ltd, London (2007)

Smith, Peter C., *Heritage of the Sea: Famous Ships* (featuring HMS *Chrysanthemum* and HMS *President*), Balfour Precisions Ltd, Huntingdon (1974)

Smurthwaite, David, *The Boer War 1899-1902*, Hamlyn, London (1999)

Snelling, Stephen, *The Naval VCs*, Sutton Publishing, Gloucestershire (2002)

Sparks, William and Munn, Michael, *The Last of The Cockleshell Heroes*, Pen and Sword Ltd, Barnsley (2007)

Stafford, David, *Secret Agent: The True Story of the Special Operations Executive*, BBC Worldwide Ltd, London (2000)

Steel, Nigel and Hart, Peter, *Jutland 1916 – Death in the Grey Wastes*, Cassell, London (2003)

Steen, Jan van der, *Scouting in Old Postcards*, European Library Zaltbommel, The Netherlands (1998)

Stenson, Patrick, *The Odyssey of C.H. Lightoller*, W.W. Norton & Co., New York (1984)

Street, Sage and Lyn, *The German Raid on the Hartlepools, 16 December 1914*, Sage and Lyn Street, West Hartlepool 1915.

Sutherland, Jon and Canwell, Diane, *The Battle of Jutland*, Pen & Sword Books Ltd, South Yorkshire (2007)

Sutton, Jack, *'Jack'* [short story on Jack Cornwell VC], YouWriteOn.com (2009)

Tarrant, V.E., *Jutland: The German Perspective*, Cassell Military Paperbacks, London (2001)

Taylor, Gordon, *The Sea Chaplain*, The Oxford Illustrated Press Ltd, Oxford (1978)

Terraine, John, *The Life and Times of Lord Mountbatten*, Hutchinson of London (1968)

Thompson, Julian, *Book of the War at Sea*, Pan Books in association with the Imperial War Museum (2005)

Turnbull, Patrick, *Dunkirk: Anatomy of Disaster*, B.T. Batsford Ltd (1978)

Wade, E.K., *21 Years with Baden-Powell*, Blandford Press, London (1957)

Wade, Eileen K., *The Chief: The Life Story of Robert Baden-Powell*, Wolfe Publishing Ltd, London (1975)

Wade, E.K., *Olave Baden-Powell*, Hodder & Stoughton, London (1971)

Wade, E.K., *Twenty-One Years of Scouting*, C. Arthur Pearson Ltd, London (1929)

Walker, Colin, *Brownsea B-P's Acorn*, Write Books CPR Ltd, Ferrybridge (2007)

Walker, Colin, *J.T. Cornwell, VC*, Write Books CPR Ltd, West Yorkshire (2006)

Walker, Colin, *J.T. Cornwell VC and the Scouts' Badge of Courage, Scouting Milestones*, Write Books CPR Ltd, West Yorkshire (2006)

Walker, Colin, *The Dawn of the World Scout Movement, Scouting Milestones*, Colin Walker (2008)

Walker, 'Johnny', *Jack Cornwell VC & TS Northampton, Milestones of Scouting* (2005)

Webb, Beresford, *Scouting Achievements*, Putnam, London (1937)

West, Nigel, *MI6*, Weidenfeld & Nicolson, London (1983)

Whiting, Audrey, *The Kents, a Royal Family*, Hutchinson & Co. (Publishers) London (1985)

Williams, C.J., HMS *Wellington One Ship's War* (1992)

Wilson, J.S., *Scouting around the World*, Blandford Press, London (1959)

Wilton, Iain, *C.B. Fry, An English Hero – A Biography*, Richard Cohen Books, London (1999)

Winton, John, *Captains and Kings: The Royal Family and the Royal Navy 1901-1981*, Bluejacket Books, Clwyd (1981)

Wood, Eric, *The Boy Scouts' Roll of Honour*, Cassell & Co. Ltd, London (1919)

Wood, Alan and Wood, Mary Seaton, *Islands in Danger*, New English (1985)

Woolgar, Brian and Rivière, Sheila La, *Why Brownsea? The Beginnings of Scouting* (2003)

Yates, Keith, *Flawed Victory: Jutland, 1916*, Chatham Publishing, London (2000)

Ziegler, Phillip, *Mountbatten: The Official Biography*, Book Club Associates – Guild Publishing, London (1985)

INDEX

References which relate to illustrations only are given in **bold**.